Durkheim and the Birth of Economic Sociology

Durkheim and the Birth of Economic Sociology

Philippe Steiner

Translated by Keith Tribe

PRINCETON UNIVERSITY PRESS

PRINCETON AND OXFORD

English translation copyright © 2011 by Princeton University Press

Published by Princeton University Press, 41 William Street, Princeton, New Jersey 08540
In the United Kingdom: Princeton University Press, 6 Oxford Street, Woodstock, Oxfordshire OX20 1TW
press.princeton.edu

Library of Congress Cataloging-in-Publication Data
Steiner, Philippe.
    [Ecole durkheimienne et l'économie. English]
    Durkheim and the birth of economic sociology / Philippe Steiner ; translated by Keith Tribe.
        p.   cm.
    Includes bibliographical references and index.
    ISBN 978-0-691-14055-1 (hardcover : alk. paper)   1. Economics—Sociological aspects.   2. Durkheim, Émile, 1858–1917.   3. Durkheimian school of sociology.   I. Title.
    HM548.S74 2011
    306.3092—dc22   2010016618

British Library Cataloging-in-Publication Data is available

This book has been composed in Sabon
Printed on acid-free paper. ∞
Printed in the United States of America

10 9 8 7 6 5 4 3 2 1

Contents

Translator's Note

Where the following text quotes directly from writings which have been translated into English, I have used the most accessible translation; and when the translation has required revision, the reader's attention is drawn to the fact that the passage cited no longer directly corresponds to the original. The existing English translations of Durkheim's writings, however, are unsatisfactory; they are often inaccurate or fail to provide appropriate information on sources and editions. While the principal writings of Emile Durkheim are currently available in useable French editions, both print and digital from the Bibliothèque Nationale, coverage in the English language is surprisingly poor and, in some cases, shoddy. This is all the more surprising given the status that Durkheim has enjoyed since the mid-twentieth century as a "founding father" of modern sociology.

Two new editions of his major writings do meet contemporary scholarly standards. Besides being a lucid and reliable translation, the Penguin Classics edition of *Suicide* (2006) includes a chronology of Durkheim's life, a helpful introduction by Richard Sennett, some further reading, and a note by Robin Buss which quite properly specifies the exact source for this translation and draws the reader's attention to the existence of an earlier one published in 1952. Likewise Karen E. Fields's new translation of *Elementary Forms* (1995) is a good and readable translation, prefaced by an informative introduction which, among other things, explains how this new translation differs from that of Joseph Ward Swain. Both of these new translations replace earlier English versions by improving on their readability and reliability, while also providing important details about the source on which the translation is based and what this implies for the final English text.

None of this, however, is true for the second translation of *Division of Labour* (1984). Nowhere is it stated that this is a translation of the revised second French edition of that work; indeed, no account at all is given of the publication history of the text. The very brief translator's note merely draws the attention of the reader to the unsatisfactory state of referencing and citation in English, which for some unexplained reason the translator was unable to remedy; Lewis Coser's introduction is vague and unhelpful, failing to provide any account of the place of the text within Durkheim's writings; and the translation, while an improvement on the 1947 Free Press edition (itself a reprint of an earlier 1933 edition), is not free from error. One has to turn to that earlier edition to find any explanation of Durkheim's revisions for the second edition, and also to find in an appendix what it was that Durkheim decided to excise from his original introduction. Similarly, in *Rules of Sociological Method* (1982), it is evident that there were two French editions of this work, but there is no mention of which edition this translation is based on, nor indeed is it anywhere stated when the book was first published, nor why Durkheim felt moved to write it.

Besides these key works, there are some other translations which are useable, if dated: *Professional Ethics and Civic Morals* (1957), which is a translation of Kubali (ed.), *Leçons de sociologie, physique des mœurs et du droit* (1950); *Sociology and Philosophy* (1953), a translation of *Sociologie et philosophie* (1924); *Moral Education* (1961), a translation of *L'education morale* (1925); and a number of collections of thematic readings. Some context is provided in contributions to *The Cambridge Companion to Durkheim* (ed. Jeffrey C. Alexander and Philip Smith), whose essays however range from the informative to the wildly speculative.

I draw the reader's attention to these points because Philippe Steiner's book examines the development in Durkheim's thinking from the 1880s to his death in 1917, and his influence on a number of students and younger collaborators. The absence of clear chronological and contextual markers from most existing English translations of his writings makes it very difficult to relate these to the arguments that the author here develops.

Keith Tribe

Durkheim and the Birth of Economic Sociology

Introduction

Durkheim's sociology is not usually considered in regard to its relationship to the economy—an economy which belongs to *la vie sérieuse* and which, together with religion and ritual (*la vie religieuse*), stands in opposition to the life of pleasure and art. Indeed, of all the classical founding fathers of sociology from the later nineteenth and early twentieth centuries, it is Durkheim who seems most removed from such a context, as compared with the work of Vilfredo Pareto, Georg Simmel or Max Weber, for all of whom this connection is both recognised and well established. It is the same for writers of the previous generation—Karl Marx, Herbert Spencer and Alexis de Tocqueville. It could even be said that Durkheim has become the representation par excellence of the sociologist who clearly distances himself from the economist, almost eclipsing Auguste Comte in this respect. Precisely because Durkheim's sociology is holistic in approach, and emphasises the common values that will programme the individual right from the very first steps that individual takes in society, it seems to be the antithesis of an economic approach founded on methodological individualism and rational self-interested behaviour.

One can almost forget that Durkheim's first work, his French dissertation, dealt with the division of labour, an economic topic if ever there was one. But saying that, it has to be admitted that the distinct message the reader takes from the book, following Durkheim's own emphasis, involves the non-economic dimension of economic relations; once again it is the opposition to economics which dominates. This reading is lent even greater weight by Durkheim's explanation, in the preface to the second edition of *Division of Labour*, that he was abandoning an extensive and ambitious research programme devoted to the historical transformations through which professional groups had passed—from medieval corporations to those forms of association engendered by the development of modern industry—in favour of a completely different programme: the sociological study of religion in primitive societies.

However, there is an unavoidable question that arises from the importance given to the economy by all the major founding fathers of social science in general, and sociology in particular, at the exact time when Durkheim was elaborating his own work: how could a major sociological body of writing emerge during this period *without* confronting questions arising from the disruption of contemporary economic change? This was after all an issue that preoccupied all other great thinkers of the time.

How could the study of social facts, the study to which Durkheim attached both his name and his work, simply disregard the abundance of facts arising from modern economic activity, whether the latter is conceived in terms of capitalism, industrial society or, of course, the division of labour? Can we believe that a sociologist who claimed in the strongest terms that sociological research was not worth one hour of his time if it did not allow him to better understand the present would be capable of *not* closely studying the functional economic conditions of modern societies?[1]

By turning our attention to the way in which the economic dimension bears upon Durkheimian sociology, we are not merely examining one dimension among others of his work, but one of the most important. This was something Durkheim had in common with contemporary classical sociologists.

But does Durkheim's change of perspective, placing the sociology of religion first among his preoccupations, not imply an abandonment of any sociology of the economy? We do not think so. Weber proved that an interest in the sociology of religion was in no respect contradictory to a strong interest in the sociology of the economy. We will demonstrate that the reorientation of Durkheim's work after *Suicide* did not mean that he ceased thinking about the economic dimension of social life, for this reorientation led to a new and original approach, linking economic sociology, the sociology of religion and the sociology of knowledge.

Sociological reflection on the economic conditions of modernity takes the form of two research programmes in Durkheim's writings. The first outlines the contours of a critique of economic categories, expressed either as an epistemological critique and a sociology of knowledge or, positively, as the development of an economic sociology of contract and forms of socialisation within the economic sphere. The second research programme deploys the sociology of religion to renew the functional understanding of modern societies, and especially of the categories within which members of these societies think about economic processes. The initial focus of this book is upon a presentation of these two programmes.

Is it possible to deal solely with Durkheim when considering Durkheimian economic sociology? Not at all. The contribution made by François Simiand and Maurice Halbwachs is essential, since they were after all the principal contributors to the "Economic Sociology" section of the first two series of *L'année sociologique*, and then later to *Annales sociologiques*.

---

[1] "[W]e consider that our studies would merit not one hour of trouble if they were only of speculative interest . . . It will be seen [in this book] that science can help us to discover the manner in which we have to orient our conduct, so that we might determine the ideal towards which we confusedly tend." (Durkheim 1893/1984: xxxix).

The extent of their contribution makes consideration of their work indispensable. But, in so doing, there should be no misunderstanding: it is not that, failing to find anything of great substance in Durkheim's own economic sociology, we turn instead to the writings of his disciples. To do so would be quite inappropriate, for Durkheim clearly expressed his aim and scholarly practice in a letter to Marcel Mauss of 15 July 1897: "my true ambition is to see some young people of merit, like those [Célestin Bouglé, Simiand, Paul Lapie], following me not unquestioningly, and freely using the results of my work" (1998: 98).[2] Durkheim strongly believed that it was important that the different branches of scientific knowledge work closely together, and he hoped to form a group, a team of "workers", dedicated to the proper development of the sociological approach that he advocated.[3] The group which formed around the *Année sociologique* produced a remarkable range of sociological work and established a moral unity in which Durkheim obviously took great pleasure, even if there were recurrent crises within the group, whose members found the constant labour of reviewing very demanding (Besnard 1998: 18–20). While the work of Halbwachs, Mauss and Simiand is given the most prominence in what follows, there is no intention of neglecting the work done by other members of the team such as, for example, Bouglé, Hubert Bourgin, Georges Davy and René Maunier, even if there were differences between them and they rejected this or that thesis of Durkheim.[4]

[2] In the following letter Durkheim returned to the subject in a more composed way: "I have no other ambition than to see that my work is not unfruitful. I set no great store by my talent, or my style, but only that the pains I take be used and that I know of it. If, as you tell me, this satisfaction will not be withheld from me, I will consider myself well-rewarded. I took hope this evening from reading the article by Simiand that will appear in the *Revue de métaphysique*." (Letter to Mauss, July 1897, in Durkheim 1998: 80–81). In 1930, when his candidacy for the Collège de France was under consideration, Mauss came back to this characteristic of the Durkheim School: "We were not simply a school of disciples blindly gathered around a master. Of course, Durkheim was full of ideas that had a major impact. But what brought us to him was that we knew he was a thinker [*savant*], that his methods were very sound, that his knowledge was extremely extensive and scrupulously substantiated." (Mauss 1930: 210).

[3] Following Besnard (1979, 1993, 1998), the collective dimension of Durkheimian sociology must be emphasised. It is also remarkable, and uncommon, to see a great thinker forming, during his lifetime, a school within which thinkers as brilliant as Halbwachs, Mauss and Simiand were able to develop, all of whom would end their careers in the Collège de France.

[4] Referring to the existence of theoretical differences between Durkheim and Maunier (the rejection of holism and of the emphasis placed upon legal norms), Alain Mahé (1998: 47) argues that Maunier should not be treated as one of Durkheim's disciples. Such a view is an error. Being a Durkheimian means being one of the group formed around the *Année*, so a Durkheimian like Bouglé was no less distanced from some of Durkheim's holistic principles, as his interest in Simmel's formal sociology makes clear. Similarly, and as will be discussed in detail below, when Durkheimians such as Simiand and Halbwachs attributed

This argument also applies to the team that reunited around the short-lived second series of *L'année sociologique* and, to a lesser extent, to those who worked on *Annales sociologiques*.

Once we have extended the field of enquiry to include Durkheimians, what becomes of the two research programmes that Durkheim had in view?

As we follow the writings of Simiand, from the numerous reviews that he published in *L'année sociologique* to his major works of the 1930s, it seems that his virulent critique of economic categories followed closely the line already taken by Durkheim when reading contemporary economic writings during his work on the *Division of Labour*. In other words, Simiand's work does not appear out of nowhere: its structuring principle is the methodology put forward by Durkheim in the *Rules of Sociological Method*, and he went on to develop a critique of economic categories for which Durkheim had laid the initial foundations. Moreover, in Simiand the sociological critique of economics quickly led into the elaboration of sociological concepts which were, in his view, necessary to overcome the defects to which he drew critical attention in the writings of a broad range of economists; the empirical work of Simiand, his "positive economics", consequently makes a contribution to the first Durkheimian research programme regarding the sociology of the economy.

What of the second research programme? The intertwining of Durkheim's work with that of Mauss has been clarified by Camille Tarot (1999), but when we come to the relationships between the economic and the religious we enter an area less clearly marked out than the first. One has to return to the basic material and emphasise that Mauss's noted essay *The Gift* and the works leading up to it over a quarter of a century are part and parcel of Durkheim's economic sociology. The pages in which Mauss successively presents his conclusions concerning "moral codes", "economic sociology and political economy" and "general sociology and ethics" represent those points where he invokes the existence of Durkheim's second programme of research into the sociology of economics, laying claim explicitly to this relationship at the very point where the sociology of religion and the sociology of economy are so vividly reunited. Moreover, Mauss's work is placed within a sequence including Davy's thesis (1922) and Maunier's studies of exchange rituals in North Africa (1927, 1933). By recognising the significance of Mauss's economic sociol-

---

importance to the motives and actions of agents in their economic sociology, they made no attempt to conceal the fact that they here broke with a point central to Durkheim (Halbwachs 1930: 11–13, 473). But who would claim that Bouglé, Halbwachs and Simiand did not belong to the Durkheimian school?

ogy, and making the necessary connection to Durkheim's second research programme, Durkheim's economic sociology gains a resonance that it has hitherto been denied.

The presentation of these two aspects of the work of the Durkheimians —the critique of political economy on the one hand and reflection on the foundations of religion on the other—forms the second objective of this book.

The plan of the book is as follows.[5] The first two chapters outline in turn Durkheim's two research programmes. Chapter 1 examines the nature of the critique of political economy developed in texts originating during the period that Durkheim was preparing his thesis and reaching up to the publication of *Suicide*. The second chapter is directed to the origin and characterisation of the second research programme: beginning with his reflections on the ideal, Durkheim relinquishes politics for religion as the counterpoint to the economic. The sociology of knowledge becomes an essential intermediary for the relationship between religious sociology and the sociology of economy. Overlooked right up to the present, this completes and augments the first, better-known perspective; it lends the Durkheimian approach, quite original on this point, a brilliance that neglect had dulled.

Chapters 3 to 6 show how these two programmes are taken up by Simiand for a critique of political economy and by Mauss for the relation between religion and economy. Chapters 3 and 4 show how Simiand and Halbwachs deploy the sociological critique of economics, whether as an epistemological critique of the categories and methods employed by contemporary economists or through the elaboration of an original approach to economic sociology, refined in terms of empirical studies of prices, wages, consumption and money. Chapter 5 is devoted to the connection between religion and economy. First of all Durkheim's own preliminary thoughts on the subject are dealt with; then the emphasis turns to Mauss's economic sociology at work in *The Gift*, as well as in the various essays that he published in the early twentieth century, especially his writings on change and Bolshevism in the 1920s. Finally, chapter 6 shows how these two research programmes, largely independent of each other in their initial phases, came together in the most thought-provoking writings of Mauss and Simiand—in *The Gift* once more, and in *La monnaie, réalité sociale*. In these works, the dialogue between the two Durkheimians, whether direct or indirect, is a valuable means for an understanding of the importance

[5] Throughout this book, I will use masculine pronouns to refer to the generic human individual, as this usage reflects that of my sources. It is to be understood that this "he" includes individuals of both sexes.

of their joint ambition. Here one can most clearly see how the sociology of religion and economic sociology are blended through the medium of the sociology of knowledge.

These six chapters primarily constitute a history of sociological ideas. The final two chapters are addressed to an examination of that which continues to be of relevance in Durkheimian economic sociology.

Chapter 7 seeks to isolate the specificity of the Durkheimian critique when directed to the manner in which economic categories and representations are disseminated, especially among a growing public of experts, managers and engineers—categories which are at the roots of the diffusion of "economic belief" (*croyance économique*), to use Frédéric Lebaron's (2000) striking term. Attention is then turned to the writings that Durkheim devoted to the sociology of the schooling system, which mesh perfectly with the sociology of knowledge and lay the foundations, in Durkheim, Halbwachs and Simiand, of a sociology of economic knowledge.

Chapter 8 will show that there is a convergence with Weber's problematic on the question of social mechanisms—in Weber, confirmation before members of a sect; in Durkheim, the process of scholarly competition initiated by the Jesuits—where the attempt is made to explain the emergence and increasing power of the economy in seventeenth-century Europe. We will see that the Durkheimian sociology of knowledge and of the schooling system can be employed to go beyond Weber's investigations, given that the latter tells us nothing about the manner in which the ideal motivations orienting interests and economic activity are produced and diffused after Puritanism is transformed into pure utilitarianism. Hence, the way in which Durkheimian sociology of economic knowledge is anchored in the sociology of the schooling system provides us with a crucial perspective upon the construction, the diffusion and the organisation of the economic understanding of the world that we moderns have; an understanding that, one can say, contributes more than any other to a very particular illumination of present-day society.

CHAPTER ONE

Durkheim and the Critique of Political Economy

Durkheim's interest in political economy seems to have been quite slight; he wrote nothing that could strictly speaking be described as "political economy", and he contributed to all sections of the *Année sociologique* save that dedicated to reviewing new work in economic sociology. Moreover, as a letter he wrote to Célestin Bouglé in 1896 shows, he declared himself to be disappointed by his reading in political economy, even if he did imply that the use of history and statistics would open the way to worthwhile discoveries in the field:

> I hope that the reading of economists serves you better than it has me. When I began, fifteen years ago, I too thought that I would find here answers to the questions that concerned me. I spent many years with such reading and have learned nothing more than that which a disheartening experience teaches. All the same it is true that this domain is wide open for exploration. No doubt one could make some interesting discoveries here with the help of statistics and history. (Letter of 16 May 1896, in Durkheim 1975 II: 392)

During the closing decades of the nineteenth century, sociology took shape as a new discipline, and political economy was academically institutionalised. The relation of Durkheim to political economy cannot be understood without taking these changes into consideration, together with shifts in the nature of political economy during this period. His writings from 1887 to 1893 show that he made a real effort with respect to political economy following which, from 1895 to 1896, a progressive but definite distancing from such work occurred. This distancing did not derive from any lack of interest in the economic dimension of social life; it was related to dissatisfaction with the way that economists went about their work. Durkheim's relationship to political economy is essentially a critical one: critical of the method practised within this social science, and critical of the categories in whose terms economists thought about the functioning of society. Nonetheless, within this work of critique Durkheim developed an economic sociology by considering how it might be possible to go beyond the academic economic knowledge of his time: for economic facts are social facts, and can be approached sociologically by taking into account collective representations and, more generally, social institutions.

If we are to grasp the various aspects of Durkheim's relation to political economy, the following questions have to be answered. First of all, how extensive are Durkheim's references to economists and political economy? Second, given that his borrowings from German economists are openly acknowledged, and their precise location known, what limits did Durkheim set himself in these borrowings? Third, what criticisms did Durkheim make of economic theory? And finally, how did economists react to these criticisms?

DURKHEIM AND THE ECONOMISTS OF HIS TIME

We can obtain a better idea of Durkheim's writings by sorting them chronologically into three phases. First come the reviews and articles he wrote during the years from 1885 to 1890; these are the years before the completion of his thesis, the period of his intellectual formation. This is followed by a period in which three texts are produced: *The Division of Labour*, *The Rules of Sociological Method*, and the course on socialism, to which should also be added two contemporary articles (1895; 1897b). It was during this period that the initial programme for the sociology of political economy was developed. Finally, we have the texts that followed the publication of *Suicide* in 1897, after which Durkheim had his "revelation" concerning the importance of religion in social life. We can use this simple framework to register the number of references made to political economy and to economists and group them by tendency or nationality. These references can be summarised as shown in table 1.1.[1]

The greatest number of references fall in the years 1885–89, representing 47% of the total; and if the period is extended to 1893, we get a total of 59%. By contrast, during the period from 1900 to 1915 the frequency of such references tails off and they provide no more than 17% of the total. This chronology substantiates the statement made to Bouglé about a distancing with respect to economics and economists. We can refine this initial finding by examining Durkheim's references in terms of a few broad groups.

---

[1] The authors are grouped as follows: eighteenth century—Jean-Joseph Louis Graslin, Jacques Necker, Ferdinando Galiani, etc.; Classical—Adam Smith, David Ricardo, Jean-Baptiste Say, John Stuart Mill, etc.; socialist—Marx, Simonde de Sismondi, "professorial socialists" (*Kathedersozialisten*); French—Charles Gide, Paul Cauwès, Maurice Block, Gustave de Molinari, Emile Levasseur, etc.; German—Gustav Schmoller, Albert Schäffle, Adolph Wagner, Karl Bücher and all "German economists"; foreign—Henry C. Carey, W. J. Ashley; generic—terms such as "economists", "economism", economic science", "political economy".

TABLE 1.1
Economists Cited in the Principal Works of Durkheim

	Pre-DL	DL	Rules	Socialism	Post-Suicide	Total
Eighteenth-century	0	0	0	12	0	12 (3%)
Classical	5	6	1	17	11	40 (9%)
Socialist	14	1	0	31	6	52 (12%)
French	17	19	1	10	1	48 (11%)
German	96	9	0	3	12	120 (28%)
Foreign	1	2	0	0	1	4 (1%)
Generic	67	15	10	15	43	150 (35%)
Total	200 (47%)	52 (12%)	12 (3%)	88 (21%)	74 (17%)	426 (100%)

Eighteenth-century authors appear to be very marginal, and reference to them is for the most part to be found in the course on socialism. Necker and Graslin are introduced into the third and fourth lectures of the course when Durkheim deals with the foundations of socialism. That concludes their role. The classical economists have a more sustained presence, even if a modest one, apart from the lectures on socialism (19%). They are not here dealt with in any detail but serve to represent the orthodoxies criticised by Sismondi and Henri Saint-Simon. Things are not any better for classical economists in the *Division of Labour*, where they serve only to establish the problem (five or six references being made in the introduction).

Among the authors classed as "socialist," Sismondi is cited *solely* in the fifth lecture of the course on socialism. Marx is cited often enough—twenty-five times, nearly half of all the references for this group, and chiefly in the period covered by the lectures on socialism. Reference to professorial socialists (*Kathedersozialisten*—usually referred to as "socialists of the chair") is principally to be found in the first period (nine instances), following which it more or less entirely disappears (three instances). Apart from the German economists, the only foreign economists cited are the English economist W. J. Ashley and the American Henry Carey.

We now come to those economists who were Durkheim's contemporaries. There are more than twice as many references to German as to French economists (28% of the total and 11% respectively), but four-fifths of these references are made in texts predating 1889, and of these two-thirds (sixty-eight instances) concern Schäffle alone, leaving Wagner (twelve instances) and Schmoller (five instances) far behind. After gaining two mentions in the *Division of Labour*, Schäffle entirely disappears, Schmoller and Bücher then predominating among Durkheim's German references. From 1893 onwards, references to French economists become more frequent than those to German economists (thirty-one instances against twenty-four), most references being to Levasseur (sixteen instances) for his writings in economic history, with four references each to Cauwès and Emile de Lavaleye, two economists who are close to German historicism. Only eight references are made in all to liberal economists (Block, Molinari, Paul Leroy-Beaulieu) and their journal, the *Journal des économistes*.

Durkheim often refers to political economy or to economists in general terms, and this occurs for the most part when talking of liberal economists. Such general references are always frequent (at around 25%), but during the final period their importance increases, reaching 63%. So not only did Durkheim have a diminishing interest in economists, but he increasingly referred to them in generalised terms, which means that he ceased taking an interest in any doctrinal or theoretical differences that there might be among them.

These findings raise a series of questions. What significance should be attached to the prominence of references to the German Historical School, and their subsequent disappearance? What status should be assigned to the omnipresence of Schäffle in the period before the publication of the *Division of Labour*? What is the significance of generic references? We will deal initially with the first two questions, then turn to the third, which involves Durkheim's critique of political economy.

During the entire period in question, the same strong elements appear in the way that Durkheim accounts for the development of social science and of political economy during the nineteenth century (Durkheim 1886a, 1888a, 1909a; Fauconnet 1903). Classical political economy, with its emphasis on a positive conception of economic laws, serves as the point of departure; this is followed by a critique of the limitations of this form of political economy, and the contributions of Auguste Comte, German economists, and also Alfred Espinas and Herbert Spencer are cited by way of contrast. This history finally ends with a presentation of the system of the social sciences according to Durkheim. This structure is typical of the early texts, but later texts are not so different, apart from the greater emphasis on the role of Saint-Simon and Comte.[2] Throughout these reflections on the social sciences, the status of political economy is special: in contrast to other domains, political economy was an autonomous science that required reintegration with those sciences to which it properly belonged. How might this outcome be achieved, allowing (in the language of the articles of the period 1900–15) the replacement of political economy by an economic sociology?

This is where the German economists come in, and we need to examine carefully the role Durkheim attributes to them, since commentators have not given entirely satisfactory accounts of this. Paul-Laurent Assoun (1976: 957) maintains that the reference made to German economists is not merely one among many but introduces a theoretical model critical to the realisation of a social science (ibid.: 968; see also Jones 1993: 36–37). The position taken by Bernard Lacroix and Béatrice Landerer (1972: 164; see also Filloux 1977: 29) seems better founded: they talk of the simultaneity or the similarity in the two approaches and note that the reference to German economists implies an opposition to economic orthodoxy (ibid.: 171, 181). But both of these interpretations remain at a very general level and fail to provide answers to the following questions: firstly, was the reference to German economists inevitable, or might Durkheim have found another way of introducing their perspectives into the domain of the social sciences? Secondly, what is the exact nature of the reference made to German economists, and how does it fit in among the other references that Durkheim made in his writing?

---

[2] The boundaries and nature of sociology developed and hardened over time in Durkheim's thinking. In 1886 he thought that sociology was made up of three separate sciences (1886a: 213): the study of the state; the study of the regulatory function of the law, morals and religion; and the study of economic functions. To these he added a general sociology and a pathological sociology. Durkheim modified this schema in 1888 by dividing sociology into four domains (social psychology, moral science, legal science and a renewed political economy), each of which was to be studied by a physiological approach (the study of social functions) and a morphological approach (the study of social structures) (1888a: 101–4). He then gave his thinking a more or less definitive form in elaborating the classification employed in L'année sociologique. He reversed the approach adopted in 1888, transforming the two approaches into two domains: the sociology of social morphology (the study of the social substratum) and the sociology of social physiology (the study of social functions). The latter is made up of special sciences distinguished by Durkheim according to categories of fact: religious, legal, and moral facts, then language, custom and the economy (1900b: 26–27). It was the task of a general sociology to synthesise the facts so distinguished (ibid.: 36). He will return to this more systematically in 1909, with the difference that a sociology of aesthetics will take the place of a sociology of custom (1909a: 153).

According to Assoun, Durkheim could only think of social science in terms of the model given to him by German economists, since they connected ethics with political economy and had an extended conception of the social sciences. The evidence for this argument is weak. In the first place, and this is something of which Durkheim is aware (1887: 269), it is wrong to suggest that classical and liberal economists were uninterested in connections between ethics and political economy,[3] although it should be said that the way in which they showed this interest was, for a sociologist, unsatisfactory. In the second place, German economists were not the only ones to put forward a model capable of sustaining the kind of general social science to which Durkheim aspired: others who might have played this role would be Saint-Simon and Comte. In 1885–86, the year in which Durkheim was in Germany, the *Methodenstreit* was at its height and would leave its mark upon all economists right up to the world war. At this time either Durkheim was unfamiliar with Saint-Simon's work or his knowledge of it was meagre—this would alter in 1895. But Durkheim did not ignore the work of Comte and what it might offer him as a point of departure. The real question is, therefore, why did Durkheim play down any reference to Comte and refer instead to the German economists? Our hypothesis here is as follows: German economists offered Durkheim the possibility of taking a position within the field of social science not available from the standpoint of Comte.

Economic opinion of Comte's work and of his sociology was then so low that Durkheim would naturally have favoured alternative intellectual filiations. Clémence Royer wrote an article against Comte in the *Nouveau dictionnaire d'économie politique*[4] so vitriolic that a note was added to it stating that, while not wishing to diminish this "remarkable" article in any way, the editors were not completely of the same view as its author. André Liesse for his part revealed his aversion to the sociology associated with Comte's name in writing that "it would be foolhardy to claim that, in sociology, one has arrived at even the most modest of scientifically acceptable conclusions" (1891: 894). Only Mill and Spencer escape the disaster which has befallen positivism and sociology, no doubt because of their knowledge of political economy. It might also be noted that, at this particular time, reference to the work of Comte was not especially common among sociologists themselves. With the partial exception only of René Worms, none of Durkheim's "rival" sociologists, such

---

[3] Many French liberal economists were interested in this issue, among them Henri Baudrillart, a well-known author of the period who devoted a large part of his work to it (Baudrillart 1883: 1891; Breton 1991: 395, 404).

[4] The views of Block (1897: 62–66) or of Henri-Charles Mailfer (1883) are not fundamentally different from those that can be found in the *Dictionnaire*.

as Gabriel Tarde and Frédéric Le Play, either conducted their research, or more generally placed themselves, under the banner of positivism.[5]

And so if sociology was a body of knowledge of fragile intellectual status, lacking institutional recognition, reference to the German economists would have been both necessary and useful to Durkheim, enabling him to enter an important debate among economists over the nature of political economy and its relation to social science and, ultimately, to mark himself off from liberal economists. It should be remembered that the German historical school was in the late nineteenth century at the height of its prestige, and it had an international audience; its work was everywhere discussed, and Durkheim could neither ignore it nor fail to talk about it. In addition, if Durkheim did for a moment think that liberals were losing momentum, he quickly abandoned this hope and acknowledged that, in France, the orthodox school retained an influence that had been lost abroad (1887: 268). Durkheim was therefore able to draw upon the German economists of the historical school at the precise time that divisions were appearing among French economists,[6] making use of an approach that had an important resonance for the presentation of his own perspective on the social sciences. This hypothesis helps us understand why, when references to German economists receded after 1890, references to the ideas of Saint-Simon (Durkheim 1909a/2004: 11–17) and above all to Comte moved in to replace them (Durkheim 1900a: 118–21; 1900b: 34; Durkheim & Fauconnet 1903: 125, 129–30; 1909a: 140–47). We will even see that Durkheim (Durkheim & Fauconnet 1903; Durkheim 1909b) could present a penetrating defence of the Comtean position on political economy.

We now have to examine the nature of the references to German economists. Here his 1887 article, "La science positive de la morale en Allemagne" is quite crucial, since it shows that economists are not the only Germans referred to: there are also references to legal scholars (Rudolf von Ihering) and to a moral philosopher and psychologist (Wilhelm Wundt). Durkheim stayed for a time in Wundt's laboratory, and Wundt made a particular contribution to the formation of Durkheim's sociological problematic. We should be wary of the idea that Durkheim only paid attention to economists. This article also demonstrates that Durkheim differentiated

[5] "Comte's disciple, Emile Littré, had sought to encourage the autonomous development [of sociology] in the pages of his journal *La philosophie positive* (founded in 1867) and through a short-lived *Société de sociologie* (1871–1873?) formed in Paris during the Commune. However, in 1875 sociology was still defined as a branch of positivism whenever it was not taken for socialism" (Geiger 1981: 345). See the study of Yamashita Masayuki (1995) for an account of Comtean sociology between Comte and Durkheim.

[6] This point is emphasised by Lucette Levan Lemesle (1986: 232–33; 1991: 366) and Yves Breton (1991).

between the work of Gustav Schönberg, Schmoller, Wagner and Schäffle, and that he criticised *all of them*.

Durkheim characterised German economists by the connection they made between ethics and political economy (1887: 269–70), although he recognised that simply making this connection was not enough, for it could easily involve sentimentalism and theoretical confusion—here Durkheim was close to Menger, adversary of the historicists in general and Schmoller in particular. One could not therefore just connect ethical facts and economic facts; Durkheim maintained that it was also necessary to show that they were of the same nature, as had Wagner and Schmoller (1887: 272). And that is the principal merit of Wagner and Schmoller: conceiving society as a real entity and studying economic functions as social functions. The second merit that Durkheim saw in them related to method: by taking account of history and accepting a degree of relativism, these writers were studying man himself, and not a logical man, the pernicious abstraction upon which the constructs of orthodox economists are based. Durkheim therefore put his finger on the essential difference between orthodox economists and professorial socialists: the place given to reform. Without rejecting the ideas of the reformers,[7] he exposed two difficulties in their ideas: first, they had constructed a conception of the plasticity of economic facts which erred in thinking this to be more developed than it really was; and secondly, they placed too much weight on deliberate action by the legislator in the transformation of social facts (1887: 280–82). This is where Schäffle comes in; but Durkheim presents him both as if he lacked these faults and was at the same time under their influence, in particular when Schäffle ascribes too great an importance to knowledge (1887: 284). Finally, Durkheim emphasised the merits of Hermann Post—the only writer to devote himself to the study of "details", that is, the study of institutions such as the law and the family—from which he derives a new general criticism: "The great defect of all the works which we have analysed up to now is their extreme generality" (1887: 337). And so, even in this article, written at the very moment that Durkheim's understanding of the presence and role of German economists in the field of social science was maturing, a fine balance was struck.

Schäffle has an overwhelming presence in Durkheim's references to political economy during the period 1885–90. This cannot be explained by any adherence on the part of Durkheim to Schäffle's principles, since

---

[7] Durkheim is close to the viewpoint of the German economists. Schmoller's book (1900), which Durkheim read, highlights many similarities between the two writers—even if, of course, one cannot conclude from this that it was *only* in Schmoller that Durkheim found these ideas.

Durkheim criticises him in the same terms as he criticises Schmoller or Wagner. The primacy lent to Schäffle is instead explained by the fact that, when Schäffle was heavily criticised by Leroy-Beaulieu (1884) and Arthur Raffalovitch (1885) Durkheim defended him in the pages of the *Revue d'économie politique*—a journal established in opposition to the orthodox liberal school.[8] Indirectly this critique bore on him too, since he had drawn from the work of Schäffle in his opposition to orthodox economists; but above all Durkheim felt the need to disengage himself from a critique argued in terms of "collectivism" or of "authoritarian socialism". It was wrong, he wrote, to take a minor work like the *Quintessence of Socialism* (Schäffle 1874) as the last word of an author, for his real doctrine was to be found elsewhere. Here Durkheim distinguished a political question (the opposition between socialism and individualism) from a scientific question: the "hypothetical and objective" study of socialism and, above all, how "collective activity" could combat "the dispersive tendencies that engendered the practice of individualism" (Durkheim 1888b: 378–79). By defending Schäffle in this way he therefore defended *the formulation of his own intellectual project* as it had developed during the years 1881–83 (Filloux 1977: 14–15) and was subsequently reworked for his thesis. This is apparent in the way that he formulates the central question of the thesis:

> As for the question which was the origin of this work—it is that of the relations of the individual personality to social solidarity. Why is it that the individual, while becoming more autonomous, depends ever more closely upon society? How can he be at once more individual and more solidary? (1893/1984: xxx [trans. revised KT])[9]

This defence did not mean Durkheim was uncritical of Schäffle. In the same year that he called Schäffle's *Bau und Leben des socialen Körpers* a

---

[8] Founded by Charles Gide, the *Revue d'économie politique* opened its pages to German economists and published several translations of articles by Lujo Brentano, Bücher and Schmoller. Gide tended to have a benevolent attitude toward Durkheim and the Durkheimians; moreover, Gide was a byword in the cooperative cause, and in this he was at one with the political ideas of eminent Durkheimians such as Mauss and Simiand (Pénin 1998; Mauss 1920b).

[9] Mauss made some valuable comments that help us understand the way in which Schäffle influenced Durkheim's thinking while he was formulating his thesis: "Durkheim devoted himself to study of the social question from the time that he was at the *Ecole normale*. To begin with, he conceived this in a quite abstract and philosophical way, as the 'relations of individualism and socialism'. In 1883 he defined this more exactly: the relations of the individual and society were to be his subject. From this point he progressively developed his thinking and his analysis of facts, from the first outline of the *Division du travail social* (1884) and its first draft (1886), until he saw that the solution to the problem belonged to a new science: sociology" (Mauss 1928: 504–5).

"genuine treatise of positive sociology" (1888a: 98), he reproved Schäffle for lending clear ideas too great an importance, for his emphasis upon logical developments in social life, for his doctrinal eclecticism and, finally, for a lack of rigour in observation. Wagner also disappeared relatively quickly from the Durkheimian corpus: both Wagner's methodological orientation[10] and his political conservatism explain Durkheim's low level of interest in his writing. Bücher cropped up rather later in Durkheim's references, but as we have already seen, Bücher never became a prominent point of reference for Durkheim; his attention was caught by Bücher's classificatory economic schema, even if the theoretical framework was somewhat indeterminate (Durkheim & Fauconnet 1903: 157). Durkheim credited Schmoller's *Grundriss der allgemeinen Volkswirtschaftslehre Bd. I*, published in 1900, with the presentation of "a complete sociology from the economic point of view" (ibid.: 158–59). But Durkheim could not accept Schmoller's argument that the scientific community should devote one or even two generations of research to descriptive empirical work (Schmoller 1883: 144, 148; 1894b: 137). In his *Rules of Sociological Method*, Durkheim questioned why it was so necessary to concentrate on monographic studies of selected societies and only afterwards compare them and seek to make some generalisations (1982: 109–10) If this approach were taken seriously, it would "defer the study of sociology until [an] indefinitely distant time" (1982: 110), when historical research had been completed. This perspective, which Schmoller had defended against Menger, was rejected by Durkheim:

> But in reality the circumspection is only scientific in appearance. It is untrue that science can formulate laws only after having reviewed all the facts they encompass, or arrive at categories only after having described, in their totality, the individuals that they include. The true experimental method tends rather to substitute for common facts, which only give rise to proofs when they are very numerous and which consequently allow conclusions which are always suspect, *decisive* or *crucial* facts, as Bacon said, which by themselves and regardless of their number, have scientific value and interest. (1894/1982: 110)

---

[10] Wagner wrote in 1892: "If the deductions that one makes from the prime motivating factor [personal economic advantage] are correct, and taking exact account of the three hypotheses [the isolated abstraction of a single motivation, recognition of one's interest and of the possibility of its realisation], the results produced by the method together with these three hypotheses are *entirely exact*. The deductive method is therefore the only one which can be called exact in political economy. . . . The political economy that develops upon this basis itself becomes an exact science which is *rigorously theoretical wherever deduction is employed*, and can with good reason be compared with pure mechanics, or to mathematical physics" (1892 I: 251). As we shall see, Durkheim rejected this principle.

To go beyond this ineradicable character of the real, it is necessary to create a limited number of social types, and so provide oneself with the means to construct *series* of facts that would allow the inference of one explanation of a social fact from other social facts. This criticism was extended in chapter 6 of *Rules*, where Durkheim explained how proof might be "administered" thanks to the method of concomitant variations:

> As soon as we have proved that in a certain number of cases two phenomena vary with each other, we may be certain that we are confronted with a law. Since there is no need that they be plentiful the documents can be selected, and what is more, studied closely by the sociologist who makes use of them. (1894/1982: 153 [trans. revised KT])

ECONOMIC ACTIVITY AS SOCIAL FACT AND THE CRITIQUE OF POLITICAL ECONOMY

When Durkheim addresses "economists" in a broad and undifferentiated manner, he does so in criticism of their science; most of his formulations lend emphasis to the fact that it is not for him a matter of this or that particular issue in economic theory but rather of its methodological foundation.

From 1886 onwards Durkheim was critical of the reductive perspective of political economy. This critique was directed to one particular feature of political economy: political economy, mistakenly, sought to achieve the status of an independent science by separating itself off from moral and social perspectives. This faulty approach is related to the education and training of economists, who, as lawyers, businessmen or public officials, were unfamiliar with biological and psychological knowledge and so lacked the kind of scientific training required to create an economics in the mould of other natural sciences (1888a: 85–86; 1900b: 34). Accordingly, Durkheim placed emphasis upon the "great economic error" (1886a: 208) of "reducing society to no more than the simple juxtaposition of individuals", so that "man and society as conceived by economists are pure imaginary entities without any correspondence to the real [*les choses*]" (ibid.: 212). This conception prevented economists from properly defining their object and led them to overlook the role, importance and conditions of existence of social solidarity. Hence the problem presented by the status of abstraction in the social sciences and in political economy.

To avoid having to deal with facts that were too complex, economists isolated economic facts from other facts; they isolated the economic activity of a "logical man" from the entirety of actions performed by a "real man" immersed in society (1887: 279). Durkheim did not question the procedure of abstraction itself, which he thought legitimate (ibid.: 274; 1886a: 212) and which he defended several times during his career;[11] but he objected to the way that economists made use of it:

> To abstract is to cut out of reality one part which one isolates: it does not involve the creation of an entire rational being. But man and society as conceived by economists are pure imaginary entities, without any correspondence to the real [*les choses*]. (1886a: 212)

Durkheim contrasted two kinds of abstraction: that which is a legitimate instrument for scientific work and which isolates one part of reality so that it may be studied according to the principles of experimental science; and that which, on the pretext of isolating a part of reality, substitutes for that reality ideas that one is seeking to render coherent. He rejected this latter procedure, since it did not deal with a problem but simply substituted ideas for reality.

> Whether one likes it or not, whether it is a good thing or a bad thing, societies exist. Economic activity takes place within constituted societies. Logic is powerless if confronted with a fact that complicates a problem, but which cannot be excluded by abstraction. (ibid.: 208)[12]

In 1888 Durkheim clarified his critique by emphasising that *homo œconomicus* is the outcome of a dual process of abstraction:

> To simplify things economists have artificially impoverished matters. Not only do they abstract from all circumstance of time, place, and country in imagining the abstract type of man in general, but in this ideal type itself they have neglected everything that does not relate to a life that is strictly individual, so that this abstraction from an abstraction leaves them nothing more than the cheerless image of a purely selfish self. (1888a: 85)

Economists have therefore denatured their contribution to the creation of the social sciences—the conception of an economic law as a natural law—as a consequence of this process of faulty abstraction:

> Economic laws, and more generally, social laws, are not therefore very general facts that the scientist derives inductively from observation of

---

[11] This can be seen in the conclusions to the *Elementary Forms* (1912/1995: 424–25, 443), as well as in his course on pragmatism (1913–14: 80–81), where he takes a firm stand against what he considered the vague arguments of American pragmatists and of Henri Bergson, who overestimate notions of movement and flux.

[12] Albert Hirschman (1984) raised this idea of greater complexity to the status of a research programme.

societies, but instead logical consequences that he deduces from the definition of an individual. The economist does not say: things happen in the way established by experience; but instead: they have to happen like this because it would be absurd if it happened in any other way. The word *natural* has therefore to be replaced by the word *rational*. (ibid.)

Experimental science rests upon a work of abstraction that permits the scientific construction of the social fact, bracketing-out common sense and necessitating the consideration of all the facts that enter into the framework so constructed. This phase of rupture is quite central for Durkheim, as it is in the epistemology of Gaston Bachelard and Pierre Bourdieu. It facilitates the initiation of a genuine scientific procedure constraining the scientist in his interrogation of social life that is, according to the *Rules*, external to him—like an object in the natural world for the scientist working in the physical sciences. In later texts Durkheim explains that the concept is the means of communication between individuals and of the cumulative nature of knowledge (1912/1995: 491). The concept is rooted in a way of thinking, as a collective phenomenon; in this respect it is filled with reality and has an impact upon the actions of individuals through the intermediary of representations that it conveys and which are transmitted through education. Thus Durkheim rejects the abstraction put forward by economists on the grounds that it does not involve a break with common sense or, more exactly, dresses up this renunciation as an abstract figure that is both illusory and deceptive. *Homo œconomicus* can rightly lay claim to abstraction, and it will be seen that, much later, the Durkheimians will not ignore its virtues; but what this abstraction holds out is the possibility of remaining at the level of a rationalisation of common sense. According to Durkheim, this is at work from the moment that the economist, starting from this abstraction, proceeds through a process of introspection to deduce from the assumed behaviour of the *homo œconomicus* what it will be useful to do, deducing then from this a complete rational understanding by setting these assumptions in logical order. In the closing parts of his course on pedagogy, where he was not directly considering political economy, Durkheim did acknowledge that this abstraction process had some merit, in that it had furthered the role of rationalism in the European intellectual world mediated by theoretical individualism:

That in particular is where the abstract human individualism of eighteenth century writers comes from, the atomistic conception of society, their disregard for history. Does that mean that this error is not offset in any way? No, of course not. The very simplicity of the idea almost necessarily led to rationalism, and the power of reason is itself a power. (1904–5: 316)

Durkheim never repudiated scientific rationalism; proof of this can be found in the course on pragmatism, which was conceived as a warning of the dangers that this philosophical trend held for the social sciences (1913–14: 45–53, chs. 16–18). This remains unaltered by the fact that he found the rationalism of Galileo, Descartes, Leibniz and Newton wanting, scientifically superseded. This classical rationalism sought to reduce everything to simple elements, a procedure no longer fitting to complex biological and social facts, where such a reduction did not simplify but instead destroyed the fact to be explained (life or the social):

> This supreme rationalism [of the seventeenth century], this rationalism that rested only upon an illusion—the illusion that complexity is only superficial appearance—this rationalism is only the inferior form of rationalism. Reason has to acquire strength sufficient for it not to doubt itself, while being aware that matters are complex, and this complexity is real. (1904–5: 317)

The second chapter of the *Rules* opposed ideological analysis to science, arguing especially that science has to divest itself of common-sense notions that arise in social life through the need for action. This break had to be made because science (unlike the arts) had failed to respond to needs arising from immediate practice, and because science (unlike ideological analysis) did not establish itself by adopting prenotions, or the ideas we have formed about a social fact, but instead by taking the social fact itself as the object of study. However, ideological analysis played havoc in two particular branches of sociology: ethics and political economy.[13]

Durkheim takes issue with Mill's definition of political economy: the study of social facts primarily, or exclusively, in terms of the amassing of wealth. The existence of such a sphere of social activity is postulated rather than demonstrated, and as a consequence, "the subject matter of political economy so conceived is made up not of realities which may be precisely pointed to, but merely of possible ones, pure conceptions of the mind. They are facts which the economist *conceives* of as relating to the purpose under consideration, and facts as he conceives them" (1894/1982: 67; 1895–96: 52; 1909a: 158). Durkheim is certainly a little hasty here, for Mill constructs the economic fact through the intermediation of *homo œconomicus* and a generalised notion of wealth. But there is something else behind this rather misplaced criticism. Taking as his example the theory of value, Durkheim maintains that economists fail to adhere to the procedural sequences that he advocates: definition, observation, classifi-

---

[13] The same argumentative structure is set to work in the critique of pragmatism, a stream of thought that Durkheim criticised for its non-empirical, hypothetical character and its logical utilitarianism (1913–14: 139–51).

cation, explanation and then the formulation of laws that generalise the results. Instead of that, he argues, for definition and observation of economic facts the economist simply engages in introspection, coupled with a few facts selected for illustrative purposes. Consequently, scientific procedure as understood by Durkheim is largely absent from the economist's practice, while art—by which is here meant the normative character of reflection—is preponderant. Durkheim then takes up the law of supply and demand, a principle that is never established inductively, which is never subjected to comparative methods that might demonstrate that things actually happen in this way:

> All that could be done, and has been done, has been to demonstrate by dialectical argument that individuals should act in this way if they perceive what is in their best interest; any other course of action would be harmful to them, and if they followed it would indeed constitute an error of logic. . . . But this entirely logical necessity in no way resembles the one that the true laws of nature reveal. These express the relationships whereby facts are linked together in reality, and not the way in which it would be good for them to be linked. (1894/1982: 68–69; see also 1900b: 34; Durkheim & Fauconnet 1903: 125)

These criticisms are important and, for the most part, well directed, but they are in need of some qualification, since the critique of Mill leaves a great deal to be desired (Petit 1995b: 81–87). Firstly, he accuses Mill of failing to define the precise object of political economy, although he then goes on to employ a definition which is imprecise for reasons very close to those of Mill.[14] Secondly, it is erroneous to accuse Mill of thinking that preliminary definitions or basic principles come first in the order of investigation, as they certainly do in the order of exposition. Mill was aware of this difficulty. Presenting his essay on the definition of political economy, he made clear that first principles in truth come last (in the order of discovery), and that "what are called first principles, are, in truth, *last principles*. . . . Though presented as if all other truths were to be deduced from them, they are the truths which are last arrived at" (1844: 311).

The method that Durkheim sets to work is *not* a method of this kind, for what he calls his experimental method is coupled with the construction

[14] In the second lecture of the course on socialism, he apologises for not having defined what an economic object or function might be. This can be attributed, he says, to the economists, from whom he had taken their fundamental concept just as he had found it. Does this matter? According to his response, it does not seem to: "There is no great difficulty with this since if we have a rough idea of the actual limits of the economic domain one has a general understanding of the nature of the essential objects included, and that is enough for us for the time being" (1895–96: 52). Mill says much the same thing in his introduction to the *Principles of Political Economy*.

of the object of study, of the classes within which they are located and, finally, of a small but carefully selected number of experiences. Thus, in *Suicide*, he begins with a definition of how he conceives suicide before, faced with some methodological difficulties that need not detain us here (Gane 1988: 21ff.), explaining that he is reversing his usual method: he deduces the types of suicide from his theory of socialisation. The classification and definition of facts is not the result of inductive elaboration but depends upon a series of abstractions, just as it does for economists (Steiner 1994; Cherkaoui 1998).

His reflections on method involve a second orientation—what we call an informal critique—raising the question of the social nature of economic facts. Are economic facts accountable to the terms of the definition of the social supplied by *Rules of Sociological Method*—ways of acting, thinking, and feeling external to individual consciousness that are imposed upon individuals? Durkheim does not think it possible to exclude economic facts from the domain of social facts (Durkheim & Fauconnet 1903: 130) or to neglect the contribution of political economy to social science, that is, to the understanding of modern society; he rejects Simmel's approach precisely on this point because of the mistakes made by Simmel when dealing with economic theory in his *Philosophy of Money* (1900b: 17). That being so, the definition of the social cannot fail to confront particular problems when economic facts are involved. The constraint at work in economic matters—as with language—is only indirect (1982: 57, 65–66); economic facts have a much greater plasticity than social facts, such as legal or moral laws. The difficulty raised by economic facts relates to their lesser degree of social crystallisation, their lesser resistance to transformation and change (1900: 29). This is not without methodological consequence, since Durkheim suggests two ways in which social facts might be identified: either by their general social character (power of coercion, evidenced by the sanctions employed where a rule is not respected), or by their diffusion within the group. This second possibility, far easier to put to work, is associated explicitly with the economic fact (1894/1982: 69–70).

Much later, Durkheim suggested a way of getting around the difficulty by establishing a relation between the economic and opinion. He argued during a session of the Society for Political Economy that the difference between the facts treated by sociology and those treated by political economy amounted to the former being for the most part objects of opinion, since religious, moral and legal sociology and so forth dealt in ideas and representations: "wealth, which was the object of political economy, consists of things which are apparently essentially objective and seemingly independent of opinion" (1894/1982: 230; see also 1906: 82). Is it impossible to conceive of a sociological approach to economics? No, said

Durkheim, for economic facts were themselves dependent upon opinion; the value of goods depended upon opinion, as is the case with Islamic religion and pork, or with the minimum wage, or again in the diffusion of particular forms of production (1894/1982: 231).

Durkheim thus envisaged the economic fact in the same terms as the social fact, in that it could be invested with an institutional form, the crystallisation of opinion, and assume a moral character: the two ideas being closely related. The first characteristic found its origin in a methodological principle according to which the study of the social had to be centred upon that which was most heavily freighted, on that which was more permanent in social life—crystallised social facts as against the varying trends of social life (1894/1982: 45). Fauconnet and Mauss suggested that these crystallised social facts be called institutions (1901: 150), and Durkheim immediately incorporated this into his preface to the second edition of *Rules* (1901b/1982: 45), and then into his 1909 definition of economic sociology in terms of economic institutions:

> Finally, there are the economic institutions: institutions relating to the production of wealth (serfdom, tenant farming, corporate organization, production in factories, in mills, at home, and so on), institutions relating to exchange (commercial organization, markets, stock exchanges, and so on), institutions relating to distribution (rent, interest, salaries, and so on). They form the subject matter of *economic sociology*. (1909a: 150)

The second characteristic is explained by Durkheim's general way of thinking, for the term "social" was for him identified with morals. That is why, for instance, he approached the division of labour as follows: "In this case, indeed, the economic services that it can render are insignificant compared with the moral effect that it produces, and its true function is to create between two or more people a feeling of solidarity" (1893/1984: 17). This moral characteristic in the definition of the economic requires emphasis, since for Durkheim the useful and the moral are very clearly separate and distinct: if economic activity is only considered from the perspective of utility, from that of the increase of production, it lacks all moral content, it is part of the domain of ethical indifference (ibid.: 21). Durkheim also related the economic fact to the social fact through social solidarity, or the theory of socialisation.

The theory of socialisation distinguishes social integration from social regulation. The first involves the manner in which a social group draws in an individual; this process works through frequent interaction among members of the group, through the existence of similar passions within the group, and ultimately through the pursuit of common ends (Besnard 1987: 99). The second involves a different process in that it is a matter

TABLE 1.2
The Socialisation Process according to Durkheim

	Integration	Regulation
Morphology	Interaction between agents	Social hierarchy
Social physiology	Uniformisation of passions	Moderation of passions
Representations	Common ends	Justice and legitimacy of the hierarchy

not simply of integrating individuals but also of harmonising the behaviour of one with respect to the others. Regulation works through the existence of a social hierarchy, through passions socially fitted to one's place within this hierarchy and ultimately through the justice and legitimacy of this hierarchy. This theory of socialisation is summarised in table 1.2.[15]

We can now examine how the division of labour intervenes in the process of socialisation and how Durkheim deals sociologically with the economic fact. The chapter in *Division of Labour* where Durkheim distinguishes organic solidarity from Spencer's contractual solidarity is critical in this respect.[16] According to Durkheim, Spencer's thesis is that industrial society is based upon the relation of exchange between individuals, a relationship that takes the form of a contract:

---

[15] We reject the arguments put forward by those who, following Talcott Parsons (1949, 1959), erased the difference between integration and regulation; here we follow those, like Besnard (1987), who have drawn attention to the importance of these two processes in Durkheim's theory. We will have occasion to show below that, for economic sociology, this distinction is *analytically indispensable*. In the table we distinguish between three levels for the application of the two processes of socialisation and follow Durkheim's own analytical hierarchy. The primacy (at least at the methodological level) of morphological facts—the modes of social being—leaves no doubt on this in Durkheim, and we link to this interactions between agents and the hierarchy in which they are placed. Coming then to the modes of social conduct or physiological facts, socialization involves on the one hand rendering passions uniform and on the other the moderation of these passions according to the place occupied in the hierarchy. As far as the representation of agents is concerned, this involves their relation to common ends and to justice. The importance lent by Durkheim to justice, and to the sentiment of justice, is constant throughout his work; it also represents a focal point in Durkheim's theory: "Generally, we consider that the sociologist has not completely discharged his task if he has not penetrated the deepest recesses within the individual before linking the institutions with which he is dealing to their psychological conditions. In truth, man is for us less a point of departure than a point of arrival" (1909b: 184–85).

[16] This opposition to Spencer had not escaped early commentators, and mostly they found it unconvincing (Puynode 1893).

This social solidarity would then be nothing more than the spontaneous agreement between individual interests, an agreement of which
contracts are the natural expression. The typical social relation would
be the economic, stripped of all regulation and resulting from the entirely free initiative of the parties involved. In short, society would be
no more than the establishment of relationships between individuals
exchanging the products of their labour, without any social action,
properly speaking, intervening to regulate this exchange. (1893/1984:
151–52 [trans. revised KT])

Durkheim shows that the market does little to secure socialisation. But
since so much of Durkheim's work is contemporary with that of Walras,
a brief comparison of these two classical writers (who most certainly ignored each other)[17] sheds light on the differences in thinking of the sociologist and the economist at this time. Both of them demonstrated a degree of perseverance in constituting their chosen domain as a science, and,
despite profound differences, there was a remarkable similarity in the
definition of facts that both espoused. The Walrasian definition of price
was very close methodologically to the Durkheimian social fact:

Wheat costs 24 francs a hectolitre. Let us note to begin with that this
fact has the character of a natural fact. This value of wheat in money,
or this price of wheat, is the outcome neither of the will of the pur-
chaser, nor of the will of the seller, nor of any agreement between them.
(Walras 1900: §28)

This natural quality of the social fact "price", its quality of being external
to consciousness yet all the same a constraint, does not enter into the
Durkheimian conception of market socialisation—for two reasons. Firstly,
there is no place in Durkheim for the idea that the deliberate behaviour
of agents, through aggregation, leads to a social result that is imposed on
these agents themselves. Rejecting explanations that he called "finalist"
because of the way they made use of the motivations of ends pursued by
actors, Durkheim blinded himself to understanding that individuals acting according to an economic end (maximising the utility of an initial
endowment by offering a certain quantity of goods at a certain price)
could be subject to the emergent effects of the system formed by their actions. Secondly, if prices give information on relative scarcities but contribute nothing to a process of socialisation, we are led to conclude that
Durkheim would no doubt apply to the Walrasian market what he also

---

[17] As far as Walras was concerned, Franklin H. Giddings was the leading sociologist
(Walras 1990: 5), while Durkheim and the Durkheimians had little time for Giddings's
Principles of Sociology (*AS* I 1: 144–52).

said about the rules relating to real property (those which link objects to individuals):

> It is not a true solidarity, having its own existence and its special nature, but rather the negative side of every kind of solidarity. The first condition for an entity to become coherent is that its constituent parts should not clash discordantly. But this external accord does not bring about cohesion; on the contrary, it presumes it. Negative solidarity is possible only where there exists some other kind of positive solidarity, of which it is at once the resultant and the condition. (1893/1984: 75 [trans. revised KT])

Durkheim presents exchange in the following way:

> Sometimes the social relations that give rise to the division of labour are treated solely in terms of exchange, consequent upon a misrecognition of what exchange implies and what follows from it. In fact, exchange involves two beings whose mutual dependence results from their respective lack of completeness, and it does no more than translate this mutual dependence into an external relation. It is therefore only a superficial expression of an internal, and more profound, condition. Precisely because this condition remains constant, it entirely sustains a mechanism of images which function continuously in a manner that exchange does not. The image of the other who completes us becomes inseparable from our own, not only because of the frequency with which it is associated with our own, but above all because it is its natural complement. Thus it becomes an integral and permanent part of our consciousness, to such a degree that we can no longer do without it and seek by every means possible to increase its energy. That is why we enjoy the company of the other the image represents, since the physical presence of the object the image expresses, by making it a state of present perception, marks it out more clearly. (1893/1984: 22 [trans. revised KT])

Durkheim here considers the incompleteness of agents engaged in exchange for the satisfaction of their various needs to be superficial, even where this incompleteness is the material foundation of an economic interdependence obliging individuals to relate to one another. The more profound condition, in which the system of exchange is related to the division of labour, is constituted by a "mechanism of images"—by a set of representations, or opinions as he will later say—characterised by a durability that exchange itself does not have and by the frequency with which these representations are refreshed. Later, Durkheim will place these images in the context of the scale that runs from simple sensations to concepts, arguing that unlike concepts that are separated off from those emotions tending to action, images "have a close connection with tendencies to action" (1913–14: 169). Whence, finally, comes the possibility at the socio-psychological level of solidarity among those parties to exchange, prompting the emergence of sympathy among them. In place of the economists' "weak tie" of commodity exchange conceived according to the logic of an anonymous market, Durkheim substitutes a "strong" tie—strong with regard to durability, frequency and emotional intensity—relating exchange to social representations.

Durkheim asks, Can one agree with Spencer when he considers commodity exchange stripped of all social regulation as the typical form of social relations?

> If this were so, one might reasonably doubt their stability. For if interest draws men together, it is never for more than some few moments. It can create only an external bond between them. . . . For where interest alone reigns, since nothing emerges to check the interplay of egoism, each ego finds itself in a state of war with every other, and any truce in this eternal antagonism would not be of long duration. Self-interest is the least constant thing in the world. Today, it unites me to you; tomorrow, it will make me your enemy. (1893/1984: 152 [trans. revised KT])

Durkheim concludes from the exacerbation of passions in the commodity relation that it is not possible for exchange to secure the stability and continuity required for social solidarity, because of the failure to respect the principles of social regulation.[18]

With a passage from Smith's *Wealth of Nations* in mind (1776: 18–19), Durkheim examines the nature of social relations in regard to the degree of development of the division of labour. A society in which the division of labour was barely developed could circulate goods by relying on interpersonal relations such as kinship, friendship, political domination or, more generally, benevolence. By contrast, in a society in which the division of labour was advanced the individual could not rely on personal relations to obtain what he needed, since the progress of specialisation would mean that he would have to relate to far more individuals than was sociologically possible. Impersonal exchange appeared as *an economy of social relations* adapted to the functioning of a society based on the division of labour.

---

[18] This is not specific to Durkheim; it can also be found in Max Weber when he deals with the foundations of the regularity of social activity: tradition, custom and interest. This last produces regularity and continuity in activity more stable that that based upon obligations or norms; while Weber sees here the foundation of political economy as a science, he plays down this type of regularity *when it is a matter of defining the social order*, since the order based on interest is less stable than that based on custom or that based on prestige (Weber 1922: pt. 1 ch. 1 §4.3).

Durkheim was not satisfied with this interpretation of exchange:

> Thus it is necessary for the allocation of both rights and obligations to
> be prescribed in advance, but this cannot be done according to a pre-
> conceived plan. There is nothing in the nature of things from which
> one can deduce that the obligations of either party should reach a par-
> ticular limit. Every decision of this kind can only result from compro-
> mise, midway between the rivalry of interests involved and their soli-
> darity. It is a position of equilibrium that can be found only after more
> or less laborious trial and error [après des tâtonnements]. It is, how-
> ever, quite evident that every time that we enter into some contrac-
> tual relation we can neither rerun this process of trial and error, nor
> restore this equilibrium at additional expense. (1893/1984: 160 [trans.
> revised KT])

What Smith thought of as a social economy of time cannot really be
considered as such so long as one has to negotiate, tâtonner,[19] constantly
to establish exchange contracts. It is necessary to institute social procedures, in the absence of which exchange, on account of prevailing conflicts of interest, will take up as much time as any other way of circulating
commodities. But such time is lacking, argued Durkheim:

> Most of our relationships with others are contractual. If it were nec-
> essary each time to start all over again, to repeat the negotiations
> necessary to establish clearly all the conditions of agreement for the
> present and the future, we would be paralysed. For all these reasons,
> if we were bound together only by the terms of our contracts as agreed,
> only a very precarious solidarity would result. (ibid.: 161 [trans. re-
> vised KT])

This explains the comment that is at the root of the sociological solution
put forward by Durkheim: "We cooperate because we have wished to do
so, but our voluntary cooperation creates for us duties that we did not
want" (ibid.: 161 [trans. revised KT]). Which leads to the well-known
statement:

> In sum then, the contract is not sufficient in itself, but is possible only
> thanks to the regulation of contracts, which is of social origin. (ibid.:
> 162 [trans. revised KT])

Durkheim extends his consideration of exchange into the problem of
justice:

---

[19] Note the use in the foregoing quotation of Walras's trademark conception of tâ-
tonnement, the iterative process by which parties to an exchange find their way to an agreed
price [KT].

The advent of the consensual contract, combined with the development of sentiments of human sympathy, leads minds to this idea: that the contract was only moral, that it could only be recognised and sanctioned by society on condition that it be *just*. But mark this: this principle was a *new principle*. (1898–1900: 231, my emphasis)

THE SOCIOLOGICAL APPROACH TO THE ECONOMY: SOCIAL JUSTICE

The question of justice is central in Durkheim's sociological approach to the economy, and it was this that brought together German economists, such as Gustav Schmoller, and French economists, like Charles Gide, who were open to reform (Grimmer-Solem & Romani 1998; Nau & Steiner 2002). He outlined his ideas through discussion of abnormal forms of the division of labour, then developed them when discussing anomie in modern society in his book on suicide. This highlighted the problem of social passions and their regulation through a legitimate hierarchy and socioeconomic ideals.

His argument was based upon "social value", on the collective representation by means of which the consequences of exchange are thought to be just or unjust.

> In any given society each object of exchange has, at any moment, a determinate value which we can call its social value. It represents the quantity of useful labour which it contains. By that must be understood, not the embodied labour that it might have cost, but the part of that effort capable of producing useful social effects, that is, effects which correspond to normal needs. Although this magnitude cannot be mathematically calculated, it is none the less real. It is very easy to perceive the principal conditions in relation to which it varies. They are, above all, the sum of efforts necessary to produce the object, the intensity of the needs which it satisfies, and finally the extent of the satisfaction it brings. Moreover, it is around this point that average value oscillates. It deviates from it only under the influence of abnormal factors, and, in that case, public consciousness generally has a more or less clear sense of this deviation. Public consciousness finds unjust every exchange where the price of the object bears no relation to the trouble it cost and the services that it renders. (1893/1984: 317 [trans. revised KT])[20]

[20] One can find this line of argument at several points in Durkheim's writings (1898–1900: 233–35, 239; 1897a: 275–76, 277–79); it later marked Halbwachs's economic logic when he examined the impact of worker representations on their purchasing behaviour (1912: 402ff.; 1909: 387–89, 393–94).

From the point of view of economic theory, this could definitely leave a rather mixed impression, as can be seen in a review by Saint-Marc published in the *Revue d'économie politique* (1893), where he mocked a definition of value accepted both by Bastiat and Pierre-Joseph Proudhon.[21] Durkheim defines economic justice by balancing agents' aspirations with their place in the social hierarchy on the one hand, matching the payments attached to these functions with the social value that the collective consciousness attributed to their contribution on the other. When the system of markets did not meet this dual equilibrium typical of organic conceptions of society—and there was no reason why it should do so given relative scarcities and the prices derived from the workings of supply and demand—Durkheim thought that abnormal forms of the division of labour arose.

Let us take the case of the relation between workers and capitalists in large-scale industry, about which Durkheim wrote: "For the division of labour to engender solidarity, it is thus not sufficient that each have his task; it is necessary that this task be fitting to him" (1893/1984: 311 [trans. revised KT]). The division of labour develops spontaneously in such a way as to allow the free deployment of the capacity of all, whereas the constrained division of labour begins at the point where rules are no longer adapted to custom and practice but rest on force. Under what conditions does this spontaneous development occur? This requires that equality has been established in the external conditions of exchange, which is, he writes, incompatible with the transfer of wealth through inheritance or with any asymmetry in the relation between parties to exchange; they must be able to freely select the most favourable time to complete a transaction. Given the necessity to feed himself and so forth, the worker has to sell to the capitalist his productive services without delay; he is in fact subject to a constraint not shared with the capitalist, who finds himself in a dominant position. A contract is only fair if the services exchanged have an equivalent social value; if the values are not capable of an equilibrium, this demonstrates that external force has been added to the balance:

> The necessary and sufficient condition for this equivalence to be the rule governing contracts is that the contracting parties be under externally equal conditions. Since the assessment of matters cannot be determined a priori, but arises from the exchange itself, for the labour of those individuals involved in the exchange to be properly assessed they must

---

[21] In the political economy of the era, it was usual to contrast two theories of value, one based upon labour and the other on utility or, in Bastiat's language, on services. In the latter part of the passage cited above from the *Division of Labour* the two conceptions are mingled through a reference both to services and to "trouble", or pain.

have no force other than that which comes from their social worth. In this way, the values of things exactly correspond to the services that they render and the trouble that they cost, for every other factor capable of making them vary is, by hypothesis, eliminated. (ibid.: 318 [trans. revised KT])

Let us now examine how the anomic division of labour relates to the unfolding of the "universal market". This theme recurs in works other than the *Division of Labour* (1898–1900: 55, 234; 1895: 105, 244–45; 1897a: 283–85); it is close to one initially developed by Sismondi and subsequently taken up as a theory of crisis by liberal economists, amongst others. This unsettling phenomenon is attributed to the existence of a market whose extent exceeds the capacity of an entrepreneur to have first-hand knowledge of it; and in the absence of such direct knowledge, the entrepreneur produces not in terms of directly ascertained needs but instead according to the quantity of capital that he can set to work (Sismondi 1826: 245–60). For Cauwès, to whom Durkheim is here very close,[22] lowering the rate of interest favours the growth of production and the development of speculation. But if the stock of capital does not grow quickly enough to satisfy the growth of production and consumption, then both prices and profits will rise, and the increase of the latter will feed the demand for credit. This is the period of confidence, of speculation, of irrational exuberance. Crisis will then follow from a check to consumption, from the inadequacy of the capital stock or from the instability of sales. Durkheim, for his part, thought that the specialisation of functions required social institutions that would coordinate these functions, but this continuity is caught out by the emergence of the universal market:

So long as the segmentary type of society is strongly marked, there are nearly as many economic markets as there are different segments. Consequently, each of them is very limited. Producers, being very close to consumers, can easily estimate the extent of needs to be satisfied. Equilibrium is therefore easily established and production regulates itself. By contrast, as the organised type of society develops, the fusion of different segments involves the fusion of the markets into one single market, and gradually involves almost all of society. This becomes more widespread, tending to become universal. . . . The result is that each industry produces for consumers who are dispersed over the length

---

[22] Cauwès had outlined his position in his *Précis* (1881 I: 606) without however making any reference to the question of a "world market". Durkheim knew this source since he cited from it in another context (1893/1984: 293 n. 10), and he considered Cauwès to be a representative of a new form of political economy (1886: 205).

and breadth of the country, or even over the entire world. Contact is then no longer sufficient. The producer can no longer take in the market at a glance, nor think of it as a whole. He can no longer understand its limits, since it is, so to speak, limitless. Accordingly, production becomes unbridled and unregulated. It can only trust to chance, and in the course of a process of trial and error [*tâtonnements*], it is inevitable that the mean and the proportionate will be exceeded, as much in one direction as in another. From all this come the crises which periodically disturb economic functions. (1893/1984: 304 [trans. revised KT])

One should not believe that Durkheim regretted the passing of a previous social order; the universal market is not an evil in itself (1898–1900: 234), but, all in all, the modern economy has abolished crises of food supply only to replace them with commercial and industrial crises quite as monstrous as their predecessors (ibid.: 55). Competition, and the fixing of relative prices, do not play the regulatory role that economists believe—commercial crises are the proof of it—failing to prevent malfunctioning and the collapse of equilibrium (1893/1984: 303).

The rapid changes that had provoked the growth of the division of labour rendered the older process of socialisation no longer adequate. This topic then took up a great part of Durkheim's thoughts in presenting his course on socialism, in his work on professional ethics and in his book on suicide, as well as in the preface to the second edition of *Division of Labour* in 1902. The immense research programme that Durkheim had conceived with regard to forms of professional association highlights the manner in which his economic sociology was developed.

Durkheim proposed that a new social institution be created, a professional group (*corporation de métier*), in which he saw the means of resolving two problems in the socialisation process. First of all, a better way of integrating individuals was needed: the creation of a new social group which would cover working life and would provide the greater degree of cohesion needed by rendering passions more uniform. Secondly, since each would know to what he was entitled, passions would be moderated. Finally, the creation of professional groups would provide a principle of justice (1902a/1984: xxxii; 1897a/2006: 277, 440; 1898–1900: 106, 154, 237–38). In this reform proposal Durkheim made the institution a major element in his thinking about the economic social fact. The professional group would structure the activities of individuals in a particular domain while at the same time rendering them part of the constitutional cadre of democracy, since it would allow for the expression of political opinions and reengage the citizen with political life (1898–1900: 98–99, 129–30, 136–38). It would permit the institutionalisation of some aspects of economic facts, lending them regular form, stable over time, a normal social form. The search for what is "right" was at the heart of his thinking on social evaluation,[23] both in the mode of exchange relations between capital and labour[24] and in the changes that he proposed to economic organisation.[25]

More than the arguments used in 1908 at the meeting of the Society for Political Economy, the idea of "social value" shows how the economic fact is a social fact:

> Economists protest in vain: it will always scandalise public sentiment that an individual can make use, in absolutely superfluous consumption, of an amount of wealth that is too great, and it seems that this intolerance relents only in times of moral disturbance. There is therefore a genuine system of regulation that, while not always taking legal form, unceasingly sets with relative precision the maximum of comfort which each class of society can legitimately seek to attain. But a scale set up in this way is in no way immutable. It changes as collective income rises or falls, and with changes occurring in the moral ideas of society. (Durkheim 1897a/2006: 276)

On this point Durkheim found himself at one with Tarde. These two authors, whose differences are well known, agreed on the importance to be given to the introduction of justice when it came to the renewal of political economy through economic sociology. Tarde attached great importance to the notion of the just price and its influence on the prevailing price:

[23] "Insofar as appetites are not automatically contained by physiological mechanisms, they can only be halted by a limit that they recognise as *just*. Men will not consent to restrain their desires if they believe they can exceed the restraint set upon them. Only this *law of justice* can effect this, they do not know how to impose it upon themselves for the reasons stated. They therefore have to accept an authority that they respect and to which they spontaneously assent. Only society is in a position to play this moderating role, whether directly as a whole, or through the intermediary of one of its organs" (1897a/2006: 275, my emphasis).

[24] Durkheim wrote in the *Division of Labour*, with regard to the constrained division of labour: "But this constraint, which prevents us from satisfying freely our unchecked desires should not be confused with that which deprives us of the means of obtaining *the just remuneration for our labour*. . . . In short, for the obligatory force of a contract to be complete, it is not sufficient that it be the object of an expressed assent. It must also be *fair*, and it is not fair by the mere fact that it has been agreed upon verbally," (1893/1984: 318 [trans. revised KT], my emphasis).

[25] "That does not mean, however, that the professional group is a sort of panacea for everything. The crisis through which we are passing is not rooted in a single and unique cause. To put an end to it, it is not sufficient to regulate it where necessary; more, it is necessary that regulation be what it must be, that is to say, *just*" (1893/1984: lv [trans. revised KT], my emphasis).

And how can the impact of the idea be denied, by which each era, or each country, forms its own idea of justice with regard to prices? To what kind of consumption is morality entirely alien, if by morality one understands the higher and profound rule of conduct guided by the convictions and major passions that lead life? And, if one abstracts from these convictions and dominating passions which, spoken or unspoken, are the prime social and individual forces, what does political economy explain at all? (Tarde 1902 II: 37)

The principal problem posed by this theory of social evaluation is not so much its static quality, as Filloux believes (1977: 208), since Durkheim recognises the shifting nature of this evaluation; nor is it the overdetermination of commodity exchange such that it is entirely subsumed by the idea of the free market (Beckert 1997).[26] The difficulty is rather that Durkheim never sought to establish with any precision how this scale of value was formed, how it worked and how it evolved (1898–1900: 233).

From these reflections on exchange, the division of labour, and justice, it appears that the socialisation process ran into difficulties in the domain of economic life. On all evidence, the division of labour and the multiplication of exchange associated with it led to frequent interactions between individuals, so the emergence of acute problems at this level of social integration are not to be expected. It is the same for the creation of uniformity in the passions, brought about through the fixing of the rates of exchange between commodities and through freedom of contract. In general, peaceable exchange resulting from the opposition of interests (the buyer wants to give less, the seller wants to gain more) leads to a price which harmonises passions, providing that the exchange is not constrained in any way. Difficulties are encountered instead with the common ends associated with the division of labour. Durkheim is not explicit on this point: should one understand him to deny to the growth of production the status of a common aim, once this is no longer seen to be a cause of the division of labour? Should the common end be sought in the ideal of the modern man, where each has to strive to achieve a true specialisation as a means of realising his social being? Or again, would the common end be sought in a greater harmony of the different parties making up economic life, as, for example, in the relations between capital and labour?

---

[26] As with the scholastic theory of the "just price" (Lapidus 1992), social evaluation is a moral norm that permits one to assess the *difference* between the prevailing market price and the price which society (collective conscience) or a person representing it (a judge, local administration, etc.) considers to be just. Far from being a theory of price, social evaluation is a sociological appreciation of the results advanced by economic theory as an explanation or justification of "market justice", or of commutative justice.

In the following chapter we will see how much importance Durkheim gave to this problem of an ideal, but also how this major topic led him off into a different research programme.

It is the regulation process that raises the greatest difficulties. The existence of a hierarchy in the economic world was not a matter for doubt, and Durkheim elegantly took its measure in his work on "social value". But, as has been seen, Durkheim had doubts about the manner in which this hierarchy coincided with the principle of social justice that he espoused. In addition to this, it is plain that the two other levels of the regulation process went to the heart of the difficulties. Passions could not be moderated because of the social opacity arising from the development of the universal market, the conflicts which arose with the development of large-scale industry, and the inequalities reproduced by the process of inheritance.[27] More seriously, the question of economic justice was a problem in what Durkheim called the constrained division of labour and, on a larger scale, in the commercial and industrial world (1898–1900; 1897). Hence, the first conclusion from Durkheim's thinking here is that there exists, within modern society, a profound impairment, a defect in social regulation.

To sum up, with these arguments we can see a quite original perspective taking shape in Durkheimian economic sociology: the idea is to draw upon the *social representations* that form "social value" to show how economic facts are conditioned by "ways of doing, thinking and feeling" —in other words, by the ways in which conceptions of the economic world are formed and shaped. Durkheim lent an organisational foundation to these representations by relating them through professional groups to new forms of the division of labour. In taking account of these social dimensions and of economic behaviour at a precise historical moment in European societies, Durkheim is searching for a way of overcoming the abstraction and imperfection of political economy. It is for this reason that he develops towards a rationalism capable of dealing with the real complexity of the social, a rationalism that upholds the ideal of clarity and precision first developed by the simple rationalism of the seventeenth century.

---

[27] This objection to inheritance was first raised by the Saint-Simonians and by Jeremy Bentham; Mill, placed at the centre of these cross-currents, took up this objection in his large book on political economy, albeit in attenuated form (1848 I: 215–25). He declared himself opposed to this form of transmission of property, his opposition bearing upon both property and the family, two pillars of liberal society; and in this he was joined by liberal economists throughout the nineteenth century (Garnier 1880: 231–34, 695–96; Baudrillart 1883: 249–72; Leroy-Beaulieu 1896: 590–600), as well as by those who were critical of liberal economists (Cauwès 1881 II: 204–8).

The Reactions of Economists

It was Durkheim's first book that had the greatest impact on economists.[28] The reviews were unanimous in praising the forceful thought of the author and the great interest of the work. This was no longer the case when *Rules* was published. Saint-Marc compared *Division of Labour* with the articles published on the subject by Schmoller, which he thought better documented historically. Schmoller, for his part, regretted that Durkheim had barely integrated social and economic experience and reproved him for his failure to pursue the question of the division of labour according to social classes, as he himself had done. All reviewers latched on to fact that Durkheim wanted to deal with ethics and the manner in which the division of labour related to ethics (and Puynode considered that the book was as important as Molinari's *De la morale économique*). All thought that Durkheim had not written as an economist, which was then said to be a pity since he consequently made a number of important mistakes of substance. Criticism was focussed on the final part of the *Division of Labour*, dealing with abnormal forms of the division of labour and the proposed solution to this offered by professional groups. Schmoller expressed his reservations about the last section of the book since he thought that here scientific objectivity had been abandoned. Saint-Marc objected to the idea of abolishing inheritance since he thought that this endangered individual property, and, as has been seen above, he castigated Durkheim's theory of social evaluation that ran together two different conceptions of the theory of value. Puynode condemned all the economic sections of the book: there could be no question of regulating the relationship of capital and labour since, according to Puynode, these relations were just if freely established in the market. Such objections are, of course, unsurprising. Free traders would never admit that the justice resulting from the market could be questioned; while Schmoller, sharing a position similar to that of Durkheim, raised criticism not of his argument but of the manner in which it was made. When it came to *Rules* the economists had greater reservations: Durkheim's method struck them as rigid and abstract, and, though no one said so directly, it is apparent that they all found it very difficult to swallow what Tarde had called Durkheim's "scholastic realism" (Tarde 1893: 62).

Henceforth the debate between Durkheim and liberal economists allied with the *Journal des Economistes* and the Society for Political Economy would take a different turn. The sense of distance that Durkheim

---

[28] Taking account of the reactions of economists to Durkheim's writings must not be allowed to obscure the fact that the work of other sociologists was of greater interest to them: Spencer and Tarde had a far greater impact.

noted in his letter to Bouglé was returned in kind by a rejection no less complete on the part of liberal economists of the first Durkheimian programme for economic sociology. By contrast, the new generation of economists associated with the *Revue d'économie politique* were far more open to the arguments of Durkheim, since they could see their similarity with positions defended by Schmoller and Schäffle. This opening with respect to Durkheimian economic sociology was then implemented after 1918 when first Simiand, then Halbwachs, became members of the editorial committee of the *Revue*.

CHAPTER TWO

Politics, Economy and Religion

The relation between economy and religion in Durkheim's writings is something of a curiosity. During the period of his intellectual formation, and then in the work that led up to the writing of *Division of Labour*, Durkheim looked to economists for answers to his questions relating to social cohesion. But he progressively lost interest in political economy, to the point where he abandoned the economic sociology he had developed in his first writings. This reorientation is no minor issue in his intellectual itinerary; it is quite central to my argument.

Professional groups have an important place in Durkheim's thinking about modern economic institutions—in his 1893 dissertation, in the lectures on socialism (1895–96) that are so closely related to the question of economic regulation, in *Suicide* and also in the courses of lectures on the sociology of law and of customs that he gave in Bordeaux between 1896 and 1900, then repeated in Paris (Lukes 1973: 617–20). But in the new preface to the *Division of Labour*, he broke with his methodological approach to political and economic institutions. We need to evaluate the significance of this change. If professional groups had provided for the moralisation of economic life, regulating it by creating a social hierarchy, moderating passions and legitimating this hierarchy, one needs to ask exactly what the sociology of religion might offer a sociology of the economy that could not have been provided by a continuation of the initial programme of economic sociology.

My hypothesis is that the problem of the ideal leads Durkheim to shift the balance of his studies towards religion, and towards the social conditions for the formation and diffusion of knowledge and belief. But does this mean that he abandons an economic sociology? One might think so, but I will show that this would be misleading; for within *The Elementary Forms of Religious Life*, he formulates a second research programme, directed to the religious foundations of the economy.

The "Revelation" of 1895

> It was only in 1895 that I clearly understood the leading role played by religion in social life. It was in this year that, for the first time, I found a means to approach the study of

religion sociologically. This was a revelation to me. The 1895
lecture course represents a clear divide in the development
of my thought; all my past studies had to be reviewed and
revised so that they might be harmonised with these new
conceptions. (Letter to the editor of *Revue néo-scholastique*,
8 November 1907, in Durkheim 1975 I: 404)[1]

This passage from Durkheim's correspondence is one of the clearest statements that he made about his own sociological itinerary, and because it
appeared in a letter to the editor of a periodical, it became part of a polemic, while also being public in character.[2] The terminology of "revelation" can be related to the arguments of Thomas Kuhn, who described
such changes of scientific vision as analogous to an aesthetic or religious
"conversion", the different scientific paradigms involved being incom-
mensurable (1970: 117ff.). This explains why scientists, when describing
the moment of their paradigmatic discovery, make use of a language far
removed from rational explanation, as Durkheim did too (ibid.: 122–23).
Durkheim's terminology should not therefore be taken too literally; it is
"normal" in the sense used in the *Rules of Sociological Method*. His terminology should instead be related to a dual dimension of continuity and
change. On the one hand, as I will try to show at the end of this chapter,
and then in chapters 5 and 6, the thread linking Durkheim's initial interests to those which dominated his work after 1895 remained unbroken;
but on the other hand, the importance of this juncture should not be
played down, since the way in which it substantially redirected Durkheim's
research programme cannot be ignored. The preface to the second edition of *Division of Labour* provides a solid basis for assessing the reorientation in his research, a reorientation which is evident in the work that
he published soon afterwards (Durkheim 1902b; Durkheim & Mauss
1903).[3]

"Some Remarks on Professional Groups": this is the title that Durkheim
gave the new preface to the *Division of Labour*, outlining how he had

[1] The course to which he refers is that of 1894–95 on religion (Lukes 1973: 618), notes
for which have since been lost.

[2] Durkheim wrote to Mauss in December 1897: "Apart from its substantial interest,
L'année sociologique must have a definite orientation. Essentially, the sociological importance of the religious phenomenon is the outcome of all that I have done; and it has the
advantage of summarising our orientation substantively, more concretely than in the formulations I had previously employed" (1998: 91). While this public stance may be somewhat
dramatic, this letter to a very close colleague is clear evidence of Durkheim's reorientation.

[3] No doubt that explains his reticence when preparing the new edition of *Division of
Labour*: "Following a great deal of hesitation, I have decided to go ahead with a new pref-
ace and without any internal rearrangement, except for cutting the argument on morals"
(Letter to Mauss, 14 May 1901, in Durkheim 1998: 283).

been progressively led towards conclusions he drew in his book *Suicide*. In the second paragraph of the new preface he immediately highlights the particular character of his argument; what then follows has to be read as an account *of how he would have proceeded* had he not been diverted by more urgent tasks:

> If originally we only touched obliquely on this problem [the role of professional groups in social organisation], it is because we were intending to take it up again, making it the object of a special study. Since other preoccupations have arisen to divert us from this project, and since we do not see when it will be possible for us to carry it out, we would like to take advantage of this second edition to show how this question is linked to the subject dealt with in the rest of this book, indicating the terms in which it is posed, and attempting especially to dispose of the reasons that still prevent too many minds from comprehending the urgency and importance of the problem. (1902a/1984: xxxi).

The following three pages recount the importance that Durkheim ascribes to the legal and moral anomie which suffuses economic life. While there is a morality shared by professionals such as doctors, lawyers or professors, there is nothing of the sort among the growing mass of workers, employees and managers who people modern large-scale industry and bureaucracy. In the absence of rules,[4] social functions cannot spontaneously adjust to each other, and conflict and disorder "of every kind of which the economic world affords so sorry a spectacle" (ibid.: xxxii) takes the place of such adjustment. We might note that the origin of this "sorry spectacle" is to be found in a profound characteristic of the human being in society: the want of a limit to passions, or the "malady of infinity," which only morality is capable of containing, inasmuch as the theory of socialisation remains at the level of uniformisation (the process of social integration) and the differential moderation of passions (the process of social regulation). Durkheim devotes so much attention to legal and moral anomie in the economic sphere because this is a major dimension of modern society: from being secondary, the economic sphere now becomes central. Creating professional groups would provide a morphological foundation adequate to moral industrial life, allowing those involved in industry to develop moral rules regulating competitive behaviour.

But Durkheim suggests only *what he would have to do* to show why a social institution, once linked by the Constituent Assembly to the *ancien régime* so that it might be all the more easily written off and buried, is

---

[4] In fact of *norms*, as Durkheim clarifies a few pages later: "Nor indeed is a rule merely a customary manner in which to act: it is above all *an obligatory manner of acting*, that is, one to some extent not subject to individual arbitrariness" (1902a/1984: xxxiv).

again part of the present. Many detailed historical studies would have to be undertaken, employing a comparative method capable of demonstrating the role played by ancient guilds, the void left by their elimination and the need to create again an institution capable of filling this void. In the absence of such studies, and despite his general condemnation of "sociological essayism", Durkheim considered that "it is not impossible, even now, to catch a glimpse, although only in its most general traits" (ibid.: xlvi) of the sociological nature of this institution, studying a past of which one has only passing glimpses and for which the sociologist "need only indicate its general principles as they appear to emerge from the facts just stated" (ibid.: l). These general principles are to be seen in the history of guilds since the Middle Ages, that is, in the development of social and economic activity which itself led to the loss of this institution's useful function—hence the discredit into which they fell before their suppression at the time of the French Revolution. For modern industry, a new institution was needed to structure this growing segment of social life to match the extension of the commercial sphere (ibid.: li).

This new preface embodies the reformist dimension of Durkheimian sociology. True, it is less apparent than in chapter 3 of *Rules of Sociological Method*, and it no longer involves the argument that science will provide a programme that politics has then to implement. Instead of precisely defining the exact institutional form of the professional group, Durkheim considers the moral forces that could do so: "How much more important it is to set to work immediately on constituting the moral forces which alone can give the professional group substance and shape!" (ibid.: lvii [trans. revised KT]).

We can, therefore, strike a rather surprising balance. Durkheim had elaborated a research programme within which a sociology of the economy had a central place, to the extent that it had its own objects (division of labour, professional groups, social justice) and also its own questions to pose (the nature of modern social relations, the improvements to be made to these relations). He had certainly assembled a great deal of material and to some extent assimilated this in his research.[5] How can one take account of such a renewal, and what does the project for an economic sociology become in the new domain in which Durkheim is now working?

Firstly, we shall show that that it is possible to explain how the "revelation" had its origin in the elaboration of his theory of socialisation and in

---

[5] Proof of this will be found in the lectures on the development of teaching in France, where it will be seen that Durkheim had studied in great detail the role and function of the university corporation from the thirteenth to the eighteenth centuries (1904–5: 94–100, 150–51, 191). Similarly, the courses of lectures on law and custom (1898–1900) make many allusions to professional groups and outline the political role that they might assume.

his apprehensions concerning the adequacy of economic socialisation. Secondly, we shall see how the sociology of the economy is entirely renewed when related to the importance of religion in understanding the functioning of social life.

Economy, Politics and Forms of Suicide

Durkheim argued that it was not necessary to make progress responsible for the height of the suicide rate; it was not the fact of progress, but its rhythm, that was at stake. Durkheim introduces a normative viewpoint: "normal" progress can only take place slowly. By definition, progress brings about changes in social morphology, that is, in social facts that endure over time (1894/1982: 52). When such changes happen more quickly than the flexibility of institutions permits, the functioning of these institutions is altered and the socialisation process that depends upon them suffers as a result. Nor does Durkheim hesitate to describe this situation as a morbid *effervescence*, a pathological state, or a state of crisis and imbalance (1897a/2006: 412–13), leading to surges in suicide which are reflected in the statistics. The arguments presented in the body of the book regarding egoistic and anomic suicide highlight the architecture of Durkheim's thinking on this important point.

In regard to egoistic suicide, Durkheim studies the religious, familial and political spheres of modern life. The same model is presented in each case, articulated as a long-term condition which is said to be "chronic", together with short-term phenomena which are called "crises". The model is constructed as follows: starting with a prior historical phenomenon, he identifies a condition of failing social integration; on this basis arise crises, which explain some statistical exceptions or which are themselves the starting point for a new spike in the suicide rate, indicative of a deterioration of social integration in the short run, cumulatively progressing into the long run. The chronic phenomena that affect each of the three social spheres (religion, family, politics) are Protestantism, the decrease in density within families and the widening gap between the citizen and political life.[6] This chronic situation forms the backdrop against which Durkheim

---

[6] The first two of these phenomena are familiar, and clearly developed in *Suicide*; only the third needs further explanation. Despite the importance of politics to Durkheim's sociological project (Lacroix 1981), he did not systematically deal with political questions; however, he did adhere to the view expressed by Benjamin Constant (1814) that the modern citizen was removed from political life. In his lectures published under the title *The Physics of Custom and Law*, Durkheim represented sociologically the rupture between the citizen and politics and sought to show how professional groups could contribute to an amelioration of this rupture.

places the short-term phenomena affecting the social rate of suicide. An asymmetry between the three spheres of activity here emerges. For religion and the family, Durkheim takes no account of short-term social phenomena which bring about breakdowns in equilibrium, although according to Durkheim these are the foundation for a sociological explanation of suicide (1897a/2006: 205, 267). For politics it is different, since electoral crises, revolutions and wars do have an impact upon the rate of suicide.

During these political crises, social integration, enfeebled by the distancing of citizens from political life, is reinforced because "political passions [are] at their height" (ibid.: 219), but "as soon as . . . [the crisis ends] . . . the rise that [has] been momentarily halted, resume[s]" (ibid.: 220); only wars have a more lasting impact, their effects enduring beyond the period of military operations (ibid.: 221). Durkheim thus explains the fall in the number of suicides in France in 1877 and 1889 (electoral crises), in 1830 and 1848 (revolutions), and in 1870–71 (war).

As regards anomic suicide, Durkheim considers the relation between suicide and the spheres of family and economy. The features relevant to temporality are only properly developed in respect of economic activity (ibid.: 279–80). Periodic crises, such as stock exchange crashes or a sudden rise in the number of bankruptcies,[7] have an impact upon economic activity while disrupting equilibrium in a way favourable to suicide. The impact of the crisis ends in much the same way as does that of political crises, although economic crises weaken social regulation and have an impact at the level of chronic anomie. By separating economic organisation from the regulatory powers of the state, religion or family, modern society creates a condition of insufficient social regulation, and this has an impact upon the passions and aspirations of those social classes most closely linked to economic activity. These are the individuals who suffer from this state of affairs, whence the higher number of voluntary deaths among practitioners of the liberal professions, merchants and industrialists as compared with those engaged in agriculture.

Short-period phenomena, in every case considered as social *effervescence*, can thus engender either a growth or a decrease in the number of suicides. This observation can be lent greater significance if it is added that economics or politics are associated with either of these outcomes. We have to clarify what Durkheim means by "social effervescence", then

[7] It even involves the "crises" linked to Universal Exhibitions, particularly those of 1878 and 1889. It is difficult to grasp this link between a stock exchange crash and a Universal Exhibition; it is not that clear why the latter should stir the passions of industrialists in the same way that a collapse of the bourse would. Instead one would expect a heightening of passions among the public, but this would be to leave behind the link between economy and suicide and introduce a connection between (festive) public events and suicide.

seek to understand how this social phenomenon can have such contrary effects.

When it is a matter of political effervescence (ibid.: 219–20), Durkheim maintains that electoral crises or revolutionary phenomena[8] increase political passions. But he takes a favourable view of such events because of the contribution they make to social integration; the more the level of passionate life is raised, the stronger such integrative tendencies are.[9] In terms of social integration, effervescence is a positive phenomenon since it runs counter to the distancing of the citizen from political life. However, the integration of the group depends on the existence of common goals, on passions which individuals devote to such common goals and to the regularity of social interaction. By reactivating the importance of a common political end, by increasing the level of passion with which political life is conducted and by the frequency of interactions, effervescence raises the degree of group integration and, in so doing, plays a prophylactic role in the occurrence of suicide. When the short-term political phenomenon comes to an end, political life slumps to its previous low level, and the weakness of social integration in the group comes once more to the fore.

In the case of economic effervescence (ibid.: 280), the relationship between effervescence and the socialisation process no longer takes the same form. In Durkheim's eyes, economic activity has three characteristics: an increasing autonomization of the economic sphere, which leads ultimately to an inversion of the relationship between means and ends;[10] an absence of regulation, whether it be religious or political (ibid.: 279); and finally, the competitive context linked to the increasing internationalisation of commercial relations.[11] Since the end of the eighteenth century, the evolution of modern society has led to the most forcible elimination of those structures which regulated economic activity, unleashing passions that

[8] We leave wars here to one side, since elsewhere Durkheim did so too; these are more in the nature of long-term phenomena (both in their course and then in the subsequent effects), and they are also phenomena whose political character cannot be easily characterised.

[9] "And, when society is integrated in such a way that it leaves little room for individuation of its component parts, the intensity of collective states raises the general level of passionate life" (1897a/2006: 396).

[10] "And since these theories [related to economic materialism] only express the state of public opinion, industry, no longer considered as a means towards an end which is higher than itself, has become the supreme end of individuals and societies" (1897a/2006: 280).

[11] "When the producer could dispose of his products only in his immediate neighbourhood, the moderate profit to be made could not greatly over-excite his ambition. But now that he can almost claim to have the whole world as his customer, how could it be that, faced with this endless prospect, his passions could continue to accept being restrained as they once were?" (1897a/2006: 280).

render the situation of working life very favourable to anomic suicide: "This explains the excitement which reigns in that part of society, but which from there has extended to all the rest. The state of crisis and anomie is constant in it and, as it were, normal" (ibid.: 280 [trans. revised KT]). This analysis can be linked to the criticisms Durkheim made, in the first edition of *Division of Labour*, of the way in which the development of modern commercial activity was connected to the anomic division of labour, the "unlimited" nature of market expansion, such that each producer could claim to be confronted with the totality of demand, as could all his competitors (1893/1984: 305). In this sense, economic *effervescence* is thought to have negative outcomes, since it ends in the "bad infinity" of anomie. This is therefore the reverse of the way in which Durkheim regards the domain of political life: in commercial and industrial sectors, social life is a construct of an exacerbation of economic passions, that is, the passion of riches (ibid.: 236) and the passion of well-being (ibid.: 239). The phenomena of the short-period, economic crises inflate an already intense level of impassioned activity: and this is harmful, says Durkheim, for all limits have already been removed from passions, and their further exacerbation can be nothing but distressing for individuals. There are two arguments here, which have to be distinguished. On the one hand, there is a principle that the impassioned life cannot be endlessly intensified, since ultimately the individual always suffers the consequences.[12] On the other, it is no longer here a question of social integration (the moulding of uniform passions) but of social regulation (a differential moderation of passions). That amounts to saying that the unfolding of economic activity, in the forms that it assumed in the course of the previous century, brings with it a chronic exacerbation of passions no longer subject to constraint. Crises add a new twist to the exacerbation of passions[13] and, in so doing, once more destabilise the differential moderation of passions already jeopardised by the chronic anomie of economic life. Durkheim's thinking about poverty stands four-square with his interpretation of economic passions. According to him, poverty offers a form of protection against suicide. Poverty does not just mean a low level of resources, since this does not of itself prevent individuals becoming involved in the struggles over social identity that intensify during a period of economic

[12] This principle, already present in the *Division of Labour* (Besnard 1987: 34–35), is taken up again in the *Elementary Forms* (1912/1995: 219, 227–28).

[13] "Now, it so happens that at this time the struggle becomes more violent and more painful, both because it is less regulated and because competition is fiercer. All classes are caught up in it because there is no longer any established classification. So the effort is all the greater at the moment when it becomes more unproductive. How can the will to live not be weakened in these conditions?" (1897a/2006: 278).

crisis.[14] Poverty signifies separation from a world where economic passions are constantly exacerbated, either because a "natural" norm regulates passions, as in the agricultural sector, within which economic activity generally remains more subordinated than elsewhere to ecological and biological constraints; or because a religious ideal supplies a regulatory norm.[15]

We can consider finally the problem presented by the contrary effects of the passions in the political and economic domains. Political passions endure, but at a lower level of intensity than economic passions, which are just as lasting but at a higher level. This has differential consequences for the bounds within which the life of passion unfolds, a brutal variation that intensifies the life of passion and has differing outcomes for socialisation. Secondly, this abrupt heightening of the intensity of the life of passion does not have the same significance in respect of its impact upon regulation or social integration. While positive for this second process, it is not for the first, since the problem differs: here it is a matter of moderating passions according to the place they occupy in the social hierarchy, not of rendering them more uniform and intensifying the passions animating different individuals who are members of the same social group. Where it is a matter of moderation, of setting limits to the unfolding of passions in the economic sphere, it can be seen that crisis, by working against this, adds to deregulation and an increase in the suicide rate. Professional groups can here play a role by working directly upon the nature of the relations among those involved in large industry, but they can and should also intervene at the level of the representations held by the members of the social groups in question. This intervention into the domain of representations raises the problem of the articulation of ideas and passions. Socioeconomic life—Durkheim is very precise on this—draws some of its specificity from the nature of the *ideal* to which it corresponds.

The importance of the ideal is emphasised in the first preface to the *Division of Labour* (1893/1984: xxvi); and we also know how Durkheim stressed it in his conclusion to the *Elementary Forms of Religious Life*:

---

[14] From a Tocquevillian point of view, to which Durkheim is close enough in his analysis of economic passions, poverty is, apart from extreme cases, no impediment to involvement in economic passions; it is envy that inspires the poor, just as fear (of being outdone, or of falling into poverty) inspires the rich (Tocqueville 1840/2003: 617–18). According to Durkheim, there is not a shadow of doubt that extreme poverty plunges destitute individuals into the purest fatalism.

[15] "It is not for nothing that so many religions have celebrated the benefits and the moral value of poverty. This is because, of all schools, it is the one that best teaches man to restrain himself" (1897a/2006: 278). The two phenomena can be coupled, as Durkheim does in the case of agriculture (ibid.: 282).

Thus the formation of an ideal is by no means an irreducible datum that eludes science. It rests on conditions that can be uncovered through observation. It is a natural product of social life. (1912/1995: 424)[16]

The question is, What does Durkheim think economic ideals are, and above all, do they exist in the same way that one can talk about religious or political ideals? The investigation that Durkheim initiated in the *Division of Labour* is entirely dominated by the way in which we might reconcile the imperatives of ordinary life when modern life is founded upon the imperative of economic specialisation. He begins by examining the alternatives of amateur and specialist, and the book ends by favoring the latter:

We must limit our horizons, select a definite task, and involve ourselves utterly, instead of making ourselves, so to speak, a finished work of art, one that derives all its value from itself rather than from the services it renders. Finally, this specialisation must be carried the farther the more society is of a higher species. . . . [But] [t]he rule prescribing that we should specialise remains limited by the opposite rule. We conclude that it is not good to push specialisation as far as possible, but only so far as necessary. (1893/1984: pp. 333–34)

This question is very closely related to that of the ideal: "the moral ideal, from being the sole one, simple and impersonal, has become increasingly diversified. . . . One fact, among others, reflects this view: this is the increasingly specialist character assumed by education" (ibid.: 4). Hence Durkheim presents the division of labour from both a systemic and a social perspective (Lockwood 1964). Seen from its systemic aspect, the division of labour sets social functions to work; seen from social aspect, it sets individuals to work as "agents of exchange" (ibid.: 337).

From the systemic point of view, the economic ideal harmoniously reconciles different relations and their connections one with another. This ran counter to the assumptions of contemporary economists, who adhered to a conception of spontaneous and harmonious order resulting from the free play of unchecked economic passions. The implications of Durkheim's approach became quite plain in his reading of Saint-Simon, where he linked the conscious organisation of economic functions to

---

[16] He came back to this in a letter to Bouglé: "It has so often been said to me that sociology can take no account of the ideal, that it is positivist and realist. I show that the ideal is inherent to it, because it lives and up to the present day not a word has been said about it. I somewhat regret that here in your article you did not emphasise this" (Letter of 13 October 1912, in Durkheim 1975 II: 438). Bouglé took note of this and presented this aspect of Durkheim's work in his lecture course on values and in his courses on economic sociology during the 1930s (1922: 15–17, 32–36; 1935: 12).

what he called "socialism". There is also in this perspective an economic ideal which is of the same kind as a political or religious ideal, securing the common bases thanks to which a collective consciousness creates a solidary form out of different functions and different specialised individuals. At this systemic level, the economic ideal is inescapably a political ideal. Nonetheless, the current condition of modern societies in no respect guarantees the practical realisation of such an ideal; the specialised nature of the economic domain opens up divisions between the economic interests of individuals as well as aspirations which have no clear limits. Contrary to free-trade economists, who saw the creation of spontaneous order as the ideal, the end to be achieved, in this functional economic process, Durkheim instead saw in the spontaneous order the elimination of the ideal, its repudiation; for such an economic ideal liberated the unbridled economic aspirations of different classes of economic agents, checked only by limits that were created by the clash of intensified passions. However, in the course of a critique of communistic remnants in early nineteenth-century socialism (1895: 84–85), Durkheim clearly expressed the idea that the economic aspirations of agents could never be satisfied, that their divergences could never be overcome, and that it was instead necessary to take a different point of departure: the organisation of economic functions. Only by starting with the integration of the system (the socialist economic and political ideal of the conscious organisation of economic functions) would one secure social integration (autonomous individuals as producers and traders, endowed with differentiated economic aspirations which were both unequal and unequally satisfied, but all the same contained). It was from this social dimension of the economic ideal that problems arose, and it is certainly at this juncture that Durkheim's argument concerning the socialising functions of professional groups seemed quite indispensable to him. The emergence of these professional groups would provide the social milieu from which the moral rules and the ideals specific to each profession would come, which would then regulate the polymorphous morality inhering in the modern economic sphere, that is, contain aspirations and economic passions in various ways suited to the place each person had in the social system. Hence the economic ideal, as an objective which the entire society set itself as something to be achieved, would be realised in the establishment of specific groups charged with giving life in concrete terms to the different ideals, as well as facilitating the realisation of the systemic economic ideal.

The economic ideal is not identical for all individuals since the ideal depends on the function or category to which such individuals belong—which can be seen, although in an approximate matter, with socialism as an ideal toward greater equality for the working classes (Durkheim

1895–96: 38)[17]—and in this the economic ideal diverges significantly from a religious or political ideal, defined by a common end, identical for all individuals.[18] An additional difference lies in the extent to which the definition of an economic ideal is much less clearly delineated than in other spheres.[19] In sum, it can be understood that the role of the passions differs in the political and the economic spheres. In the former, it is a matter of social integration; the ideal is collective, and it concerns the agitation of passions so that they might reach a higher level. In the latter, it is a matter of social regulation, moderating passions which are too powerful; an inversion has taken place where the economic sphere is increasingly autonomous from the rest of social life. It is also a matter of moderating such passions differentially, since effective social regulation presupposes that economic ideals will differ. In the economic sphere there consequently exists an identity (the passion for material prosperity), but it is perverted; there are differences (between the ideals, according to their place in the social hierarchy), but they are neither clearly marked nor legitimated. This opposition between the economic and the political can be represented together with the Durkheimian typology of the four types of suicide (see figure 2.1).

It seems, therefore, that economic activity has a quite specific place in Durkheim's argument. In the *Division of Labour*, he argues that the development of economic activity progressively modifies the form of social cohesion and the task given to each individual; with the development of the division of labour, solidarity has become organic, and this form of solidarity requires the specialised individual. While providing new conditions of socialisation and other significant elements for modern society, economic relations are themselves incapable of providing a satisfactory means of socialisation. This is provided by the intervention of politics,

[17] "The economic ideal assigned to each category of citizens is itself fixed between certain limits within which the passions can freely roam. But it is not limitless. This relative limitation and the moderation that results are what make men content with their lot, while at the same time giving them moderate encouragement to improve it" (1897a/2006: 273). Since morality originates in an ideal, what Durkheim called the "moral polymorphism" (1898–1900/2001: 7) prevailing in the economic sphere also supports this idea: "This feature of professional ethics can moreover easily be explained. They cannot be of deep concern to the common consciousness precisely because they are not common to all members of the society" (ibid.: 6).

[18] "[G]reat upheavals in society, like great popular wars, sharpen collective feelings, stimulate the party spirit and the national one and, by concentrating activities towards a single end, achieve, at least for a time, a greater integration of society. . . . Since [struggles] oblige men to cling together in order to confront a common danger, the individual thinks less of himself and more of the community" (1897a/2006: 223–24).

[19] Whence Durkheim's efforts to unravel these in systematic form in *Socialism* and in *Physiology of Law and Morals*.

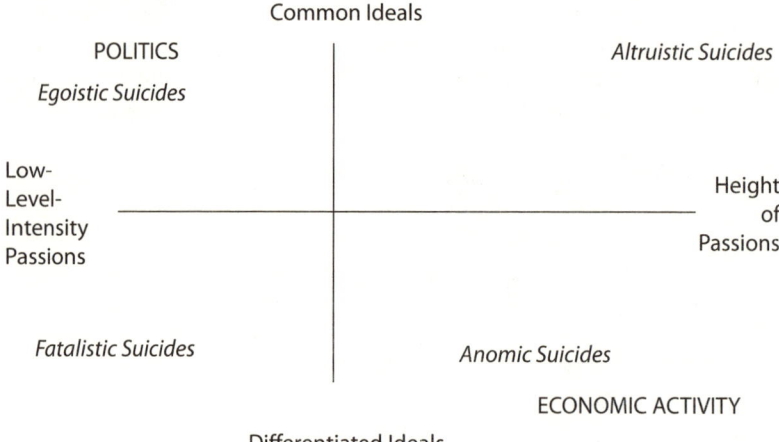

FIGURE 2.1 Types of suicide, nature of ideals and the level of passion

through reforms such as those prompting the formation of professional groups.

The economic differentiation which the division of labour introduces into the structure of democratic political organisation brings to the fore a passion that acts as a solvent on social relations: the passion for wealth, or for material prosperity. Here Durkheim finds himself on the path already traced in the second volume of Tocqueville's *Democracy in America*;[20] their arguments converge in a very striking manner when it comes to assessing the impact of passion for material prosperity[21] (taking a term from Tocqueville which they share in common). Both Durkheim and Tocqueville are concerned about the effects of the diffusion of this passion, for it distances the individual from social life and confines him within the limits of his own passions. If in America, writes Tocqueville, religion and the passion for self-government play a decisive role in connecting the man to the citizen, this does not happen in France, where revolutionary convulsions have discredited the Church and where the passion for equality erodes the idea of self-government. Consequently Tocqueville calls for a renewal of French social and political life through the "science of association", through which the impact of economic passions can be limited by linking them to decentralised political activity. Durkheim maintains

[20] One should also note that Tocqueville's argument about centralisation is mobilised by Durkheim when he seeks to explain certain features of the French educational system (1904–5: 142–44).

[21] *La passion du bien-être*—this is translated by Gerald E. Bevan in the Penguin edition of *Democracy in America* as a passion for "material prosperity" [KT].

that the connection of religion to economic activity has unravelled, as has that between the state and economic activity; in response, he suggests that one find a regulatory norm in a specific form of politico-economic decentralisation (a professional group), which he outlines in the conclusion to *Suicide*, in the preface to the second edition of the *Division of Labour*, and in his course on the physics of the law and of morals.

But one could ask, Is there not a paradox in reviving a problematic that turns on a relationship between economy and polity, the very relationship that came undone in the "revelation" of 1895? To see how Durkheim extended his thinking on the socialisation process by confronting the economic sphere with religion, we have to consider the *Elementary Forms of Religious Life*.

Religious Life and Economic Life

In his 1902 essay dedicated to the subject of totemism, Durkheim criticised the interpretation of the phenomenon made by Sir James Frazer, Baldwin Spencer and F. Gillen after Spencer and Gillen's ethnography of the Arunta. Durkheim argued as follows: these authors discounted the idea that totemism had a religious significance because they developed a utilitarian and economic understanding of the *Intichiuma* ceremony.[22] As members of a totemic clan were not able to consume their totemic animal, the increase of this animal was of no benefit to them. "From which it followed," wrote Durkheim, summarising the current interpretation,

> that such increase had to be effected in honour of and for the benefit of other clans; these were the interested parties and virtually the sole consumers of food secured to the tribe. In other words, each totemic group worked, if one can use this expression, not for itself, but for its fellows, in a reciprocal manner. There is among all clans a kind of magical cooperation whose outcome is to increase the alimentary resources of the society. . . . Understood in this way, totemism gradually loses all religious character and becomes a kind of economic undertaking. (1902b: 319)

Durkheim did not agree with this line of argument.

First of all, the totemism observed by Spencer and Gillen was an advanced form, and so the fact that it might be interpreted in a utilitarian way by the Arunta did not mean that it had had such a function originally. For his part, Durkheim reinterpreted the *Intichiuma* as a rite which

---

[22] This was an annual ceremony in which each totemic group practised rites which would allow the number of totemic varieties to increase (1902b: 318).

served the reproduction of the totemic species in the absence of which there would have been no totemic clan. Secondly, Durkheim derived from his study of the division of labour the insight that a "totemic" division of labour, if one can call it this, would be too complex to be a primitive social fact.[23] Thirdly, Durkheim argued that developments internal to a totemic religion could account for the path taken by the rites of *Intichiuma*. Traditions relating to ancestors assumed an increasingly important role, such that the totemic species was gradually displaced as a medium of religious forces. The rites themselves continued, but a new purpose was given to them:

> Nothing happens more often than to see an institution which has lost its original purpose nonetheless survive by the creation of new purposes. The totem no longer had a real religious utility; what remained to it was an alimentary or economic utility. And it is this new utility which now explains the perpetuation of the rite. And this explanation is accepted all the more easily because in the meantime the clans have merged. (ibid.: 349)

It is quite remarkable to see Durkheim strike a balance between a religious and an economic interest: if the rite loses its religious interest, it gains an economic interest. This stance highlights a leading principle emerging from Durkheim's work during the second period, quite clearly balancing religious and economic life, the sacred and *la vie sérieuse*.[24]

When Durkheim describes the social life of Australian tribes (1912/1995: 216ff.), he demonstrates the temporal dimension that lends it rhythm: the phases of dispersal driven by the imperative of finding food are followed by phases during which the tribe reassembles. This is the

---

[23] In this regard, Durkheim's essay should be compared with Maunier's article of 1909—I will come back to this in ch. 5.

[24] In his study on the morphology of Eskimos, Mauss had already developed the idea that the social life of these tribes, the seasonal succession of summer and winter, was quite different in nature in each of the two phases (dispersal/reassembly). Mauss argued that this rhythm revealed the symbiosis between these tribes and the game from which they lived (1906: 442); when such game could be hunted over a large area, the group dispersed; and when it could be hunted in a small area, the group reassembled. This alternation of dispersion and concentration of the social mass was paired with the dissociation of two kinds of activity: with dispersion went economic activity, and with reassembly went religious life: "There is, in other words, a summer religion and a winter religion, or more exactly, there is no summer religion . . . Life is as if secularised. Even magic, which is, however, most often something purely private, seems to be no more than a quite simple medical science, in which all ceremony is reduced to a very few elements. By contrast, the onset of winter is greeted with an almost continuous state of religious exaltation" (ibid.: 444). To these two regimes of social life there correspond two distinct legal regimes (in the winter, communism; in the summer, individual or familial egoism (ibid.: 465).

time when the social bond is renewed, rediscovering an intense collective life in festivals and religious ceremonies whose strongest moments are regarded as periods of social effervescence. The economic organisation of Australian tribes is not comparable in any respect with that of the modern European societies dealt with in *Suicide*; all the same, economic life is already here contrasted with that which lies at the heart of collective life. The scattering of the tribe brought about by the search for subsistence entails a social dormancy comparable with that noted by Durkheim in the case of wintering French peasants: "Gathering seeds or plants necessary for food, hunting and fishing are not occupations that can stir truly strong passions. The dispersed state in which the society finds itself makes life slack, monotonous, and humdrum (ibid.: 217). Economic passions remain in such societies at a very low level; that is easy to explain. The economic sphere is still embedded in familial relations and is not an autonomous domain, there is no inversion of social means and ends, and of course competitive relationships play hardly any role at all. As a consequence, private interests cannot engender an unfolding of passions such as Durkheim observed in late nineteenth-century Europe. But all the same, he had already seen here the corrosive work of the economic upon the social bond: each individual was absorbed in the pursuit of his own private interest, and the socialising elements of collective life faded into the background.[25]

The collective forces which make us human and which lend us strength (ibid.: 211) need, however, to be maintained and revitalised following their relegation during periods devoted to economic activity. Time has to be devoted to the rejuvenation of these forces and of collective ideas (ibid.: 349–50). This lends social life its rhythm (ibid.: 353–54), since there is no prospect of remaining assembled together permanently, for economic imperatives must also be satisfied.

When does this sacred or festive time occur, if examined in terms of the theory of socialisation? Durkheim's response is quite startling: social effervescence means that the rules of collective life are momentarily suspended, and it is at this point of suspension that the outcome which is already inherent in this effervescence can unfold and find realisation. The

---

[25] "Everyone goes about his own personal business; for most people, what is most important is to meet the demands of material life; the principal motive of economic activity has always been private interest. Of course, social feelings could not be absent altogether. We remain in relationship with our fellow men; the habits, ideas, and tendencies that upbringing has stamped on us, and that ordinarily preside over our relations with others, continue to make their influence felt. . . . Depending on the intrinsic energy of those social feelings, they hold up more or less successfully; but that energy is not renewed. They live on their past, and, in consequence, they would in time be depleted if nothing came to give back a little of the strength they lose through this incessant conflict and friction" (1912/1995: 352).

unregulated and orgiastic character of a turbulent assembly is clearly marked in Durkheim's terminology,[26] even though he is careful to suggest in the course of his discussion that social regulation exists within the framework of clan and tribe. The lack of regulation is therefore real, affecting important parts of social (especially sexual) life; but this lack of regulation plays an essential role in the intensification of passionate life, an intensification which will then be dissolved during the subsequent period of the tribe's dispersal in pursuit of economic ends. If exceptional excitation of passions of this kind necessarily involves such deregulation, it also provides a quite exceptional outcome, since it revitalises collective ends and ideals, allowing the life of passion to be intensified (strengthening social integration) and reinforcing social ideas (strengthening social regulation).[27] The exacerbation of passions occurs within a short-run framework, but its impact is nonetheless felt at two levels: in the short-run, during which the turbulent assembly actually takes place; and in the long-run, in the revitalisation of the social ideal or good with the effects linked to the creation of a new ideal. In this respect Durkheim made progress by clarifying the role of passions in relation to ideals within the framework of his theory of socialisation: loosening for a while the constraints which secured social regulation, the disorderly gathering promoted a higher degree of social integration, raising the level of passionate life immediately and providing an ideal thanks to which, in the long term, integration and regulation would be reinforced.

A similar line of argument can be seen at work in Durkheim's treatment of the transformation of pedagogical doctrine during the Renaissance (1904–5: 210–11, 218–20; Besnard 1993). Rabelaisian ideas are the archetypical rejection of all regulation, of all discipline, of all constraint, of all bounds. Society harbours a plethora of life, and brings about a revolution by introducing new pedagogic ideals. Durkheim discovered in the Renaissance, in a social institution of very great importance (the schooling system), features which glorified the creative deregulation of ideals. Within Australian tribes, as in the Renaissance schooling system, social effervescence is viewed positively as means for the creation of ideals capable of reinforcing social integration. This kind of feature remains absent from the economic effervescence whose impact Durkheim criticised in *Division of Labour* and in *Suicide*, since effervescence of this kind simply brought about an exacerbation of passions that corroded the

---

[26] Durkheim's description is couched in quite unequivocal terms: it is a matter of "vigorous passions devoid of any control", of "tumult", of "sexual relations outside the rules governing sexual relations", of "incest", of a "pathological delirium and neurosis", and so forth.

[27] Here I take up Borlandi's analysis concerning the Durkheimian definition of the social as the product of the association of individuals (1995).

social body. Furthermore, linked to free-trade economic doctrines, such economic effervescence destroyed the economic ideal as Durkheim understood it in his study of socialism, and, especially, in rejecting the idea of professional groups, made it difficult to implement a common ideal.

Here we can see the crucial role played by the notion of the ideal in the shift that led Durkheim to reconsider the direction of his work. As presented in the conclusions to *Elementary Forms*, the ideal engendered by groups in a condition of social disorder is a unifying element in social life:

> A society can neither create nor recreate itself without creating some sort of ideal by the same stroke. This creation is not some sort of optional extra step by which society, being already made, merely adds its finishing touches; it is the act by which society makes itself, and remakes itself, periodically. (1912/1995: 425)

The contemporary social problems which Durkheim had considered in political and economic terms in his previous writings are now related to their capacity to create new ideals during a period of "transition and moral mediocrity" (ibid.: 429).[28] The assessment has not altered since he wrote the conclusions of *Suicide*. The religious fact has supplanted the political fact when it became a matter of examining some major problems presented by the unfolding of the economic fact. The religious fact became central, since it facilitated the study of a decisive element in the theory of social regulation—the ideal—an element whose importance for the comprehension and the evolution of social life Durkheim had noted from the very first.

Two questions remain. Firstly, how do we reconcile this thought with the practical imperative that Durkheim claimed, both in 1893 and in 1912, to have always had in mind?[29] As has been noted (Bellah 1990), it is hard to imagine that the study of the social characteristics of Australian tribes might stand in for the study of professional groups. The moral reform and the creation of ideals proper to modern society, which is dominated by the backwash of economic passions, could hardly find anything which

---

[28] "A day will come when our societies once again will know hours of creative effervescence during which new ideals will again spring forth and new formulas emerge to guide humanity for a time. And when those hours have been lived through, men will spontaneously feel the need to relive them in thought from time to time—that is, to preserve their memory by means of celebrations that regularly recreate their fruits" (1912/1995: 429–30).

[29] Durkheim's credo in the preface to the first edition of the *Division of Labour*—"We would esteem our research not worth the labour of a single hour if its interest were merely speculative" (1902a/1984: xxvi)—is echoed in the introduction to the *Elementary Forms*: "like any positive science . . . its [sociology's] purpose above all is to explain a present reality that is near to us and thus capable of affecting our ideas and actions. That reality is man. More especially, it is present-day man, for there is none other that we have a greater interest in knowing well" (1912/1995: 1).

might be of direct utility in analyses devoted to Australian tribes. For this we would have to know which social rules might be, or would need to be, set on one side during the phases of creative social effervescence in order to reveal the ideals, representations and institutions which would facilitate stronger integration and better regulation in modern societies.

Secondly, when he addressed the French Philosophy Society in 1913 and defended his argument concerning the social origin (under particular conditions) of religious sentiment, he made the following point:

> The collective condition which nurtures religion is the communion of individual consciousness, their fusion into one which is for an instant all-absorbing. But this communion is only, and can only be, very occasional; it is one of the forms of social life, but there are others. There are social relations which do not share this feature to any extent and which, as a consequence, are not religious in themselves. Such, for example, are relations of exchange. The consciousness of parties to an exchange plays no part in their transaction. This is one of the characteristics of exchange that I emphasised in a book published twenty years ago. (1913:40–41)

Does this polar distinction of economy and religion, or again profane and sacred (Paoletti 2002a), mean that the economy escapes religion inasmuch as it is the founding domain of the social? The discussion up to this point allows us to put forward two arguments. First of all, the position of Durkheim with regard to the social role of religion privileges the integrative function in the sense that religion provides a collective ideal to all individuals belonging to one society (Pickering 1984; Isambert 1992). There is a sense in which a shift took place from the political to the religious. But at a price: one cannot find in Durkheim the type of analysis which Weber would develop in systematically relating existing social differences between the originators and bearers of religion (eminent intellectuals, aristocrats, burghers, peasants) and the salvational goods distributed by the aforementioned religions. Secondly, through the recurring opposition between a sacred and a profane time into which the social life of the tribes studied by Durkheim was divided, Durkheim introduced a structuring idea which converges with Weber's conceptualisation, so essential in the sociology of religion, of a *tension* between the pursuit of salvation and the exigencies (political, military, economic, sexual) of life in the world (Weber 2004a).

The two arguments are separately located. According to the logic that Durkheim sets to work in *Division of Labour*, the integrative dimension of religion provides a necessary complement to specialisation, a phenomenon which leads unfailingly towards anomie, to the loss of connection between social functions and social representations. The same is true of the regulatory function of religion, which is able to set limits to economic passions. In this sense religion can be thought of as overhanging the economy, and it will only encounter the latter as the fixed limit to the free unfolding of the economy, assuming the form of systemic and social ideals that it holds out to the faithful. This is not the same with regard to the tension existing between the sacred and the profane, the religious and the economic and the social rhythms thereby involved; the existence of the tension here strongly connects the two domains, a connection capable of sustaining inquiry at the junction of the sociology of the economy and the sociology of religion, as Weber demonstrated. But that was not the path that Durkheim took, for his attention was caught by the mediating intervention of the sociology of knowledge.

THE SECOND DURKHEIMIAN PROGRAMME IN ECONOMIC SOCIOLOGY

From all this we might conclude that, following the "revelation" of 1895, Durkheim entirely abandoned the terrain of a sociology of the economy in favour of a sociology of religion and of knowledge. This conclusion is not, however, a very satisfactory one.

First of all, we need to bear in mind that Durkheim thought of his "revelation" with respect both to the religious element in social life and to a supersession of the Marxist interpretation of history—the supersession of historical materialism understood as a doctrine that made the economy the foundation of human history and social life. Let us recall what he wrote to Mauss to persuade him to collaborate on the *Année sociologique*:

> You are one of the kingpins of the group and quite essential, not only because you are in Paris, but also because as I anticipate and hope, the *Année sociologique* will develop a theory which, entirely at odds with such a crude and simplistic historical materialism (notwithstanding its objectivist tendencies), will henceforth make religion, not the economy, the matrix of social facts. The role played by him who directs his attention to work on religion—even though religion must be all-pervasive, or rather because it is—will thus be very great. (Letter to Mauss, June 1897, in Durkheim 1998: 71).[30]

[30] Durkheim's approach is not so far from that of Marx when the latter states: "It is in fact much easier to find through analysis the earthly core of cloudy religious conceptions than it is to *elaborate* from given real lived relations their ethereal form. The latter is the sole materialist, and therefore scientific, method" (1867: 357 n. 89). This comment on method is not so far removed from the way in which Durkheim himself proceeded, when seeking to isolate the social conditions of the emergence of religious thought in social groups in a condition of social effervescence.

The same idea is expressed in the closing pages of a review Durkheim published in 1897 of a book by Antonio Labriola, which he considered to be a rigorous presentation of Marx's theory:

> Not only is the Marxist hypothesis unproven, but it is contrary to facts which appear established. Sociologists and historians tend increasingly to come together in their common affirmation that religion is the most primitive of all social phenomena. . . . In principle everything is religious. Yet we know of no means of reducing religion to economy, nor of any attempt at really effecting this reduction. . . . More generally, it is beyond dispute that, at root, the economic factor is rudimentary while, by contrast, religious life is rich and pervasive. How therefore could the latter result from the former and, on the contrary, is it not probable that the economy depends on religion rather than vice versa? (1897c: 253)

But one should recall that the conclusions of the *Elementary Forms* include a brief, but very important, declaration regarding the sociology of the economy. Having stated that "nearly all the great social institutions were born in religion," he appends to this a note explaining what exactly he means by this "nearly".[31] Drawing on the work of Hubert and Mauss (1904) on magic, and no doubt also having benefited from Mauss's initial studies of the circulation of goods in primitive societies, Durkheim writes:

> Only one form of social activity has not as yet been explicitly linked to religion: economic activity. Nevertheless, the techniques that derive from magic turn out, by this very fact, to have indirectly religious origins. Furthermore, economic value is a sort of power or efficacy, and we know the religious origins of the idea of power. Since mana can be conferred by wealth, wealth itself has some. From this we see that the idea of economic value and that of religious value cannot be unrelated, but the nature of these relationships has not yet been studied. (1912/1995: 421)

The amount of work that such a hypothesis requires is evident; and we know that Durkheim wrote to the editor of the *Revue néo-scholastique* that he had felt the need to review and revise "my past studies". Not only could nothing be salvaged from the first sociological approach to the economy, but there were entirely new questions that had to be answered, together with new tools for so doing.

It can therefore be concluded that a sociology of the economy remained on the Durkheimian agenda since, at the moment that the *Année soci-*

---

[31] To my knowledge, only François Héran (1988) has drawn attention to the importance of this note.

ologique was founded, the sociology of religion is conceived in terms of a critique of historical materialism. But the second programme of economic sociology is clearly stated in the above footnote to the concluding chapter of *Elementary Forms*. If, by contrast to what Marx and Marxists thought, the economy is not the foundation of social life, and if it is fitting to put religion in its place, then it becomes necessary to demonstrate the existence, and the nature, of the connection that establishes a relationship of the economy to the religious. Taking account of the close connection that Durkheim saw between the sociology of religion and the sociology of knowledge, the second Durkheimian research programme into the sociology of the economy would involve a sociology of economic knowledge.

Durkheim did not fully develop the potential of this second research programme, which in the *Elementary Forms* remained buried in a programmatic statement of intent.[32] But, in 1912, the end was near. War, sorrow and illness would not allow Durkheim the possibility to go further. We have to turn to the Durkheimians to establish whether, and up to what point, the two programmes of economic sociology that Durkheim had sketched would be capable of bearing fruit.

---

[32] In his critical discussion of pragmatism, a doctrine already presented in the conclusion to *Elementary Forms*, the economic is not even mentioned when Durkheim considers the forms of thought and action involving religion: "The religious life, for example, is rich in many forms of thought, and activities of all kinds. As thought it contains: 1. myths and beliefs; 2. an incipient science; 3. a degree of poetry. As action one finds there: 1. rites; 2. morals and law; 3. arts, aesthetic elements, songs and above all music" (1913–14: 191).

CHAPTER THREE

Simiand and the Critique of Political Economy

The foundation of *L'année sociologique* coincided with Durkheim's decision to abandon his first research programme in economic sociology.[1] Simiand assumed responsibility for the section devoted to economic sociology, and under his direction it took shape as a sociological critique of the economy conforming to Durkheim's own programme of work. This programme, guided first by Simiand and then by Halbwachs, was subsequently developed into a distinctive body of work within French interwar social science. During this period, economic sociology sought to elaborate, in Simiand's words, a "positive method [which] will be necessarily and simultaneously a sociological method" (1912: 206).

There was nevertheless a duality within the sociological critique of political economy as conceived by Simiand. He was, above all, a brilliant critic of the errors and limitations of orthodox political economy, subjecting them to minute and unsparing examination. To this was added a more constructive economic sociology, the elaboration of an alternative theory being, ultimately, the best kind of criticism one could make. This constructive aspect of Simiand's economic sociology—or positive economics—is the subject of the next chapter. It will become apparent that the connection between the two paths of Durkheimian economic sociology was secured by the role that Simiand and Halbwachs assigned to social representations in explaining economic behaviour and, ultimately, the formation of economic magnitudes (prices and quantities).

ECONOMIC SOCIOLOGY IN *L'ANNÉE SOCIOLOGIQUE*

L'année sociologique was from 1895 to 1898 the title of a section published in the *Revue de métaphysique et de morale*, introduced in response to a suggestion by Bouglé (Besnard 1979: 8). The publication of a new journal under this name was then the work of both Bouglé and Durkheim: Bouglé played the essential role of intermediary and organiser, while Durk-

---

[1] This journal has been the object of several studies directed to better understanding of the group around Durkheim (Besnard 1979; Clark 1968; Heilbron 1985; Karady 1976, 1979). Details of the content of the first series can be found in a dissertation by Yash Nandan (1974); see also the special issue of *L'année sociologique* (1998).

heim played a more clearly intellectual role, especially in the coordination of the team of contributors throughout the first series (1898–1913).[2] After the First World War, Mauss succeeded only in staging an incomplete revival of the journal—the second series published only one complete volume in 1925, the following volume breaking off in the middle of an article and appearing in this incomplete state. The journal arose from the ashes again in 1934 under the title *Annales sociologiques*, whose five series (general sociology, sociology of religion, legal sociology, economic sociology and social morphology) were entrusted respectively to Bouglé, Mauss, Jean Ray, Simiand and Halbwachs.

Section 5 of the original *L'année sociologique* was dedicated to economic sociology and edited by Simiand. Principal contributors were Hubert Bourgin (volumes 4–12), Georges Bourgin (volumes 8, 10, 11 and 12), and Halbwachs (volumes 8–12). Durkheim made no contribution to this section, although he wrote pieces at one time or another for all other parts of the journal.[3] The second series brought the same contributors together, but its brief existence provides scant foundation for any analysis. In the four numbers of series D of the *Annales sociologiques* the work of three members of the original group (Simiand, Halbwachs and Georges Bourgin) assured a degree of continuity, providing most of the reviews and contributing three out of the seven original essays. The new contributors were less involved; none who contributed to the first volume in 1934 published anything in the succeeding numbers. After the death of Simiand in the spring of 1935, it was Halbwachs, his most faithful collaborator, who took responsibility for economic sociology within the Durkheimian group of writers. He wrote many pieces for the journal and was also judicious in his choice of works for review or précis—notable here is the importance he gave to the writings of John Maynard Keynes. But all the same, there is a gradual decline in the energy that he put into such writing. This can be explained by two factors: Halbwachs did not have Simiand's drive nor the acuity of his economic analysis. Secondly, the group of economic sociologists writing for the *Annales sociologiques* was volatile, lending substance to Heilbron's view that Durkheimian sociology had

[2] The frequency of publication altered with volumes 11 and 12: it ceased annual publication and appeared once only in three years. Its content also changed; it ceased publishing new original work. As Durkheim wrote (*AS* I 11: ii), these changes were related to the overwhelming burden of reviewing undertaken by contributors, leaving them insufficient time for their personal research (Besnard 1979: 25).

[3] The correspondence between Durkheim and Simiand shows that Durkheim took a close interest in the composition of Simiand's 1902 essay and that he thought well of it (Letter from Durkheim to Simiand, 18 December 1901, in Durkheim 1975 II: 441ff.). He later cited Simiand's study of wages and Halbwachs's essay on needs as realisations of the project of economic sociology (Durkheim 1915: 11).

some difficulties during this period (Heilbron 1985). Only with the last two volumes, published in 1938 and 1940, was a degree of continuity established by Robert Marjolin and Raymond Klee.[4] The journal suffered another blow with the outbreak of war and the dispersal of contributors. After 1945 the third series of *L'année sociologique* was launched with new contributors. Two older writers, Georges Bourgin and Georges Lutfalla (the latter having been a contributor to series D of the *Annales sociologiques*), were assisted by Jean Lhomme and others whose contribution was discreetly noted; among these were Charles Bettelheim, Edouard Dolléans and Georges Duveau. During the 1950s the section dwindled and then disappeared altogether.

THE INITIAL PROJECT AND ITS REALISATION

Simiand's prime interest was to determine how political economy related to the wider social sciences, since "the general problems of economics, the significance of its framework, its method—these are of general interest to social science, which might benefit from them" (*AS* I 1: 457). But that was not a simple matter: "What foundations are essential to economic science as a social science? Is it the original and fundamental science, economic life being the basis and condition of all social life; or is it simply one part of the social sciences? We might even ask: in what sense, and under what conditions is it a social science at all?" (ibid.: 458). Simiand adopted the programmatic statement that Durkheim placed in the first issue:

> We believe that sociologists have a pressing need to be regularly informed about studies conducted by specialist sciences, the history of law, of customs, or religions, moral statistics, economic sciences, etc., because it is there that are to be found the materials upon which the sociologist works. (Durkheim, *AS* I 1: i)

And Durkheim added that the work to be done was not simply a matter of providing information; in a passage directed to political economy, he suggested that "it can help bring about a convergence between sociology and particular special social sciences which have held themselves aloof, to their own cost and to ours" (ibid.: ii) To this dual objective Simiand

---

[4] Simiand and Marjolin worked on the explanation for economic cycles—a theoretical question central to interwar economic policy. Drawing on Swedish work, Marjolin presented an interpretation of the cycle very different from that of Simiand (Marjolin 1938, 1941), and he clearly distanced himself in respect of method (Marjolin 1941: 303–60; Damalas 1947: 236–37).

added a third: the assessment of historical materialism. This is hardly surprising in view of the stance Durkheim adopted toward Marxism at the time he founded *L'année sociologique*, evident in his review of the book by Antonio Labriola as well as in his correspondence with Mauss. But in fact this question was touched on elsewhere in *L'année*.[5]

If we itemise the contents of the journal systematically, the extent of the work done by Simiand and his collaborators quickly becomes apparent: no fewer than 1,862 books and articles were dealt with over a period of fifteen years. This took up 1,300 pages and made up around 29% of the periodical.

A large minority of the work reviewed was French, accounting for 27% of the items; *L'année sociologique* was therefore very open to foreign publications. If we compare this with the *Revue d'économie politique*, the significance of this is emphasised: of the 1,417 books reviewed in the *Revue* from 1897 to 1912, the 499 foreign publications account for only 35% of the total. In *L'année* German works predominated in the "Economic Sociology" section, accounting for around 50% of the reviews; American and English work by comparison only accounted for something like 10%.

This prompts two comments. First of all, as with Durkheim himself, this preponderance of German references should not be a cause for surprise; for this period it would have been surprising if there were not such a prominence. Secondly, the proportion of books in the German language is not uniformly distributed within the section. Under the heading "Method and General Works", they are not strongly represented and over time gave way to Italian, English and, to a lesser extent, American books. Under the heading "Value, Price and Money", their proportion is high and also stable; while the headings "Production Organisation" and, even more, "Production Forms" were dominated by German works (58% and 76% respectively). The explanation of these variations has to be sought in the principles of classification that Simiand developed.

Principles of Classification

Reconsideration of the contribution and position of economic science requires that an appropriate form of classification of economic facts be

---

[5] We can trace it in the reviews directed to the economy that are not in the fifth section. Despite the range of authors, the argument advanced is nearly always the same: the materialist theory of history lacks validity when it comes to explaining general social facts, and, *a fortiori*, particular social facts. On this point one can consult, among others, Durkheim's own reviews (*AS* I 1: 327–28; *AS* I 2: 317), those of Gaston Richard (*AS* I 2: 418–20), Parodi (*AS* I 5: 132; *AS* I 6: 141), Halbwachs (*AS* I 10: 493–94) and above all, Bouglé's pieces (1908b, 1936: Lectures 1–4).

created. This is how Simiand put it when introducing the fifth section of *L'année sociologique,* volume 2:

> The sociological method in economics encounters serious difficulties as soon as it goes beyond explanation of general and theoretical problems from a social perspective. These difficulties relate to the conduct of scientific research into the concrete material presented to it, which is complex, quite diverse and infinitely varied. . . . What principle of abstraction should be followed? Current practice, more or less well thought-out, diverges considerably here. No one particular approach has been so successful that it has been possible to eliminate others. It is possible that several systems might co-exist, even be superimposed on each other, or combined in such a way that this reality might be properly expressed. Would it not at least be prudent for the time being to establish consistently an initial degree of abstraction, a (perhaps significant) restriction in time and space? (*AS* I 2: 439)

Simiand states that the real problem is neither that of information (disseminating the findings of special sciences among sociologists) nor of using the "social perspective" to illuminate the economic approach, but rather the elaboration of an economic science as a component part of sociology. Behind the problem of classification, Simiand encountered a major methodological problem, that of the principles of abstraction constitutive of an economic sociology.

The heading "Conception of Economic Science, General and Theoretical Economics" appears (sometimes with variant wording) in all volumes of *L'année,* but in the second volume there are three other principal sections: "Economy of Primitive Peoples", "Classical Antiquity and the Occidental Middle Ages" and "Modern and Occidental Economy". But as the lengthy and amorphous fourth section shows, this classification was not capable of resolving the problems with which he was concerned.[6] It was not until the fourth volume that a definitive structure was created, with the classical distinction of production and distribution being associated with concepts of systems, forms and regimes. Subsequent volumes simply refine this classification by introducing the distinction between institutions and representations. Simiand presented a synthesis of his classification in 1912 and then used it for the first volume of the second series (1925: 720-23), in constructing his teaching at the Conservatoire national des arts et metiers (1929–31) and in presenting his work on wages (1932a II).

---

[6] This is also true of later statements by Simiand, when arguing that the idea of the economic fact as independent of the social was of recent origin (1932a II: 582–84).

The classification scheme first distinguishes production from distribution, and then within each of these introduces a further distinction between representations and institutions, these last being examined at three distinct levels in terms of the triptych system/regime/form. By *economic system* is meant "the collection of economic relations and institutions that characterise the economy of a society" (*AS* I 4: 503). Simiand illustrates this with Schmoller's distinctions (family economy, urban economy, regional economy and national economy) or those of Bücher (economy without exchange, with direct exchange and with indirect exchange). By a *production regime* is meant "the institutions of economic production defined and classed with regard to the legal and social relations characteristic of them" (ibid.: 514), while by *form of production* is meant "the institutions of economic productions defined and classed with regard to the technological and morphological relations characteristic of them" (ibid.). Simiand makes clear that his definition of production is extended to include the domain of commerce; and that, in addition, there is no simple relationship between regimes and forms, that is, between law and technology, since one form can be found in several regimes, while one regime is compatible with many forms of production. In the tenth volume, the notion of *type of production* is introduced, there being however no explicit definition of this category; it involves the classification of economic facts, such as the distinctions between agriculture, commerce and industry, or the classification of forms according to their products (*AS* I 12: 628n; see also Simiand 1912: 157).

The classification of the sphere of distribution took longer to arrive at its final form. The first two sections, "economic classes" and "elements of distribution", distinguish institutions from representations. The subdivisions within distributional institutions are then "institutions of distribution" (later, "organs of distribution") and "morphology of distribution".

This classification has similarities with that advanced by Durkheim towards the end of the first chapter of *Rules of Sociological Method*, where he distinguishes levels of social reality according to their temporality (morphological or physiological facts) and their degree of consolidation, from structured organisation to the "free currents of social life" (Durkheim 1982: 58). Here Simiand transforms the distinction by linking physiology to the law, and morphology to technology on the one hand, to demography on the other. Then, remaining at the level of institutions, Simiand introduces the notion of type that Durkheim had used in chapter 4 of *Rules* to clear a path between Comte's grandiose appeal to humanity in general and the narrow perspective of historians familiar only with the particular. Simiand's types of production play the same mediating classificatory role, especially when related—as Bourgin does explicitly (*AS* I 12:

TABLE 3.1
Principles of Classification in the Section "Economic Sociology"

	Production	Distribution
Institution from a global perspective	SYSTEMS TYPES	ECONOMIC CLASSES (according to social status, wealth, economic function)
Organic	REGIMES	ORGANS (according to economic and legal characteristics)
Morphological	FORMS	MORPHOLOGY (location, migration etc.)
Representations	VALUE, PRICE, ELEMENTS OF PRICE, MONEY	ELEMENTS (patrimony, income, wages, interest, rent)

628–29) in the twelfth volume—to the *evolution* of types and to the morphology of production. There remains only the question of the classificatory contrast between institution and representation. In Durkheim, a representation is not "a simple image of reality, a motionless shadow projected into us by things. It is rather a force that stirs up around us a whole whirlwind of organic and psychological phenomena" (1893/1984: 53). Later, discussing pragmatist philosophy, he will go so far as to suggest that collective representations have the power to create social reality (1913–14: 173). Simiand demonstrates great originality in taking up this concept of representation and applying it to those objects which are central to economic theory: prices, price formation, money and the variables of distribution. We shall see at the end of this chapter that the determination of prices and of the variables in distribution (e.g., wages) depends upon the representations of agents.

Following the example of Durkheim and Bouglé, Simiand took a lively interest in the work of Schmoller, and for the most part gave his writings a warm reception. However, once Simiand had registered the way that Schmoller's thinking escaped the accepted framework for economic theory, he became more critical (*AS* I 4: 494–95; *AS* I 8: 518), finding Schmoller's propositions too vague, too centred upon doctrine and marred by a teleological perspective.

We can examine this issue in the context of Simiand's review of Sombart's *Der moderne Kapitalismus*, a review which turned on the problem of classification. Having listed at length the many distinctions made by Sombart, Simiand gave his reasons for finding them unsatisfactory. He thought the classificatory criteria used by Sombart—human motives, intentions, the spirit of human subjects (entrepreneurs)—to be inadequate on three counts. Firstly, Sombart did not construct his classification using objective characteristics (as Bücher had done). Secondly, he employed a priori propositions that were not based upon an analysis of facts. Thirdly, Sombart was said to employ a criterion which had no logical priority in the analysis:

> In a word, isn't the capitalist spirit a product of capitalism, rather than capitalism being the product of a capitalist spirit? In truth, general theses of this kind are not amenable to positive proof and form no part of sociological explanation strictly understood. Sombart's thesis and the Marxist thesis share the same defect (of claiming to provide a single global explanation of very complex circumstances); but Sombart's explanation does not even have the coherence and objectivity of the Marxist explanation. (*AS* I 6: 483)

The critique of the German historical school in *L'année sociologique* was conducted in reviews of monographs in the section "Forms of Production", written in the tenth, eleventh and twelfth volumes by Hubert Bourgin, who questioned how it might be possible to go beyond the unstructured and unimaginative collection of material on forms and sectors of production.

Bourgin thought these monographs to have very many deficiencies. He argued that the terms employed were imprecise, and that use of the term "system" should conform to that elaborated in *L'année sociologique* (*AS* I 10: 579). The same went for the terms "form" and "regime", so that the confusion of technological and legal relations might be avoided. In addition, the monographs under review did not focus precisely enough upon economic questions and became too easily mired in biographical and administrative considerations. Finally, since there was a lack of rigorous classification, no interpretation of results was possible; there was no real assembly of materials that might render possible the study of causes, which was "the true object of the work" (ibid.: 585).[7]

Bourgin refines his criticism in the twelfth volume, building on Simiand's own critique of the "historicist historians [*historiens historicisant*]" (Simiand 1903, 1906). He writes that the monographs produced by such historians are characterised by their monotony, the deadening repetition

---

[7] Here we find a problem that Durkheim had raised in the final chapter of *Rules*, a problem that had led him to oppose Schmoller's strategy: science meant the establishment of *laws*, and to do this, in the social sciences, it was necessary first of all to establish a series of rigorously selected facts before examining them with the aid of the method of concomitant variations, so that one could derive a *proof* in the explanation of the social by the social.

of the same framework, their limited perspectives, their "bureaucratic formalism". He explains the status which has been attributed to these German works and the reasons for his growing dissatisfaction:

> This fastidious repetition of the same tasks, lacking any personal initiative, its impulses channelled and measured by rational direction, is not unique to the seminar, nor more particularly to German researchers. It is almost universal, and indeed French works, because of their inferior coherence, fall below the gross yield that German works achieve through their discipline and rigorous enthusiasm for research. (*AS* I 12: 646)

The solution to the problem lies in the abandonment of this kind of economic historiography, based as it is on a sterile empiricism, in order to deal with *problems* which restructure the material and open out experiences "founded upon the comparison of statistical data, on variations of social facts" (ibid.: 649).[8]

This critique is never without interest and vigour, but at the same time it reveals the limitations of the bold classificatory enterprise upon which *L'année* embarked in the fifth section. Constructing a new classification implied reorganisation of the structure of research and/or of teaching; there was therefore an institutional stake in this, and it could be that the economic sociologists associated with *L'année* lacked the means to realise this on their own, and certainly not in the short term. The editors—here Hubert Bourgin, but it was the same for Simiand—found themselves faced with the fact that work in progress, as well as publications, did not fit easily into the framework that they were developing. This would explain why the section "Type of Production" remained vestigial: it fell to six items in the tenth volume, rose to sixteen in the eleventh, and in the twelfth volume there was what amounted to a confession: "We place here a number studies or monographs on industry which do not, strictly speaking, deal with types of production but which by their title, by the subject of study, do contribute to such work and provide a suitable framework" (*AS* I 12: 630). It was the same with the section "Morphology of

---

[8] The reference to "problems" is a direct echo of the criticism that Simiand had directed at the *historiens historisant*, when he accused them of simply piling up facts that were useless because unrelated to a problem (1903: 162–65). Bourgin's repetition of this criticism rings a little oddly since his own writing is more *historicist* than that of the German *historians* whom he criticises. His article and book on the meat trade (1905, 1907) are quite certainly very carefully done and organised with respect to *L'année*'s classificatory scheme, but they lack breadth and their significance is more historiographic than substantive. Bourgin did acknowledge this in the conclusion to his book (1907: 177). His more theoretical work on market and industry (1924) did not present any findings that one could say added to Durkheimian economic sociology in any significant way.

Distribution", which, for lack of any works to review, could not be initiated before the twelfth volume, and then included only two studies. The Durkheimians here found themselves at an impasse: lacking the power to impose their classification on other scholars, they could only wearily repeat their methodological precepts or let themselves be drawn away from their reviewing activities into work that allowed them to demonstrate the validity of their method and of their classification. Simiand recognised the problem when editing some of his contributions to *L'année* for a book: "In social science there has been rather too much discussion of method in advance of actually doing anything, or rather, instead of doing anything" (1912: 2). Nonetheless, this was the point from which Simiand began, recognising that though one did not have to remain at the level of methodological criticism, it was not possible to bypass it.

ECONOMIC SOCIOLOGY AS A CRITIQUE OF POLITICAL ECONOMY

The critique of the German historical school which ran alongside the elaboration of the classificatory scheme for the "Economic Sociology" section of *L'année* was accompanied by vigorous criticism of "traditional" or "orthodox" economics. The choice of articles made by Simiand in 1912 shows that he directed his attention to different currents of the latter (1912: 5–6) and no longer to the historical school. "Traditional" economics meant for Simiand French liberal economics (for instance, Clément Colson), the Austrian school associated with Eugen von Böhm-Bawerk (dealt with in a critical article on Adolphe Landry), Schumpeter, and the new, mathematics-based economics of Vilfredo Pareto, Irving Fisher, Stanley Jevons and Alfred Marshall. The main thrust of his critique is methodological; Simiand found himself following the route taken by Durkheim from 1885 to 1897, but he had an understanding of the material to which Durkheim had never laid claim and which even Halbwachs could not rival.

The Methodological Critique of Political Economy

The critical aspect of Simiand's economic sociology is very important to the approach which he fostered in *L'année sociologique*. This is closely related to the Durkheimian allegiance to scientific practice, a practice that Durkheim had exemplified in *Rules* and which Simiand sought to introduce into economic sociology. The measure of this is the importance attached to statistics as a means of verification, an approach linked to the title of the final chapter of *Rules*: "Rules for the Demonstration of Sociological Proof". This was acknowledged by his contemporaries, and after

Simiand's death both Durkheimians (Bouglé 1935: Lectures 7–8; Bouglé 1936; Halbwachs 1936) and sympathetic economists (Marjolin 1941: chs. 7–8; Damalas 1944: 195–214) on occasion emphasised Simiand's painstaking approach to questions of method.

The various contributions that Simiand selected for his 1912 book on method are organised around three closely related themes. First of all, Simiand criticises the abstractions used by economists and the way in which they introduced them. Secondly, he denounces the bogus deductions which economists make from their excessively restricted hypotheses to account for the range of observed behaviours as well as the way in which their theories are matched to such behaviour. Thirdly, he insists that economic theory is normative and performative in character.

Taking the first level of this critique, Simiand argues that economists have eliminated social and historical dimensions from economic reality; this is really one of the principal criticisms that Durkheim had already directed to economists, a criticism that others had also raised. Through this Simiand demonstrated the existence of two strong and implicit hypotheses made by economists. The first concerned the existence of the material world and knowledge of it on the part of economic agents. The second concerned the hypothesis of perfect foresight. Whether political economy involved the hypothetical case of Robinson Crusoe on his island or the laws of supply and demand, Simiand opened up for examination everything that economists assumed about social life, knowledge of objects and their qualities, expressed in the classroom examples of which economists were so fond: "He [the ideological theoretician] is compelled to assume an island for Robinson Crusoe, and then on this island trees, coconuts, a river for the canoe made from a tree trunk, etc." (1912: 69). These assumptions took a more institutional turn with exchange: "this theory assumes: prior appropriation, alienable property, alienable according to the wishes of proprietors, the institution of contract to mediate between such wishes, and especially of the contract for exchange and for sales" (ibid.: 92; see also 200–203). Simiand adds to these remarks a series of others concerning the knowledge of the world that the behaviour attributed to the *homo œconomicus* demands. This cognitive socialisation, one might say, concerns the capacity attributed to individuals so that they might be able to assess without problem firstly the quality of the objects with which they are surrounded and secondly the future. In short, these two important dimensions of the social are treated as transparent for the agents involved. Taking an example from daily life, Simiand raises the problem of the appreciation of the quality of a product:

> What precisely will be, for the consumer, the best quality? Of the many elements which go to make up the quality of a good, many are such

that the ordinary buyer is entirely incompetent to appreciate them. . . . The real properties of a chocolate, for example, are already difficult or delicate enough for the average consumer to sense. (ibid.: 16)

It is the same when *homo œconomicus* seeks to look into the future:

But why not include in the hypothesis the man who does not know whether his needs will decrease or whether his resources will increase? . . . So it is said that the case is unreal? On the contrary, it is something that can be observed on a daily basis; but that is of no concern to this method. It is said that nothing new will appear? That is to be seen. That nothing in this case can be foreseen? But is not this lack of determinacy exactly what the theory of interest should deal with? (ibid.: 64–65)

These are telling criticisms, since economic theory would be significantly modified in the course of the twentieth century by introducing uncertainty as regards the qualities of a good on the one hand and in respect of the future on the other. If to this is added the arguments made by Simiand on the sociopsychological phenomena related to the use of money, it is even possible to discern the outlines of a critique whose terms are very close to those employed by the regulation school. Here orthodox economic theory stands accused of reintroducing the social and cognitive foundation which had previously been stripped from economic agents, invoking common knowledge, the acceptance of a material environment and a probabilistic future without any kind of socialisation or understanding between selfish individuals being possible (Aglietta & Orléan 2002: 20–23, 62–63; Orléan 2002: 207–11).

Simiand goes on to criticise the way in which abstractions are generated within economic theory. The economist makes assumptions so that the models with which he works might function, but how to know why these assumptions are introduced and not others? Why does the ideological theorist stop short with a particular model when an infinity of alternative models exists? Simiand suggests that this happens because the economist arbitrarily reintroduces social and historical reality when selecting possible hypotheses, choosing those which, in his view, coincide most closely with the stylised reality which he wishes to explain:

[The ideological theorist] takes up cases that spring to mind from a vague acquaintance with the facts which come to our attention in mere everyday life and become part of our thinking; he takes instances that are self-evident, "that speak for themselves"; or he adopts those cases that other theorists have already used and which have become part of the tradition of so-called "abstract" economics; or he might make casual, unmethodical observations, never securing a complete and objective investigation. (1912: 70)

From that Simiand infers the pseudo-scientificity of economic theory: confounded by the prospect of an infinity of all possible hypothetical cases, economists make a definite but arbitrary selection on an implicit basis which is not susceptible to any assessment of its relation to empirical reality. Since this is the case, writes Simiand, "we ask them to reconstitute their work with all the rigour that scientific experimentation demands" (ibid.: 71). This explains his choice of a different method of abstraction, respectful of the experimental imperative that takes account systematically of empirical data:

> All scientific knowledge proceeds on the basis of abstraction . . . and experimental method is itself, in this sense, abstract whenever it opens out a relation. The nature of the method is not therefore determined by the use of abstraction, but rather by the type of abstraction employed. Instead of abstractions of experimental method ceaselessly seeking to model or shape themselves according to concrete reality, constantly submitting themselves to the control of correspondence with facts, validated only to the extent that such correspondence can be verified, the abstractions in this case [in orthodox theory] are ideas. (ibid.: 57–58)

From there we come to the question of deduction and the confrontation with empirical reality constructed by ideological theory. Simiand argues that the theory of action to which economists adhere is too limited to take account of observed behaviours. Starting from the idea that the qualities of products are not the simple, easily identified givens that economists suppose them to be, and also taking account of the fact that agents can be sidetracked in their comparative evaluations by alternatives in which advantages and disadvantages cannot be disassociated, Simiand argues that self-interested behaviour finds itself confronted with very many possible options. Which will prevail? The economist has no way of deducing this from his premises without making use, once more, of uncontrolled allusions, allusions that do not satisfy the criteria of experimental science (ibid.: 21–22). Simiand consequently characterises orthodox economic theory in the following terms:

> The abstractions that are here at issue are *ideas* formed without restraint in the writer's mind, lacking any immediate concern for their correspondence with the facts; these are defined, modified, combined, guarding only against formal contradiction but with no concern for experimental verification, employing only the rational faculties of deduction, presumption, imagination. . . . The conduct of research will

consist in defining interest according to the characters thought to be analytically fitting, and posing this or that question in terms of the idea of interest so formed . . . seeking to resolve the questions formed in this way through logically correct arguments whose premises are provided by the definition of interest or by analogous definitions, or by the introduction of general postulates of an equally conceptual form. This method should not therefore be called "abstract", but "conceptual" or *ideological*. (ibid.: 58–59)

This therefore raises the question: *how should one go about criticising this ideological construction*? Simiand outlines both empirical and theoretical critiques, showing that both are equally ineffective, and that it is instead necessary to adopt an experimental approach which puts the relation to facts first so that one might then construct a positive economics, or an economic sociology.

Simiand was too familiar with contemporary theory to overlook the fact that economists did seek to confront their formal results with empirical facts, but he thought that this confrontation was inadequate and, above all, biased methodologically. For example, when Irving Fisher endeavoured to verify the quantity theory of money developed in *The Purchasing Power of Money* with statistical and historical studies, Simiand objected that the statistical framework was too narrow (just thirteen years) (*AS* I 12: 715), and that he was indiscriminate in his use of historical material:

> In the work considered below Mr. I. Fisher presents a verification of his theory of interest based upon facts. But he thinks that, in such a case, one should consider oneself satisfied if the facts roughly fit the theory; for the theory is sufficient unto itself, and there is no need to expect an exact conformity for the theory to be considered true; and that if the theory were really false, even a superficial review of the facts would be enough to undermine it. But either theory is sufficient unto itself and facts prove nothing, neither for nor against; or it is not so sufficient, and it needs, if it be judged to be true, to show a conformity with the facts, and not merely compatibility with them. (*AS* I 11: 532–33)

It is in this insulation of theory from facts that Simiand sees the origin of the "methodological scandal" propagated in the economic literature and by mathematical economics: what exercises him especially is the strategy of protecting theory against attempts to falsify it:

> The observation of facts, of or some facts, does it coincide with theoretical principles? If yes, then [ideological economic theory] benefits and proves its worth. Do these facts not so coincide? Then the problem lies

in the complexity of phenomena, the difficulty of making observations that really conform to the theory, the part played by the arbitrary or the contingent that lies in all concrete reality. (1912: 59; see also 187)

But in contrast, Simiand took no comfort from Henry L. Moore's proposal to establish a statistical economics in which pure mathematical theory would draw upon factual elements. He was certainly in favour of the employment of statistics which should "enter into fruitful relations with economic science" (*AS* I 4: 498; *AS* I 5: 473), but he intended to give statistics a role other than a subsidiary one, limited to verifying the abstract theories of political economy developed in isolation from it. It was for this reason that he found Moore's proposed "statistical political economy" or "substantive mathematics" unconvincing.[9] To go further than simply revealing statistical relationships, it was necessary to have an explanatory theory, and Simiand chided Moore for simply adopting traditional theory, without himself seeking an explanation of facts (*AS* I 12: 788). In sum, he accused Moore of failing to develop a genuine positive economics in which theory was faced with facts from the very first and maintained this confrontation of theory with fact; although the price to be paid was of course nothing other than the abandonment of orthodox theory.

This abandonment was also justified by the vacuity of any theoretical critique of economic ideology. Is it enough to maintain that there is no formal contradiction within the theory and that its arguments are all logically correct? No, said Simiand, and in any case few economists were content with such a criterion (1912: 61); he himself responded to this with a stronger argument concerning the explanatory significance of rational argument—the real possibility of a reality that is conceptually contradictory—but this line of argument remained undeveloped.[10] Does criticism have to demonstrate the incompleteness of a given theory for that theory to be completed in a progressive and systematic fashion? The-

[9] Beginning from the idea as stated by Pareto in his *Cours* (1896–97: §§580–81), Moore sought to associate statistical work with the equations of the Lausanne School's pure economics. His interest in the project dated from his work on wages (Moore 1911), and it can be found in more developed form in his book *Synthetic Economics*: "There are three special characteristics which I should like the name *Synthetic Economics* to imply: (1) the use of simultaneous equations to express the *consensus* of exchange, production, capitalization, and distribution; (2) the extension of the use of this mathematical synthesis into economic dynamics where all of the variables in the constituent problems are treated as functions of time; and (3) the still further extension of the synthesis to the point of giving the equations concrete statistical forms. With these implications *Synthetic Economics* is both deductive and inductive: dynamic, positive and concrete" (Moore 1929: 6).

[10] "It remains to be shown elsewhere that these contradictions and conceptual oppositions involve existential impossibilities." (1912: 43).

ory would then be definitive in one respect and deductive in another (ibid.: 61–63). However, Simiand had already noted that the theory in question was incomplete and that all possible deductions were not considered. Perpetuating the "play of theory" in this way, aimed at producing conceptually possible worlds, was purely a vain, Sisyphean task.

Simiand finally characterises orthodox theory in terms of the sociology of knowledge. There has existed since the nineteenth century a scholastic tradition in economics which economists have never been able to untangle (ibid.: 98) and which amounts to a normative position:

> The problem that lies, explicitly or implicitly, at the root of all theories is of the form: what is the most economical way of organising production, and how can it be achieved? The best form of distribution? How are we to obtain more products with less elements of production? How can the greatest possible number of individuals be assured the greatest possible sum of goods? (ibid.: 181)

This normative imperative overturns the principle founding all experimental science. According to Landry, who built upon the Austrian theory of choice, the optimal distribution of income over time is that which equalises the marginal utility of income spent in each period. Simiand questions the significance of this assertion. Does Landry mean that agents will act in this way? No, Simiand discovers, since Landry admits that agents do not necessarily recognise their own self-interest, or may fail to take the trouble to calculate their own interest, and that they pursue rather arbitrary rules in the temporal allocation of their incomes. This really enrages Simiand:

> That which is "arbitrary"—at least from the perspective of an economic science which claims to know and explain reality—amounts, without further argument, to a declaration that the *actual*, *real* rules are *arbitrary*, rules which the positive science must quite rightly make the object of its investigation and the substance of its laws. (*AS* I 8: 585)

The purely logical analysis of ideas based upon an a priori conception of economic behaviour seems quite empty to Simiand so long as it remains locked at the level of this a priori conception. It defines only what might be *possible*, not realities; it represents an abstract logic, a requisite mode of behaviour, not an object actually observable and on the basis of which a positive economic science could be developed, a science capable of discovering social regularities and explaining them.[11] This is meaningless

---

[11] Bourdieu echoes Simiand's conclusion when ironically characterising the academic work of the economist in terms of imaginary variations: "Economists are interesting because they are engineers of imaginary variation, in the Husserlian sense of the term, constructing

unless one supposes that there exists a law of progress—whose existence would have to be demonstrated—which would impel individuals towards the kind of ideal articulated by the theory (1912: 133). Having arrived at this point, Simiand leaves to one side ideological and normative economics so that he might present the elements of a positive economics which takes on the experimental exigencies of modern science. We shall come back to this in chapter 7, since the perspectives that Simiand opens up are original and of lasting importance for a sociology of economic knowledge.

The Interwar Years: Continuity or Powerlessness?

After the First World War, *L'année sociologique* barely got going again, producing only one complete number. Besides containing Marcel Mauss's famous essay *The Gift*, this sole volume is marked by a strong interest on the part of Durkheimians in the work of Max Weber, an interest which is especially marked for Halbwachs. As Heilbron has noted (1985), the journal otherwise continued as before. Simiand resumed the classificatory schema that had been elaborated over the years in the first series, making some interesting innovations[12] but not altering the general structure of the section (*AS* II 1925: 720–23). After this failure, the *Annales sociologiques* became the journal of the Durkheimian school until World War II. Even though the personnel might have changed, the formula to which they worked remained the same; even the section "Mémoires originaux" (original research), which had been dropped after 1908, was revived. But Durkheimian economic sociology received a major setback with the death of Simiand in the spring of 1935.

What happened to economic sociology after the death of Simiand? It is hard to share the enthusiasm that some commentators have shown for Halbwachs's economic sociology, suggesting that he went on to develop an original critique of economic theory (Baudelot & Establet 1994; Pfefferkorn 1997). In this area Halbwachs simply repeats the ideas developed

---

formal models which run on nothing, but all the same providing instruments remarkable for their capacity to break down material evidence, requiring that ideas tacitly accepted be questioned, even if this seems quite paradoxical" (Bourdieu 1994: 195). We should note that this compliment, unusual in Bourdieu, regarding the construction of economic models, is absent from Simiand's assessment, seeking as he was to supersede economic theory with his economic sociology.

[12] Among these we might note the introduction of the topic "industrial organisation" as well as the introduction of a subsection dealing with works in which positive research is combined with axiological or normative perspectives, these works permitting comprehension of "social movements (in the sense in which this expression is used in contemporary everyday language) and the actual realities to which they might correspond" (*AS* II 1925: 723).

and already repeated often enough by Simiand in the first two series of *L'année sociologique*, and Halbwachs openly acknowledged this filiation (1936: 351–60; 1937: 398–400). Systematic comparison of the criticisms made by Simiand of orthodox theory with those of Halbwachs shows this very clearly, but two factors summarise their convergence. First of all, Halbwachs stated many times in his reviews that he did not wish to repeat familiar arguments in respect of the critique of economic theory.[13] Secondly, the proceedings of the seminar at the Centre polytechnicien de recherches économiques (Halbwachs 1937) show that Halbwachs even employed the same examples as Simiand had: reference to the choice between risky and non-risky investments, the formation of price based upon a knowledge of the price in the previous period, rejection of the conception of equilibrium in favour of a succession of disequilibria.

Moreover, Halbwachs failed to come to terms with the rise of abstract economics and, more especially, mathematical economics, fluctuating between a ritual invocation of criticisms already made in the early 1900s and expressions of bewilderment,[14] revealing his incapacity to develop a sociological account of the phenomenon. True, he was at a turning point in the development of economic theory characterized by the growing dominance of the formal approach to economics, and besides simple rejection and the resurrection of past arguments, it was naturally difficult to evaluate such a new phenomenon. But all the same, Halbwachs did not even latch on to an argument already made by Durkheim, later revived (Nogaro 1944: ch. 10), which explained the rise of mathematical economics sociologically through alterations in the educational process on the one hand and on the other by the preoccupations of those who took an interest in the study of economics. The entire period was marked by the increasing engagement of physicists, mathematicians and engineers with economic questions, seeking to find a solution to the serious issues of the day. Their methods and ways of thinking lent marginalist economics the means of taking an ever more prominent place in the academic world, increasingly frequent use of formal argument being a sign

[13] This is evident in a review of Jacques Rueff's *Des sciences physiques aux sciences morales*: "He [Rueff] seeks to present a rational exposition of the theory of classical political economy, which he calls Euclidian. . . . We come back to criticisms which we have already made, time and again, of theories from which this work nowhere deviates in any essential respect" (*AS* II 1925: 736). A similar comment can be found in the review of George and Edouard Guillaume's *Economique rationnelle* (*AS* III D 3: 44).

[14] For example: "It is in fact curious to observe at present the renewal of interest everywhere in those writers who have constructed deductive systems, often mathematical in nature, an interest especially marked in the United States, where they seem to have been discovered for the first time; such work appeals neither to history, nor to statistics, but instead deploys the remarkable qualities of a forceful and subtle dialectic" (Halbwachs 1940: 7).

of this.[15] This presented difficulties for the Durkheimians, since this approach could well have been endorsed by the kind of quantitative social economics that had been long advocated, first by Simiand and then by Halbwachs.[16]

But Halbwachs did continue Simiand's concerns; one can only praise his far-sightedness in the attention he gave to Keynes, Joan Robinson and Arthur Pigou. Keynes's *Tract on Monetary Reform* (1923) and then later his *Treatise on Money* (1930) had been dealt with at length by Simiand (in *L'année sociologique* of 1925 and then in *Annales sociologiques* in 1934). Halbwachs reviewed the *General Theory* three times,[17] French economists otherwise showing little enthusiasm for the book by the great Cambridge economist.[18] The interest that Halbwachs showed in this book is therefore far from conventional, and his foresight was commendable; but all the same, a reading of the reviews reveals the limitations of his understanding.

The two principal reviews have the same structure. Halbwachs presents Keynes's own concepts, beginning with his rejection of the usual treatment of the labour market; he then passes to the determination of the underemployment equilibrium, whose explanation relates to the inclination of the consumer either to invest or to express a preference for liquidity. What position does the sociologist adopt when faced with arguments whose novelty is clear to him?[19] Halbwachs fell back on methodology:

Decisive progress is decided on the terrain of method, and such progress involves the entire future of a science. Error here, even eclectic compro-

---

[15] The development of formalisation in economics can be dated from the years 1925–35, especially in the USA, where physicists and mathematicians took an interest in economics so that they might elaborate the still latent potential of marginalist theory, which up to that point had played quite a minor role in the university world. My study of the *Revue économique* has revealed a similar process in France, displaced to the 1960s when economists emerged who in many cases had a background in engineering; they overturned the sociological approach of the *Revue*'s founders and replaced it with an economic orthodoxy (Steiner 2000a).

[16] "In other words, these men have lived, they live in an economic milieu *which has this particularity, remarkable in itself, and which is perhaps the great mystery of political economy: here opinions take the form of quantities*" (Halbwachs 1937: 400, my emphasis).

[17] Firstly, a short half-page review in *Annales sociologiques* (AS III D 3 1937: 114); the book had also been mentioned earlier (1937: 51); secondly, a "Mémoire" in the fourth volume (AS III D 4 1940: 25–41); and finally, the substantial presentation which was included in *Sociologie économique et démographique* (Halbwachs 1940: 9–17).

[18] French economists showed little enthusiasm for the *General Theory*; it was not until the end of the Second World War that the ideas of Keynes gained a foothold in French universities (Arena & Maricic 1988; Abraham-Frois & Larbre 1998).

[19] This is certainly true of the notion of an underemployment equilibrium; and it is even more the case with the definition of the rate of interest as a price paid for surrendering liquidity (Halbwachs 1940: 14–15).

mise, condemns all who work towards this end to pointless and indefinite recurrence. (*AS* III D 4: 28)

In a way that says everything. As could be expected, Keynes did not bother to follow Simiand's prescriptions: he did not seek to base his new categories on patient interpretation of statistical facts. Consequently Halbwachs rejects his new categories as "elementary empirical observations" and "simple possibilities". In short, Keynes's method is "dialectic and abstract" (Halbwachs 1940: 9), and if Keynes did manage to capture some fragments of reality he was not entirely conscious of so doing: "What is crucial is that the theoretician is entirely incapable of dealing with that part of reality which is unconsciously introduced into his conceptions. But the real cannot be dealt with that way. It has to be taken entire, or not at all." (*AS* III D 4:41) This argument is pushed even further, for "Keynes' notions and hypotheses have only a formal precision. It is not evident to what observable reality they apply, or might apply" (ibid.: 18) Halbwachs then tries to clarify his critique by explaining what part of the real it is that infiltrates the *General Theory*. The essential difference between Keynes and the classical economists is that Keynes seeks to take account of the very real and contemporary phenomenon of unemployment. If the book is of interest, it is not because of the superior analytic ability of its author or his greater capacity to make deductions from a framework of given axioms but because of the way in which he takes account of new behaviour. What kind of new behaviour is involved?

Halbwachs's response, not without audacity, isolates differences in the behaviour of the labour force. At the beginning of the nineteenth century, when wages amounted to subsistence payments, workers tended to act rather in the way that marginalist theory would have them behave: they sought to equalise the marginal disutility of work with the marginal utility of wages. Halbwachs maintained that today this is no longer so (*AS* III D 4: 41), pointing to "an accumulation of requirements that are in some respects now indispensable" to workers; that is to say, workers now had expectations about the level of wages which rendered the mutual adjustment of the supply and demand for labour more difficult to realise.

In sum, Halbwachs failed to identify the actual points of contact between Keynes's thinking and that of Durkheimian economic sociology— such as the argumentation in terms of monetary aggregates, especially as regards wages; the importance given to the opinions, anticipations or representations of agents (especially those of the entrepreneur); and the role given to social context in understanding market functioning, especially the role of the speculator in financial markets.[20] Of course, one has

---

[20] But Halbwachs noted the curious configuration that Keynes introduced to explain the behaviour of the financial speculator: "But how are the expected returns to be determined, that is to say, future annuities? . . . This is done at most for a few months ahead, the future

to guard against being too critical of Halbwachs, but it is significant that in the first postwar number of *L'année*, Lutfalla clearly showed the convergence between Durkheimian economic sociology and the approach adopted in the *General Theory*. Lutfalla noted important modifications to the conceptualisation of *homo œconomicus* owing to the "social relevance" attached to this concept when decisions are not based upon perfect foresight, but depend instead upon market uncertainties and social opinion (Lutfalla 1948: 654–55). He suggested that this line of thinking had especial relevance to the speculator and to the formation of stock market valuations, then emphasised how this approach converged with the work of sociologists interested in collective opinion—he referred to Jean Stoetzel's *Théorie des opinions*, a book by a former student of Halbwachs—which we know how to deal with quantitatively. Later in his article, Lutfalla drew attention to the way in which economists took collective representations as given facts, an attribution not without basis since these representations became fixed for the duration of any period being studied, and he gave as an example the relative stability of needs which Halbwachs had himself discovered in respect of the working classes (ibid.: 656). He also insisted that Keynesian propensities were social representations, attributed to social groups and not to isolated individuals, and that if Keynes was perhaps guilty of the sin of introspection, his followers went on to found their work upon observation (Lutfalla 1949: 659). Where Halbwachs had simply repeated conventional criticisms which were already outmoded by Simiand's last writings (1937), in which he studied the social psychology of crises in the short run, Lutfalla, certainly with the great benefit of hindsight, opened new perspectives, some of which are now at the heart of contemporary research combining economic and sociological approaches (Favereau 1988; Orléan 1992).

Contrasting Reactions

We have outlined above Simiand's profound dissatisfaction with the state of political economy. His was by no means a lone voice at this point in the history of economic thought, but he was unique in developing an economic sociology aimed at the foundation of a new form of economic science. The work of review and of classification did not go unnoticed by

---

returns over several years remain indeterminate. Hence one relies upon the opinion of others, more exactly, upon what one thinks the opinion of others will be. It is just like one of those newspaper competitions where competitors have to choose the six nicest from ten photographs. It is a matter not of choosing those one likes best, but the six that one thinks others will like best (each of the competitors making the same assumption)" (Halbwachs 1940: 14; *AS* III D 4: 33).

economists. The section on economic sociology within the *Année sociologique* had a favourable reception. Gide saw in it a kind of annual encyclopaedia (1908), and Jean Lescure regarded the bibliography published each year as definitive. So favourable was this reception on the part of economists that the creation of an *Année économique* was mooted (Bouhet 1901), an enterprise that would find partial realisation for the *Revue d'économie politique* in the section edited by Landry in 1906 and 1907. And there was even a professor of political economy at the University of Toulouse, Léon Polier, who used the classification from *L'année* in constructing his lecture courses (Polier 1911). Simiand for his part argued that Polier used this classification out of context, that his approach was insufficiently positive and that it lacked a sociological orientation.

We can note the tone of approval in commentary where the use of statistics and the consequent results are concerned. The sustained effort to draw theoretical principles from the statistical facts patiently gathered by Simiand was very favourably received by statistical economists such as Arthur Bowley (1907) and Lucien March (1903, 1907), even if they suggested that Simiand was too exacting in his approach.

The reaction to questions of method was different however, indeed, quite negative.[21] Reacting to the publication of Simiand's dissertation in 1907, economists such as Colson, Landry and von Zwiedinek refused to acknowledge that Simiand's work might represent a refutation of the determination of wages through the workings of supply and demand. This was because Simiand used an indicator (relation of production to the number of workers employed) which was too broad and indiscriminate for his purposes, and it could also be said that his study failed to make explicit the determination of wage *rates*, since he dealt only with one isolated industry and disregarded what happened in other sectors. More brutally, in the case of Colson and Landry, he was accused of being ignorant of the theories he was attacking. On balance, these economists thought that Simiand's findings were less novel than he claimed, and von Zwiedinek cited works which, independently of Simiand's method, had shown that the supply curve for labour reverses as wages increase.

Our purpose here is to assess the significance of Simiand's positive economics in the context of other contemporary research and to assess his method. Many French economists went along with the suggestion made by Bouglé (1936) and Halbwachs (1936) that Simiand was a "rational empiricist". By this they meant that beyond the attention that Simiand

---

[21] The best reaction remains that of Joseph Schumpeter (1914), who made the error of thinking that Simiand rejected abstract theory because he rejected marginalist theory. This is therefore a very significant misunderstanding; the review is consequently extremely negative, Simiand appearing to be ignorant and pretentious in equal proportions.

gave to the observation of facts, he sought to identify regularities and explain them sociologically—rationally—in such a way that they gained the status of laws. A young economist who was not among his admirers, but who took him seriously, commented astutely:

> It is the latter [Simiand, rather than Aftalion] who at first sight seems most representative of positive political economy: his entire life is given over to the scrupulous observation of facts. He does not wish to form any hypotheses, but rather limit himself to finding in facts the regularities and relationships that are initially hidden from the observer. He was the one who set up the two antithetical formulations which we have used, characterising rational economics as "theories without facts" and positive economics as "facts without theory". But all the same, we do not find in Simiand a representative of a pure positive attitude. He likes to say that he is an empiricist. He has certainly not constructed a theory without facts, but it is not just facts from which his theory is developed. There is some degree of discontinuity between his positive study of wages and his theory of wages. (Guitton 1938: 63–64; see also Guglielmi: 1945: 350–51, 385)

The most insightful critique of Simiand's method came from the philosopher Gustav Belot's review of the *Essai sur le prix de charbon* (1901). Belot is dubious about an "experimental" method setting out to observe raw facts. Is that just empiricism, he asks? What kind of sociology seeks "to prevent all intellectual assessment prior to the consideration of raw facts" (1903: 98)? More seriously, Belot accuses Simiand of confusing the order of investigation with that of exposition and taking the artifice of the latter for the reality of the former:

> Putting some conclusions at the beginning of the article, presenting them as general hypotheses suggested by psychology and economics (but neither arbitrary nor fanciful in themselves) and then providing statistics and graphs by way of verification, I really do not see how this inversion would diminish the scientific merit of conclusions drawn. . . . More exactly, it happens that M. Simiand proceeds in this way, determining through argument what is being sought, and then asking of the statistical material an indication of reality. (ibid.: 98)[22]

The polemical exchange between Simiand and Colson in the *Revue du mois* following Halbwachs's review of Simiand (Halbwachs 1908) likewise showed up the ambiguities in Simiand's position. He finally conceded to Colson that "established psychological tendencies used in his expla-

---

[22] For his part, March thought Simiand's theory of action to be an a priori construction (March 1903: 70; see also 1907: 159), a judgement which is entirely right.

nation do not flagrantly contradict ordinary economic psychology" (Simiand 1909: 348).[23] And if he sought refuge in the argument that these psychological dispositions were not individual but social, he also acknowledged that this point was not established in his 1907 book and would have to be made the object of a later piece of work.

These comments need to be kept in mind. There are very many passages in which Simiand, like Durkheim before him, states that the use of abstraction is a necessary part of the scientific enterprise; why should it be any different with *homo œconomicus*? When Simiand criticises this concept as an abstract, a priori form employed in the arguments of political economy, he has in mind more the imprecise use of the concept than the concept itself. This lack of precision in Simiand was partly resolved by his theory of economic action, which was nothing other than a *specification of self-interested behaviour* on the part of *homo œconomicus*. A good illustration of the position that Simiand adopted in the 1930s can be found in the way he criticised the quantity theory of money.[24] When Simiand reviewed Fisher's writings in *L'année sociologique* (*AS* I 12: 704–20), he paid little attention to this theory and noted:

> The regular impact of the quantity of money on prices is effected through a number of intermediaries, a particular sequence of cause and effect, which sequence is much more complex than the simplistic quantity theory, but also much more suggestive. (ibid.: 719)

The series of intermediaries to which Simiand alluded are the actions of individuals faced with a changing context, lacking transparency, in which the understanding of behaviour rests on economic representations.[25] When Simiand discussed the question of long price cycles in his seminar of 1930–32, he had no hesitation in assigning the quantity theory an important function: an increase in the quantity of money has an impact both upon prices and quantities, on account of the actions of agents who seek

[23] Belot had again clearly stated the problem: "What difference is there between invoking 'psychological dispositions common to all of one class of men' or making assertions as is usually done with regard to the motives of *the* worker, *the* capitalist, *the* trader etc.?" (1933: 99).

[24] The quantity theory of money states that there is a direct relationship between the quantity of money (M) and the price level (P). If one takes into account the velocity of the circulation of money (V), and the number of transactions, the equation is given by $MV = PT$; the right-hand side of the equation can be written as Σpq, expressing the total value of transactions.

[25] "In this simplistic and erroneous elimination—*basically between quantities and quantities, and even between values and values, Mr. Fisher only forgets man*—man who transmutes physical quantities into values, and these values are estimated in terms of other values according to regularities and tendencies, discovery of these last being the task proper to economic science" (*AS* I 12: 720).

to profit from more remunerative productive and commercial activities during periods of high prices (1930–32: 498–501). The human action introduced by Simiand is nothing other than that of a historically specific *homo œconomicus*:

> It has to be recognised that between the original magnitudes and the subsequent magnitudes there stands the indispensable factor—*man*. And this factor is no doubt a *homo œconomicus*, but an economic man who is no longer some kind of abstract automaton, timeless and universal as with the classical economic man (ibid.: 550–51)

This modulated conception of economic man has an important place in his major work on wages, where Simiand deals with the way in which human action makes connections between the variations of nominal economic magnitudes, in other words, of money:

> We end up finding that the action of a "homo œconomicus" characterised by these [general psychological] traits already provides a direct explanatory framework . . . but the "homo œconomicus" which our objective observation of facts discloses appears to us to be the outcome of economic evolution taking place within a distinct framework, involving the formation and constitution of social groupings—workers, employers, and others. And the action of this "homo œconomicus" is determined solely by this evolutionary process, and according to precise relations inaccessible to introspection, and which are only accessible through experience analysed objectively. It does not involve an individual spontaneity identical at all times and all places, but rather a social reality formed by the facts and elements of a society of this or that type under these or those conditions. (1932a II: 500)

By placing emphasis on the way that Simiand moderated his position in this way we are not suggesting that he changed his mind and implicitly reintroduced the very positions that he had previously so vigorously criticised. It is rather a question of recognising clearly the positions that Simiand developed, and which can be found in his elaboration of the notion of economic representations as means for grasping quantitatively the explanatory elements and the consequences of socioeconomic facts.

SOCIAL REPRESENTATIONS AND THE FORMATION OF ECONOMIC MAGNITUDES

Simiand's methodological criticism has to be appreciated at two levels. Firstly, his criticism bore upon the "bad abstractions" used by economists, especially that of a *homo œconomicus*; but as we have seen, his contemporaries had doubts about the real significance of this critique, doubts which led Simiand to qualify his views in the 1930s. Secondly, and more responsive to the conduct of research, Simiand dug deeper. He demonstrated the role of economic representations, which allow the sociologist to understand social regularities, since these representations explain the manner in which individuals perceive the economic reality in which they are placed and act accordingly.

Taking account of social representations in economic affairs is critical. We have seen how they emerged as an original factor in the classificatory schema through which Simiand and his colleagues organised *L'année*'s "Economic Sociology" section. There was at work here an intuition that can perhaps be compared to the theorisation of uncertainty as elaborated by Frank Knight (1921) or to some of Keynes's ideas. In any case, this lent the critique of political economy a very particular direction. Simiand supposed that the quantitative dimension out of which social and economic facts are built, a dimension diverted by some economists into a mathematical economics (Walras 1988: §§29–30), was accessible to sociological analysis. He maintained that economic magnitudes (value, price, money, the variables of distribution) were means with whose aid the social representations of a given society might be objectified, using statistics drawn from a period sufficiently lengthy for it to become plain how these representations evolved, together with the behaviours based upon them. Let us examine the significance of this powerful assumption.

As Durkheim had already done in his *Rules*, Simiand was led into criticism of the law of supply and demand, a law of whose explanatory character he was dubious:

> Free competition is nothing more than a mechanism (whether for good or for evil is another matter) ensuring that a price will be fixed at a level such that it will be locally recognised; but it is not free competition which explains why this rate should be at this or that level. (*AS* I 12: 607; see also Simiand 1912: 202–3)

From this Simiand concludes that *the social determination of rates of exchange depends upon the social representations which organise the conduct of economic agents*. The introductory remarks to the *Essai sur les prix de charbon*, which Simiand published in *L'année* for 1902, is very clear on this point:

> When I sell or buy something, which happens very often in the system of our economic life today, and if, which is also quite usual, I give or receive money, or at least estimate in money the equivalent of what I provide or receive, I ordinarily have the feeling that the determination of this equivalent in money, or the price, does not simply arise from me

as an arbitrary individual, nor from my partner in exchange as an arbitrary individual, nor from agreement between the two. (1902: 1)

This formulation is only a plagiary of Walras on competitive price as a natural price and, therefore, as the possible foundation of economic science. But Simiand does inflect this idea, since he does not retain the Walrasian principle that the market functions as an institution of socialisation in which each agent participates, through his own supply and demand, in the fixing of a price which, in turn, is *imposed* on every market participant as a "price taker". He argues that the social nature of prices comes not from the market as a space of economic socialisation but from a level that is logically prior, constraining individuals before they even emerge on the market, and Simiand deals with the matter at this level:

> The very estimation that I make of a thing before an exchange, and which I freely consider to be carefully considered and personal, derives more or less from the established rate. The proof of that, although exceptional in our society where I know of no evaluation common across a social milieu, while being also very conscious of the individual basis for my act of exchange, my felt need and effort expended, my estimation in money is entirely undetermined, and if it is fixed, then it has the air of being fixed by pure chance. (ibid.: 1–2)

And so for Simiand it is necessary that a point of reference exists for economic magnitudes—the price in the previous period, for instance—for market socialisation to occur. This lends a social character and a social objective to the market mechanism, preserving its psychological nature in estimations and opinions. This thought explains Simiand's profound dissatisfaction in respect of political economy, which not only assumed a large number of institutional conditions to be given but furthermore presumed that prices already existed at the moment they were to be determined:

> The entire analysis is built upon the initial assumption that buyers and sellers arrive on the market with an estimated price for this object. This assumption implies the prior existence of a market price for this object. Let us consider facts as they really are: individual estimations of price are derived from a price that is known and has already been realised, they form in the mind of the individual, differing plus or minus from that which that individual knows of the value already commonly attributed to the object. The proof of this is that where a new object is concerned, or an object for which those engaged in transactions know of no established price, the estimation of values made by those involved will be entirely indeterminate, arbitrary, and even incapable of being fixed—so no notion of a definite quantity will exist. The radical

vice of this theory is ultimately that it seeks to explain a phenomenon that is social in nature through individual phenomena which precisely derive from this social phenomenon itself, and can only exist by virtue of it. (1912: 210; see also *AS* I 1: 468, 472)

To match up with a priori method, he appealed for a positive theory of need:

The material which this theory must elaborate will be found, in all the given facts that we can recover and which are becoming increasingly numerous—on consumption and the movements of consumption, on the use of incomes and the variations in such use, on household budgets for different social categories on different societies, on tendencies, the habits related to them and their variation etc. By its nature this theory will find itself on the frontier of general social psychology, and it will place itself there, without doubt, among the dominating and most powerfully explanatory theories within all economic sociology. (*AS* I 11: 708)

Halbwachs moved in this direction with his study *La classe ouvrière et les niveaux de vie*, especially where he elaborated a typology of social representations relating price and quality, as we shall see in the following chapter.

In his final works, Simiand deepened the role of representations in economic processes, especially when he took an interest in the functioning of financial markets and in monetary crises (1934a, 1937). The opinions of actors, and not only immediately evident actors, are treated as social facts of prime importance in the financial market, since they are the expression of a social belief directed to the future which determines the value of securities and of money (1937: 6). On this sociological foundation, Simiand explains that the modern market does not function in terms of real magnitudes—such and such a quantity demanded or supplied at this price on this market—but in terms of conjecture, since the market works towards the future. That also explains the growing number of experts and intermediaries in the working of the market. Then he suggests that the phenomenon of monetary crisis sets in motion groups of actors having quite different economic representations (1937: 27), which in turn leads him to boldly reformulate the question of market coordination, seeing there a problem of the "coordination of impressions" between social actors with diverse economic representations (1937: 28).

In sum, the virulence of his methodological criticism should not divert attention from the profound originality of Simiand's economic sociology: the role of social representations in economic behaviour. There are many dimensions to this perspective. We have seen the essentially critical dimension in respect of orthodox economic theory, but there is also a constructive side to it, placing representations at the heart of a research strategy in which the social representation is grasped both quantitatively and historically in taking account of social behaviour in the modern economy.

CHAPTER FOUR

Positive Political Economy, or Durkheimian Economic Sociology

Simiand, Hubert Bourgin and Halbwachs devoted a considerable amount of effort to demonstrating the general validity of their method. Whatever time remained after their extensive reviewing for *L'année* was given over to the completion of books and articles whose importance today is in need of reassessment.

First of all we will consider those domains in which Simiand and Halbwachs specialised, where they seem to have arrived at a division of labour: wage formation in the case of Simiand and workers' consumption for Halbwachs. The treatment of social representations that they developed was of great theoretical significance for economic sociology and involved the creation of a theory of economic action which they thought to have general applicability.

The increasing generality of Durkheimian economic sociology did not end here. During the 1930s Simiand and Halbwachs turned their attention to transformations in contemporary capitalism, highlighting a number of systemic modifications to its institutional structure. In examining this aspect of their work, we will seek to distinguish points of convergence and of difference between Durkheimian positive economics and the regulation school.

One terminological point must be clarified. During the 1930s Simiand thought of his work as belonging to positive political economy; there is mostly little difference in meaning between this and economic sociology. However, in French political economy, "positive political economy" is taken to refer to a methodological position where exclusive adherence to one method (whether abstract or historical) is considered inadequate (Aftalion 1938: 1–3; Denis 1938; Pirou 1939: 144ff.; Marjolin 1941: pt. 3); this position therefore follows on from the *Methodenstreit* of late nineteenth-century Germany and Austria. Simiand is one of the first among French economists to use the term in this way. But use of the term "positive political economy" should not obscure important differences among those economists who used it. Simiand was very hard on abstract theory and gave the impression that he advocated an extreme variant of positivism, concerned solely with the discovery of statistical regularities. Aftalion, by contrast, started from the concepts of Austrian theory and then moved on to empirical factors, an approach similar to that of Moore's *Synthetic Economics*, a work that Simiand had dismissed. But we need to be careful in making such a sharp distinction. At times Simiand was not entirely consistent in his use of methodological formulations. Moreover, Simiand has a theory of social behaviour through which he interpreted empirical regularities derived from history and statistics. We will call this approach Durkheimian positive political economy (or Durkheimian economic sociology), reserving the generic term "positive political economy" for those, like Aftalion and Marjolin, who retained the rationalist tenets of orthodox economic theory when dealing with the empirical facts of statistics.

When applied to empirical work, Durkheimian economic sociology can perhaps be most directly characterised by considering what Simiand's various writings have in common and turning these common factors into a set of procedural guidelines. We find the following: firstly, the economic sociologist carefully establishes the facts that constitute the empirical evidence in the absence of which there can be no talk of positivism. Secondly, the facts are arranged in series so that covariations may be studied. Thirdly, passing from statistical to causal relationships, sociological theory explains human behaviour. The law obtained in this way can then be tested on evidence from "another event". Then, finally, the economic sociologist can arrive at forecasts for the purposes of economic policy.

Sociology of Economic Action

In this chapter we shall concentrate on the third of these points. It will be shown that in no respect should Simiand and Halbwachs stand accused either of employing "facts without theories" or producing "theories without facts".

Representations, Social Conflict and Wage Formation

Simiand's dissertation contains a lengthy discussion of the quality of evidence, following which he identifies four annual statistical series:

J = number of days worked
W = average annual monetary wage
Y = total annual physical production
p = sale price per ton

Using this statistical material, he constructs annual series for the variables upon which his analysis is to be based:

$w = W/J$, average daily wage
$w_m = W/Y$, average labour cost per ton, or average wage per ton
$y_m = Y/J$, average physical production per day worked
$v = (Y.p)/J = p.y_m$, average value of production per day worked.

Simiand is able to demonstrate on this basis that statistical regularities exist and that a socioeconomic explanation can be found for these regularities. Social representations play a central role here, since they connect the information available to agents, the decisions made by these agents and observed behaviour.

First of all, Simiand identifies the following regularities. When the price of coal (p)—an exogenous variable in the 1901 study—increases significantly, then the average wage per ton produced (w_m) also rises, but to a lesser degree than the price; the average production per day worked (y_m), an indicator of the level of labour productivity, remains constant or falls slightly; and finally, the daily wage (w) rises less strongly than the average wage per ton.[1] When the price falls, the three other variables for a time continue to move as they had previously done (w_m continues to increase, y_m decreases and w continues to increase or remains constant). However, if the price continues to fall, the sign of the variations for the other three variables reverses: w_m falls at about the same rate as p, y_m increases and w remains constant or decreases, but less quickly than w_m. Having got to this point, and introducing the daily output per worker (v), Simiand emphasises the relationship w/v in which:

$w = W/Y.Y/J$, or $w = w_m.y_m$
$v = p.Y/J$ or $v = p.y_m$
and hence the relationship $w/v = w_m/p$

This relationship is treated by Simiand as an inverse index of the gain made by the owners, and he adds:

- that the variations in the increase of w and v correspond to the variations in the increase of p
- that w varies less strongly than v
- that these correspondences highlight the discrepancies over time
- that $w_{max} \leq \alpha.v^2$ [2]

[1] The argument is as follows: $w = W/J$ and $w_m = W/Y$; when w_m increases, w also increases but to a lesser extent if $w/w_m = y_m = Y/J$ is slightly decreasing.

[2] This final argument is critical for Simiand since, as we shall see below, it serves to demonstrate how, in his theory of action, one moves from one particular configuration of interactions between groups to others. The coefficient α is not defined exactly by Simiand, and the statistics that he cites display strong variations in the relationship w/v, the most extreme being 37.1% (1873) and 52.1% (1892).

How might these statistical regularities be interpreted? The answer is given in the published version of his PhD dissertation:

> But these apparent and created relationships still amount to no expla-nation. We might here use an analogy to express just where our inves-tigation has got to: we contend that a particular mechanism engages or disengages, and that then some other parts move in this or that man-ner; but we still do not know what action lies behind this engagement or disengagement, nor whether this engagement or disengagement leads to, or merely allows, the movement of other parts and, in this latter instance, what the action might be which brings about this move-ment; nor, finally, what is or are the principle(s) involved in these ac-tions and which are the scientific *causes* of the phenomenon. (1907: 188–89)

The interpretation rests on the idea that self-interested human action (ibid.: 290, 310) intervenes to create the connection between the vari-ables. However, Simiand knows that there are many ways of behaving in a self-interested manner. His theory of action is based upon the idea that four tendencies coexist within each economic agent:

T_1: tendency to continue to enjoy the same gain
T_2: tendency to increase effort
T_3: tendency to have a greater gain
T_4: tendency to diminish effort

Simiand thinks that tendencies related to gain outweigh those involv-ing effort (T_1 dominates T_2, and T_3 dominates T_4) and that conserva-tional tendencies outweigh those related to novelty (T_1 and T_2 dominate T_3 and T_4). This last point is justified by reference to the psychological phenomenon of habit, whose force is the greater the longer the phenom-enon lasts (ibid.: 300–301). These tendencies are of different weight, but their order has to be strictly observed, such that T_2 can only be satisfied if T_1 is satisfied, and so on, with the exception of T_3 and T_4, which can adjust to each other, that is to say, they can both be partially and simul-taneously satisfied. Finally Simiand suggests how these tendencies are re-alised in the relation of worker and employer: when tendencies of a dif-ferent level come into conflict, it is the highest order which prevails; and if tendencies of the same order (e.g., $T_{1.w}$ against $T_{1.e}$, where the tendency T_1 on the part of the workers clashes with T_1 on the part of the employ-ers), there has to be a trade-off which involves tendencies of a lower order ($T_{2.w.}$ and $T_{2.e.}$). This theory of action[3] is Simiand's most interesting con-

---

[3] Durkheim himself left open the option that Simiand faces here—when in *Rules* he re-ferred to psychological laws to interpret statistical regularities. This use of psychology is all

tribution, one which will now be set to work in the interpretation of the cycle, since Simiand himself did not systematically do so.

The point of departure is set with a rise in the price of coal (p) which automatically brings about a downward variation in the relationship $w/v = (w_m \cdot y_m/(p \cdot y_m))$, so there is an improvement in the index to the advantage of the employer. This amounts to saying that the tendency $T_{3.e}$ is satisfied.

If we proceed to consider succeeding periods in which the price of coal continues to increase, then we find that the daily wage (w) also increases. Simiand summarises the relationship between the variations of w_m and w and then introduces the wage rate r_w:

$$\Delta w_m > \Delta w \text{ and } \Delta r_w > \Delta w$$

The first inequality is explained by the fact that $w = w_t \cdot y_p$ and that y_p has a tendency to fall during this period. The second arises from the fact that in periods when the wage rate increases new workers are taken on for whom the daily wage is less than that of those already employed because of their lower level of labour productivity. Simiand never *explicitly* examined the determination of the wage rate—an omission that lent force to the criticisms of Colson and Landry mentioned in chapter 3; instead he appealed to the inherent conflicts of the wage relation and in justification cited statistics on strikes. During the phase in which prices rise $T_{3.e}$ and $T_{3.w}$ come into conflict and are led to seek agreement according to $T_{4.e}$ and $T_{4.e}$. Employers who, without any effort having been made on their part, were happy to see an improvement in their financial gain concede a partial satisfaction of this same tendency to workers by increasing the wage rate. This outcome is more easily achieved when there is a relative improvement in the index of employers' gains (w/v). When the period of rising prices is prolonged, new workers are taken on and this in turn leads to a fall in labour productivity, but not by enough to explain the claimed fall in productivity; this comes from action taken by the workers themselves. With T_3 satisfied and on account of "habit", workers have maintained their level of effort; but with the continuation of the phenomenon, they also come to satisfy their last tendency (T_4), seeking to reduce their level of effort, which is where the fall in y_m comes from. Tendencies T_3 and T_4 are not exclusive; after at a certain point individuals seek to satisfy them simultaneously. Simiand argues that this phenomenon occurs when the daily wage has risen by between 20% and 25%; beyond this point, pursuit of an increase in the daily wage translates into T_4 and

---

the more surprising for an author who produced the rule that when a social fact is explained by a psychic fact, one could be sure that the explanation was false (Durkheim 1982: 129).

consequently into a fall in labour productivity. From this we can see that there is a reversal in the labour supply curve when the nominal salary rises beyond a certain threshold. The fall in productivity is also the outcome of the same behaviour on the part of the employer, who satisfies his tendency T_4 by reducing efforts at mechanisation in particular. This lasts as long as the relation w/v (or w_m/y) continues to fall, or while the increase in this relationship is less than the level α by virtue of the relation $w_{max} \leq \alpha.v$.

When the price of coal falls, v also falls, and since w remains constant for a time, the relation w/v increases. The tendency $T_{3.e}$ is blocked and $T_{1.e}$ takes its place, seeking to maintain the increasing nominal gain. As a result, the striving of workers for increased wages (in fact for r_w, by means of strikes) seeking satisfaction of $T_{3.w}$ clashes with $T_{1.e}$, which does not give way. The conflict between $T_{1.e}$ and $T_{1.w}$ now runs its course: workers wish to maintain the same gain (w) while the employers seek to reduce it or, alternatively, maintain the same gain (w/v), which can be done only by reducing w since v falls in line with the fall in price p. The employers' tendency to retain the same gain is effected through a fall in the wage rate, which workers are either unable to resist or only partially able. This fall in r_w brings about in turn a *downward tendency* in w and a *fall* in w_m as a result, since Simiand makes clear that the fall in w_m conforms to the movement of the price p, the relation w/v (or w_m) becomes constant. This all being given, the tendency $T_{1.w}$ can only be satisfied by resort to the lower-order tendency $T_{2.w}$, that is, through increased effort on the part of workers. This explains the turnaround in labour productivity y_m, which also explains how, after a brief and minor fall by 5% or 10%, the daily wage w (= $w_m.y_m$) remains constant: positive variations in y_p compensate the negative variations of w_m. Simiand adds that a similar sequence occurs on the employers' side, in that it seems the fall in the wage rate is not of itself capable to affect the relation w/v, since the tendency on the part of workers to retain their gain ($T_{1.w}$), and hence increase their effort (negation of $T_{2.w}$), is limited; increased effort on the part of employers (thus a negation of $T_{2.e}$) will intervene so as to satisfy the first-order tendency $T_{1.e}$. Simiand attributes the existence of such effort to improvements in organisation (such as in the division of labour) and increased mechanisation, two factors which contribute to the increase of labour productivity.

Simiand did not in 1907 present his arguments in terms of a theory of action; but the elements were there all the same, and they would be taken up once more in his major work on wages in 1932.

Representations and Purchasing Behaviour

Halbwachs adopted and significantly developed in his dissertation on the working classes (1912) Simiand's idea that behaviours depend upon the representations that agents form regarding commercial transactions and the behaviour of others. Halbwachs started with the four laws identified by Ernst Engel regarding household expenditure:

1. the higher the income, the smaller the proportion of spending on food, although food expenditure rises absolutely;
2. the share of expenditure devoted to clothing remains approximately the same, whatever the income;
3. the share of expenditure on housing, fuel and lighting remains approximately the same for all categories of income;
4. the higher the income, the greater the proportion of spending on other items.

Engel had derived these laws during the second half of the nineteenth century, but aside from the first they did not stand up against Halbwachs's own evidence. Halbwachs emphasised two problems: first of all, these laws failed to take account of a number of relevant contingencies (1912: 291), and a sociological explanation was required for such statistical regularities.

> We do not believe that the distribution of spending follows mechanically from the size of family or of income. If, as we think, there are social representations of a particular kind (regarding in the first place this or that kind of housing, clothing, recreation), then it should be expected that families of very different structure and with varying levels of income will distribute, or will tend to distribute, their spending in the same way. (ibid.: 292)

Halbwachs reanalysed the German budget data and concluded that apparent statistical irregularities in relation to Engel's laws could be explained by the presence of representations and their resistance to sudden change. Social mobility, or even just mobility within levels of income, did not keep older representations from determining the structure of expenditure on the part of a family confronted with a new socioeconomic situation. This important factor cannot be studied in his quantitative surveys since progressive changes in professional or employment situation were not recorded. In the absence of such longitudinal evidence, Halbwachs became interested in whether there was a way of life that was characteristic of the *entire* working class (ibid.: 333). The originality of Halbwachs's work lies in his investigation of the form and nature of needs.

TABLE 4.1

Morphology of Expenditures and Transactional Representations among the Working Classes

	Infrequent Expenditure	*Frequent Expenditure*
Low Expenditure	**Clothing**: uncertainty over quality, risk of being swindled	**Food**: current price considered as a natural dimension of the good
High Expenditure	**Housing**: charge always too high, little blame attached to a failure to pay it	

As regards the form of needs, Halbwachs distinguishes three major classes, according to the greater or lesser interval between successive purchases and in respect of the significance of the sum expended on each occasion. Spending on food counts as a frequent occurrence for a small amount of money; spending on clothing is less frequent but for larger sums; while expenditure on housing is the most significant, even if paid weekly. Halbwachs argues that the amount and frequency of this last expenditure relates to a quite specific moment, that is, when individuals search for new accommodation, for it is at this point that a choice is made and the sums involved become part of a conscious decision. This can all be expressed in a table that gives the *morphology* of expenditures on the part of those with low incomes (see table 4.1).

Halbwachs here links representations to each form of expenditure. The prices of food items are treated as given, since the individual prices are modest and frequently encountered; the consumer does not haggle over these prices, according to Halbwachs, since "it seems to [the worker] that these prices are part and parcel of the commodity, and are as such 'natural'; he is quickly persuaded that he has 'something for his money'" (ibid.: 404). This attitude does not, however, carry over into less frequent purchases. Here suspicion prevails; he haggles, discusses, hesitates, since "this time he is not used to linking a definite price to a particular object, he is constantly afraid of being swindled; he therefore tries to demonstrate that he is no dupe, or hopes that he is not much of a dupe, choosing that which is of the least value" (ibid.: 405). The greatest degree of uncertainty arises when confronted with the owner of accommodation, since whatever is paid, it always seems high in relation to the service received; for many workers too "rent seems to be a sort of tax, evasion of which is not thought especially blameworthy" (ibid.: 405).

As regards the actual substance of needs, Halbwachs emphasises the system formed by the whole set of needs, differentiating them by the *social visibility of expenditures.* The consumption of food occurs in the intimacy of the home and is hardly visible at all; Halbwachs notes that it is the same for expenditure on accommodation. These observations are somewhat unanticipated, but Halbwachs states that they arise out of the relation of the worker to social life and the importance of outward appearances on the street, the space of socialisation for the worker after the isolation of the workplace, in which he faces only the material on which he works. Expenditure on clothing conveys to others the status one seeks to occupy in society. Clothing has to be new, elegant and fashionable, since as Halbwachs (sounding rather like Goffman) explains, "it is essentially from appearance that those members of society encountered when the worker is out and about make an immediate judgement" (ibid.: 438)

There is no need here to discuss further the conclusions Halbwachs draws regarding the specific nature of working class expenditure—primarily related to the low level of expenditure on accommodation—since the extension of Durkheim's interest in social hierarchies and the social representations associated with them are more relevant. Halbwachs isolates three kinds of representation. First are the representations workers form of prices and of a variety of shopkeepers. The prices they encounter are frequently considered to be no problem; an open-minded consumer capable of assessing price and quality, the worker has no special need to be wary of the shopkeeper from whom he buys his food. When an expenditure is less frequent and the sum involved larger, the worker approaches things differently. Confronted with the impossibility of his being able to assess the relation of value to price, suspicion and a fear of being duped come to the fore. As a consequence, it is more or less legitimate to avoid payments (as in accommodation), or it is preferable to buy the least expensive good since that way one loses less from being swindled (as in the case of clothing). That does not eradicate the problem, since social visibility has to be taken into account, together with the representations that buyers have of their own image, which image is reinforced by the structure of their expenditure and the goods which signify this structure. In the case of clothing, the representation of price becomes complicated since it is a matter not only of avoiding being swindled by the shopkeeper at the point of sale but also of buying clothing fit for the image one seeks to project and for the representation to others of the place one occupies in society. Halbwachs thus produces a great work of economic sociology that has resonated right up to recent studies, both in France and abroad.[4]

[4] See the recent work in economic sociology by for example Michelle de la Pradelle (1996) and Paul DiMaggio and Hugh Louch (1998).

From the Sociology of Economic Action to the Theory of Capitalism

Simiand and Halbwachs, the two principal Durkheimian economic sociologists whose first studies in positive political economy were published in the early years of the twentieth century, did not ascribe any especial importance to the United States. But during the interwar years, the economy and society of America had an increasingly significant impact upon their work.

This impact was first of all intellectual: they made contact with American institutionalism (Veblen, J. R. Commons and Wesley C. Mitchell). This contact was of major importance, and was reciprocated.[5] There is no doubt about the impact that the Durkheimians made in the United States: Simiand's writings on wages and economic cycles were known to American specialists, who thought highly of them.[6] In the early 1930s Halbwachs was a visiting professor at the University of Chicago, and the discovery of a world different to that of Europe left a clear impression upon him.

Resuming his work after the First World War, Halbwachs became interested in the studies on workers' budgets that were published in Germany and the United States during the 1930s (Halbwachs 1933a). While the German material confirmed his earlier work, this was not the case with that from the USA, where wages were higher and there was a fourth category (other discretionary spending) that was of much greater significance by comparison with Europe (Baudelot & Establet 1994). Simiand's *Cours d'économie politique* placed much emphasis upon the phenomenon of economic rationalisation in the American economy. A professor so attracted to issues involving work, mechanisation and enterprise organisation could hardly ignore this;[7] the entire second volume of the *Cours*

---

[5] Two points can be noted: firstly, Veblen's work on consumption was taken up by Simiand as early as 1899 and also became a significant element in Halbwachs's work on consumption and social classes (1905a; 1905b; 1912). Secondly, Mitchell was struck by the similarity in the criticism that Simiand and Veblen made of orthodox political economy, and he went so far as to translate passages from Simiand for his personal use (Gislain & Steiner 1999).

[6] Moore (1911) used Simiand's statistics in his study of wages—although he was careful to clearly distance himself from Simiand's method—and according to Halbwachs, Paul Douglas also thought highly of the same work (Letter of Halbwachs to his wife, 14 November 1930, Archives Halbwachs, Caen: IMEC).

[7] Simiand was named "Professor for the Organisation of Work and Workingmen's Associations" at the Conservatoire national des arts et métiers in 1919, before becoming in 1923 "Professor of Political Economy and Labour Law". He remained very attached to substantive questions related to the world of work, and from 1925 was involved with the

is devoted to it.[8] The crisis of the American economy clearly captured his attention, and the whole of the *Cours* can be read in the light of this "earthquake in the economic domain" (Simiand 1929–31: 10). Seeking to challenge the idea that his work was merely one of a number of studies directed to the American and the global crisis, he examined the American case as a response to criticisms that had been made of his major work, *Le salaire, l'évolution sociale et la monnaie*. This is entirely based on French data; is not this dedication to one national case too restrictive (Simiand 1934a: 13)? He therefore envisaged a more extensive enquiry which would take into account American data.

The second volume of the *Cours*, devoted as it was to the phenomenon of rationalisation, provided Simiand with an opportunity to synthesise his view of the American situation:

> The system comes down to this: a closed internal market, with credit and "managed" money, the incomes of different classes high enough to secure a high level of purchasing power, centralised organisation and high productivity, low costs and retail prices securing high profits. (1929–31 II: 12)

The same series of ideas are reintroduced at the end of the subsequent volume (1929–31 III: 681–89) where Simiand confronts Fisher's thinking on dollar stability with his own views on the organisation of disequilibria, the only means, he thinks, of favouring economic progress.

A vast protected market, a monetary and financial system whose organisation defied the canons of economic liberalism, production organised around productivity gains and linked to high wages which made it possible to absorb a high level of production, a non-competitive market structure: these are the five factors which characterise the American situation. They are not all given the same degree of attention: American protectionism, for instance, is barely touched on in volume 3 of *Cours*, which deals with the general movement to protectionism during the last quarter of the nineteenth century. Nonetheless, this presentation, synthetic and forceful in equal measure, suffices to typify the institutional specificity of the American case, for Simiand states that Taylorism and Fordism are not easily transferable (1929–31 II: 13)—the German case is itself a particular one, the monetary regime in particular being different—and France

---

International Labour Organization; eventually he was nominated for the chair of History of Labour at the Collège de France (Gillard & Rosier 1996: 269–73).

[8] As was his habit, Simiand did not limit the phenomenon of rationalisation to one national example but treated it on a comparative basis, using French, German and American material. He was not the only one to work in this way, as is plain from the book by André Fourgeaud (1929), but Simiand differed from Fourgeaud in emphasising the American origin of the scientific organisation of work.

has neither the scale nor the production structure that would permit it to adopt one or the other of the two models.[9]

Nevertheless, the broad lines of American economic organisation—its industrial, commercial, financial and social dimensions—emerge clearly in the *Cours*, since major functional relationships are established between the elements by means of which he characterises the social system. Three areas will be considered here: the organisation of production (that is, Taylorism and Fordism strictly speaking); the relationship between production and distribution, and the place of money and finance.

If in the nineteenth century the fall in the cost of production had been linked to the fall in wage costs (ibid.: 92–93), this no longer held: the fall in production cost was now related to the increased effort by workers and management, that is, to the rise in productivity. How is this change to be explained? Simiand argues that the emergence of scientific management took place in the USA because there had always been a relative scarcity of labour and because wages, already high, had increased even more since the Civil War. As regards the socioeconomic consequence of these relations of production, Simiand located it in the fact that, if one wished to gain increased effort from workers, it was necessary that these workers have a direct interest in this effort: "One needs to gain the adherence, the will, the goodwill of the labour force" (ibid.: 101). For Simiand, this is what is new in Taylor, alongside the scientific organisation of the workplace and workshop and the selection of workers through self-interest. He argues that, whatever the formula by which the wage is determined to maximise output, the major problem remains that of confidence between the two parties:

> Every formula when properly applied can lead to optimum output, but none of them prevent adverse effects (for either management or worker) when management does not know how to set the wage rates and establish them properly on a lasting basis. (ibid: 117)

In touching on the problem of confidence, Simiand does not fall back upon vague statements, since he suggests that only a strong workers' organisation can secure such confidence on the part of the worker:

---

[9] Simiand emphasises the role of French agriculture, which cannot be sacrificed as American agriculture had been, the large number of medium-sized firms in contrast to the giant American or German firms, and the importance of luxury production for French industry (1929–31 II: 22–24). During his first course at the Collège de France in 1934–35, Simiand also placed emphasis upon the specific character of American agriculture, where "agricultural production was conceived, set in motion and managed in terms of a commercial and industrial entrepreneurial spirit" (1937: 14)—a phenomenon which he traced back to the historical and sociological conditions of emergence of new countries (1937: 15).

It is the first condition when one asks an intelligent and careful worker what he is prepared to do for a particular payment, to be able to express this to him in such a manner that he can understand and accept the way in which it is worked out and the way it is to be applied in a number of instances. This means that for rather more complicated calculations this condition sometimes cannot be practically satisfied between worker and management or its representatives; it needs a well-founded and well-informed workers' organisation. (ibid. 117)

In other words, there has to be a solid institutional foundation for confidence in the effective functioning of industrial organisation.

Taylorism or Fordism are heavily conditional upon the size of the market, the rationalisation of commercial functions, the size of firms and the forms of competition. Market size is related to the importance of the North American continent and to protectionism, points which Simiand makes in opening his course of lectures. The commercial function seems to him a novelty linked to the phenomenon of rationalisation—he devotes an entire lecture (Lecture 9) to this issue, emphasising the psychological dimension to the commercial function, especially at the level of advertising (ibid.: 148–52). With the increase in size of firms, noticeable in the USA and in Germany, new phenomena appear: the dissociation of capital and management on the one hand and the role of financial activity on the other. The growth in scale of firms brings about a functional division of tasks within management, so that the entrepreneurial function becomes separated from the possession of capital and becomes a factor of production to which Simiand attributes great importance (Lecture 26). In respect of market structure, Simiand deals with this in the first volume, examining the nature of cartels and trusts; in the next volume, two lectures provide a theoretical treatment (not a common occurrence in Simiand) in which he criticises the idea of a maximising economic agent[10] and the theory of general equilibrium (although his account of this is faulty). He also deals with the practical importance of monopolistic competition, where producers seek to regularise the manner in which they compete and moderate both the increase and decrease of prices while maintaining the latter above that which would normally prevail in a state of perfect competition (1929–31 I: 582). Here there is the possibility that prices will fall while at the same time significant profit margins are maintained (1929–31 II: 12).

[10] We might also note in passing that Simiand casts in doubt the theory of monopoly (implicitly that of Cournot), arguing in a manner later to be elaborated by Hirschmann (1970): "the monopolist is perhaps tempted to accept a makeshift which gives him an outcome with which he is happy: perhaps he is lazy and passive in avoiding the effort (potentially quite great) of seeking to realise that which is to his greatest benefit" (ibid.: 339).

Simiand sets up a strong relation between production and distribution. These two major categories of economic analysis are quite central to the economic sociology developed in *L'année sociologique*, and in the *Cours* he elaborates them in terms of a circuit. Economic activity is characterised by the existence of two poles, production and distribution, brought together by monetary exchanges (1929–31 I: 322). The importance that he attaches to the conscious organisation of the economy and of money (what he calls "managed money") relates to what he considers to be new in the early twentieth century: conscious organisation of the relationship between the two levels of economic activity (ibid.: 323). This leads Simiand to emphasise the dual nature of the wage: it is a cost for the entrepreneur, but also an income that enables an ever greater, and hence ever cheaper, mass of products to flow into the hands of consumers.

Simiand comments upon the novelty of recent standards of consumption—with new goods such as the car, the radio, domestic goods (1929–31 III: 685) and services (1934a: 194)[11]—and consumer credit:

And I will mention here again a form of credit which has latterly spread in the United States as a characteristic feature of the contemporary economy: consumer credit. . . . From the perspective of consumption this is more in the nature of a purchasing credit; but insofar as it facilitates the greater extension of the number of buyers, it is closely connected to the production of particular goods important enough to require mention here. (1929–31 II: 268–69; III: 685; Halbwachs 1933a: 102–3)

The essential linkage is very clearly identified, but Simiand does not deal in any greater detail with this point and turns instead to a distinction between necessary consumption and consumption on impulse. Here we have to turn to the work that Halbwachs did on American household budgets to appreciate the importance that Durkheimians gave to this aspect of the transformation of the American economic system. Halbwachs summarised the situation as follows:

The considerable increase of "other expenditures" in American households after 1918 is easily understood in high wage countries where the gospel of consumption was preached. . . . Wages increased, and prices fell [from 1920 to 1921]. The increase of "other expenditure" was consolidated in the following years, up to 1929. Of course, these new

[11] Halbwachs emphasised the great increase in "other expenditures" in American budgets (an increase of 80% over a half-century, of 45% over a quarter of a century) and argued that the car had passed between 1918 and 1929 from the tenth to the first rank of "other expenditures" and that, according to surveys, it was to be found in 27%–43% of workers' households (1933a: 100, 107).

needs did not simply come from nowhere. American industry had to manufacture these goods on a large scale to meet these needs. But above all it was necessary for a large disposable surplus to exist to which a variety of credit organisations could connect. (Halbwachs 1933a: 104)

As regards wages, Simiand placed the emphasis on the role of unions (1929–31 II: Lectures 31–32). He drew attention to the new social fact that unionism had introduced: the labour contract was no longer between two individual parties but was now mediated by collective action (ibid.: 507). This was linked to the development of collective conventions, what he called "the essential method of established unions" (ibid.: 533), and state intervention, "a new feature, increasingly characteristic of contemporary economic organisation as regards the conditions of manual work: the intervention of society, of public authority, to establish the rules applicable to given groups of workers" (ibid.: 575). The role given to unionisation cannot be doubted, since Simiand goes so far as to give it an importance as great as Taylorisation and Fordism.

Having set up the institutional framework according to the logic of a liberal contract (1929–31 I: 200), what consequences does Simiand draw with regard to wage formation? He does not give a precise formulation. His analysis presupposed the behaviour of a worker with respect to a nominal wage, and the new phenomena that he raised do not fit easily with an analysis of a real wage (ibid.: 515). He argued that the American system was characterised by a relationship between the wage and the maintenance of the price level, but he did not isolate the connection between wage and productivity in the American institutional system.

During the immediate postwar era, following the crisis of 1920–21, Simiand argued that the USA was characterised by "managed money" (1934a: 214): the issue of money organised in such a way as to avoid great variations in price. What might justify such a monetary regime? Simiand reverted to the relation of production to distribution typical of Fordism:

> There is no intention of pressuring costs, production revenue, nor especially wages, nor (least of all) profits. The intention is solely the maintenance of stable prices, guarding against both increase and decrease, but at a rate that lies above the conditions preceding the previous rise. (ibid.: 214)

But this monetary regime is undermined by the active financial development characteristic of modern capitalism. The lack of connection between the holding of capital and its use is made possible by the development of financial activity and monetary creation, mediated by a credit economy nourished by banks and the stock exchange: "their task is the generation [*prestation*] of advances" (1929–31 II: 265), and in a modern economy that is done by monetary means (ibid.: 267).

The development of such monetary and financial activity continues into phases of intensive speculation. While Simiand did not remain entirely indifferent to such episodes, he generally considered this to be a quite normal monetary phenomenon, certain cases such as the USA in the 1920s excepted. Money was, in his view, a social institution in which confidence was invested—the expectation of economic agents regarding the future. We also encounter this view in his treatment of the value of securities:

> [The movement of the price of securities ahead of prices in the real economy] means that the value of these securities can derive not only from the income attributed to them, but that they also represent a current right, and more important a right over the future of the enterprise. . . . The prevailing price of securities is therefore a representation of a belief which is as rational and well-founded as it is possible for the capitalist or his adviser or his banking representative to form of current conditions, and above all, of future conditions for the economic exploitation of the enterprise to which such securities are related. (ibid.: 280)

Hence the Great Crash of October 1929 was in part simply the outcome of a speculative bull market (ibid.: 697; 1934a: 207), even if the formation and collapse of the bull market at a particular time remains a problem to be explained.

Simiand therefore does make a significant effort to define the major features of Fordism, and does not merely make a few stray remarks. This can be seen from the way that Boyer characterises Fordism:

> Fordism can be defined as a regime of accumulation combining three characteristics. It is firstly a form of *work organisation* which is Taylorist in inspiration, promoting the subdivision of tasks, the mechanisation of production processes, and a complete separation between conception and execution. . . . It is also necessary that wages incorporate a *guarantee of a share in productivity increases* other than through the random effects of labour shortages. . . . The connection of these two factors defines the Fordist wage relation. But this is not of itself sufficient, for it has to be linked to a compatible institutional form—either oligopolistic competition or a monetary regime founded upon credit. But what is essential is that the dynamic adjustment of production and demand is primarily played out within a *national state*. (Boyer 1995: 370–71)

Nonetheless, we might well ask why Simiand did not develop in a more vigorous and detailed manner his analysis of the phenomena that he had identified, even where he had drawn attention to their importance and, in some cases, their novelty within the framework of the capitalist economy of the early 1930s.

The first reason would be related to Simiand's historical position in the twentieth century. Fordism as an organisational form had not yet been generally characterised in the way it would be half a century later, and Simiand was always careful with his facts, warning those who attended his lectures of the dangers of accepting at face value the opinions, whether positive or negative, of those who had visited the USA and written about the new realities.[12] But there is a more serious reason. Simiand took an interest in the United States to show how his approach took account of new developments. In his *Cours*, as in his book on the USA, Simiand organised his work around a defence and an illustration of his conception of the economic progress resulting from the alternation of phases A and B of the cycle. He did not seek to deepen his analysis of new realities per se, realities which he had identified in the American situation and for which his method supplied the means for detailed analysis. This can be demonstrated in respect of the relation between productivity and wages.

According to regulation theory, Fordism assumes that productivity increases are divided up on an institutional basis. Simiand's very rich and original approach to wages—especially as regards his theory of conflict between groups of actors—led him to reject the kind of formulation that became part of regulation theory. This was because Simiand modelled the evolution of the distribution between wages and profit and the role of productive effort as a cycle based upon price variations, themselves in turn derived from the expectations crystallised in money. Seeking to locate this general socioeconomic mechanism, the *Cours* (1929–31 III: Lecture 11) relates variations in wages to variations in prices, not to variations in labour productivity. Simiand then proposes a complex relationship between wages and productivity in Phase A (rising prices), where the profits of the enterprise (deriving from increased productivity and a high

---

[12] Simiand argued that rationalisation was made possible by institutional conditions in the USA, and he did not think there was any imminent possibility of Fordism's global diffusion (1929–31 II: 13–14, 22–24). Nor did he think the subdivision of tasks and deskilling to be suited to generalisation, pointing to the number of skilled workers working alongside the production line as well as those needed to build production machinery (ibid.: 99). He also expressed some reservations over the quantitative importance of Fordism, even in the USA (1934a: 173, 246). These reservations coincide with more recent assessments of the limits of the Fordist model in the context of the 1920s and 1930s in the United States (Boyer & Orléan 1991; Dockès 1993).

selling price) are divided between employees and owners, while in Phase B (falling prices) there is an increase in effort expended so that a nominal gain might be maintained. He therefore sets up a causal relation running from productivity to wages in Phase A but reverses this in Phase B (ibid.: 198–200).

And so if we consider Simiand's approach in relation to the more recent treatment of these issues noted above, it appears that there are real differences. The object of modern regulation theory is to demonstrate how capitalism was transformed in the course of the twentieth century in such a way as to render comprehensible the substantial intervention of social and economic regulation that became a leading feature of the post–World War II world economy (Boyer & Mistral 1983; Boyer 1986). Simiand showed quite clearly how the capitalism of the 1930s could not be understood in the same terms as nineteenth-century competitive capitalism; after the Great War there were important changes in market structure, international trade, monetary regulation and the wage relationship. In identifying a profound alteration in regulatory mechanisms, he touched on an issue that would later be central to regulation theory, but this apparent convergence should not be exaggerated.

In the final lectures in his *Cours*, Simiand came back to the American example, noting once more Fisher's conception of "managed money" and contrasting to it his own view that there is an *alternation* between phases of low and high prices in the process of economic development, and that the maintenance of this dynamic movement is essential even for a consciously managed economy in which various economic functions have been socialised (the role of "entrepreneurial implementation" was important in his view) and in which there was abundant statistical information and more reliably founded expectations. In other words, when he completed his lectures he came back to the case of the United States and recalled the institutional features of Fordist regulation and placed this in the context of a global approach aiming "to seek and implement a technology for equilibrium" (1929–31 III: 683). The 1929 crash represented a setback to this approach, and he concluded with a lecture entitled "Economic Fluctuations and Economic Progress" in which he emphasised the rationality of such fluctuations and proposed their organisation, which was his central argument (Rosier 1996). For Simiand, therefore, a resort to history did not seek merely to demarcate major differences in socioeconomic regulation, but also to emphasise the permanence and necessity of economic cycles.

From Durkheimian Positive Economics to the Regulation School

The convergence between the two approaches is instructive, bringing to light both similarities to and differences from Fordism. This connection between two heterodox streams of French political economy can be pursued in respect of two filiations.

The first of these is methodological: each of the two approaches opposes orthodox theory, and they both share a turn to history and social relations, which in turn directs attention to economic institutions alongside representations or beliefs. The second is material: it emerges from particular features of French political economy during the 1950s and 1960s which relate directly to the professional milieu within which Simiand and Halbwachs had worked.

A Question of Method

Over almost fifty years of reviewing (1897–1942), both Simiand and Halbwachs often expressed themselves in the most acerbic terms when writing about orthodox economics. They rejected the notion of equilibrium, of a *homo œconomicus*, and mathematical formalisation; instead they put forward an approach that would draw upon empirical investigation together with contributions from history, statistics and sociology. This resonates strongly with the approach of the regulation school, as testified by the overview composed by Boyer (1986: 39–60). In the most recent synthesis, we can find the situation of orthodox theory characterised in the following way:

> These setbacks do not result from the confluence of minor errors, but from the very success of the research programme of contemporary theory, founded as it is on an aggressive methodological individualism, the minimisation of collective elements in economic life, the rejection of history and of structural transformations in the name of the autonomy of a pure economics which should concern itself neither with social movements, nor with the complexities of the political process. (Boyer & Saillard: 11)

Each of these two approaches is anchored in historical and sociological sources. Moreover, we find the same idea motivating Durkheim's own early work, before he lost interest in political economy; and it was also set to work by Simiand and Halbwachs throughout their work in economic sociology. Simiand said as much in his essay on the American economy: one had to be wary of overenthusiastic commentaries on rationalisation, standardisation or the 1929 crisis—often little more than hasty socioeconomic journalism; instead, explanation of such phenomena required their location, as one moment in a rationally constructed history. History is not a more or less convenient supplement which the theoretician draws upon whenever it might suit, but rather an indispensable element of economic analysis. In his *Cours*, Simiand systematically embedded the phenomenon to be explained within a developed historical context so that one might grasp it intellectually and identify a solution. At the end of his first lecture he asked:

> Where might a better-founded solution [to the crisis] be discovered? It can only be found in what I suggest as a general theme of economic research, for a course of lectures such as this as part of positive scientific study, but only on condition that it is sufficiently expansive, not merely based on one country, nor on the continental scale originally envisaged, *but extended in time, going back far enough to gain understanding*. (1929–31 I: 15, my emphasis)

But how might this historical inscription of the phenomenon be best served? Simiand's approach begins from Durkheim's sociology and involves the quantitative dimension of his works.

The first of these two points directs attention to those institutions (the organisation of production, the distribution of income, monetary and financial organisation) by which economic relations are structured. The Durkheimian conception of the institution aims to locate and study "ways of doing, thinking and feeling" imposed upon agents, who are, in other words, "instituted", to use the term introduced by Fauconnet and Mauss (1901). The temporal connections which the institutional system imposes upon agents forms an essential dimension for the understanding of social regularities, first of all their permanence and then their transitions when the institutional environment alters. The institution condenses the socio-historical framework of economic action; the institution permits the construction of an explanation free of the errors of orthodox economics. Durkheim's sociology is sometimes subject to misapprehension, but here the insistence on the institution, and the instituted agent, does not mean that innovative action and related dynamics are absent. Durkheimian sociology lays great emphasis upon the process of institution and the instituted. This is true of the theory of money that Simiand develops (1934b), founded upon expectations, the anticipation of future outcomes, or even on the religious idea of faith. Simiand connected banking activity to price cycles (1929–31 II: Lecture 17), arguing that the issue of money on the part of banks is at its highest at the turning-point between Phase A (peaking prices) to Phase B (falling prices) of the economic cycle. He explained this by applying his theory of economic action to those holding financial products: in Phase A there is an increase in invested capital linked to an increased nominal income and a high rate of return. When prices fall, and when the rate of return therefore also falls, the bearers of financial assets increase their investment activity in the attempt to maintain their nominal income, and that is financed by an increased issue of money provided by the banking and financial system. Expectation and anticipation of the outcome, money is therefore a reality whose instituting dimension is very marked, especially when coupled with the conflicts inherent in the determination of wages (Simiand 1907, 1932a) and to the business cycle (Simiand 1937). In short, there is quite certainly a structure that constrains and orients the economic behaviour of individuals, but there are also individual rationalities and collective actions through which institutions reproduce and transform themselves.

To that must be added the quantitative nature of the socioeconomic fact (Simiand 1932 II: 576). The material with which the sociological economist works is made up of quantitative entities, most often monetary magnitudes, through which agents establish contact with the economic world. The Durkheimian economic sociologist also investigates statistical information, weighing merits and the limits before revealing social regularities and explaining them sociologically. This is what happens in all of Simiand's major texts (1907; 1930–32; 1932a; see also Halbwachs 1912, 1933a), and, according to the stenographic record of his lectures at the Conservatoire national des arts et métiers, his audience was regaled with numerical detail. Closely related to this statistical approach was Simiand's rejection of the abstractions of pure theory; he did not even accept Moore's idea (1929) that the validity of pure economics should be confirmed through its linkage with statistical reasoning. Simiand did not understand the positive approach as a handmaiden to pure theory; its purpose was not to validate abstract concepts but rather to furnish the material with which *original analytical categories might be constituted*, the better to guide empirical investigation.

This position subjected him to much misunderstanding and criticism, so that he was thought to advocate the view that facts speak for themselves,[13] and can therefore be interpreted without the intervention of analytic construction on the part of an investigator. The vehemence of Simiand's polemics wrongfully distracted attention from the reality of his work.[14]

[13] When André Marchal makes reference to Simiand he places him as a "pure empiricist", while at the same time emphasising that his two principal disciples, Marjolin and Charles Morazé, were far removed from this position (Marchal 1953: 173–74; 1952–55, I: 171–76). This appreciation of Simiand's work is extremely unsatisfactory, since it conceals the theoretical dimension of Durkheimian economic sociology.

[14] In his *Cours* the analysis of the American situation is structured by the notion of an economic circuit (and not by a system of interdependent markets) and problems directly related to this: the initial move within a circuit ("entrepreneurial implementation"), the

Above all, it concealed the fact that Simiand drew upon established sociological theory, as was the case with his conflict theory of action between social groups, or his theory of price, which was founded upon the social representations structuring the behaviour of agents. Nonetheless, Simiand's insistence on the difference between positive economics and orthodox economics supplemented by econometrics or statistics represented a significant difference between his own work and that of Aftalion, who used the statistical tool simply to validate or invalidate this or that part of orthodox theory in respect of its capacity to take account of economic events.[15] The price paid in all of this was either to appear to be always one step behind the systematic nature of pure theory[16] or to exhaust one's efforts in its critique;[17] that was the case with Simiand, and the same goes for regulation theory.

Pirou, Rist, Aftalion and the Revue économique

From the history of ideas we can infer that the existence of theoretical or intellectual problems is capable of generating traditions that transcend substantive relationships between individuals or schools of thought. None-

---

problem of the origin of surplus within the circuit, the role of monetary movements between the different poles of the circuit—these and other aspects show that his approach is structured quite solidly according to a definite theoretical perspective.

[15] See, for example, his approach to the quantity theory of money or the theory of exchange. There is also a difference when it comes to statistical tools: by contrast with Aftalion (1938), Simiand made hardly any use of statistical techniques (adjustments by least square differences, or March's coefficient of covariation) that went beyond a simple average. This seems to have been deliberate on his part, since as president of the Parisian Statistical Society he would have been aware of relevant techniques developed by his colleagues; and he could not have ignored March's coefficient since March applied his statistical tools to the results that Simiand had presented in his dissertation and discussed their significance (March 1907: 157–58). Halbwachs was more open to statistical technique and explained the regression coefficient in the Annales sociologiques (AS III C 2: 141–44) while questioning the use of this coefficient when seeking to establish causal relationships.

[16] The opposition between a formal rigour on the part of pure economics and the confrontation with empirical phenomena runs through all modern economics. It was this opposition between two forms of economic knowledge that prompted Simiand's critique, even if some elements of both were congenial to him (Pirou 1939), as is the same with the regulation school (Cartelier & de Vroye 1989).

[17] This dilemma is captured by Olivier Favereau when he distinguishes the strategy of conventional economics from that of the regulation school: "The objective of the regulation theory is to construct a new economic theory as an alternative to orthodoxy—the purpose is a change of economic theory. The philosophy of the school of economic conventions is different: long and bitter experience shows that every attempt to reconstruct economic theory by a complete rejection of the given dominating orthodoxy has failed. The capacity of orthodox theory for adaptation and renewal has always outrun the capacity of criticism to confront and reconstruct it" (1995: 512).

theless, it is important to locate the material connections through which any one particular filiation can be established and maintained. Here we might propose a conjecture regarding the role of French economists whose formative period was the interwar years and who continued their careers during the 1950s. The *milieu* which was created around the *Revue économique* represents an interesting case in point.

Simiand is not an isolated writer. He was a professor at the Conservatoire national des arts et métiers, then at the Collège de France, and a member of the editorial committee of the *Revue d'économie politique*. He also enjoyed the friendship of important professors such as Pirou, who had been his student at the Ecole pratique (Pirou 1932: 1265), and also of Charles Rist, who played an important role in the French university system, especially in relation to the teaching of political economy.[18] Rist was more interested in monetary theory and worked in the Institut scientifique de recherches économiques et sociales, which was a kind of research seminar (Jeanneney 1996: 268). Pirou, on the other hand, had a larger audience, by virtue of his position as a professor keen to offer general conceptions of political economy to his students but also because of his seminars at the Ecole pratique des hautes etudes, where he kept a close eye on new developments in economic theory, developments which in some instances, like American institutionalism, were close to positive economics (Pirou 1937, 1938). His powerful institutional position led him to edit a large collective work, *Traité d'économie politique*, a survey of contemporary economics in which Simiand had, before his premature death, been announced as the author of the volume devoted to economic cycles—a volume which was eventually written by Guitton.

However, Pirou reacted more favourably to the approach of Simiand—who had kept Pirou abreast of his latest work by sending him copies as they were published—and differentiated his work in important respects from that of Aftalion,[19] even if he did not entirely take on board Simiand's approach and had critical reservations about what he called Simiand's "social monetarism" (Pirou 1932: 1285–87). Likewise, he defended the importance of Simiand's positive economics when Guitton subjected in turn rational economics, positive economics and synthetic economics

[18] "As a student of the Paris Faculty of Law preparing for a doctorate in the economic sciences, I followed the teaching of François Simiand from 1933 until his death in 1935, encouraged by Gaëtan Pirou and Charles Rist, professors in the Faculty of Law, who were my supervisors" (Jeanneney 1996: 267).

[19] "[I]t would be instructive to make a comparison between the writings of Mr. S[imiand] and Mr. Aftalion. Each of them is an advocate of the positive method, but their practice of this method diverges. Some prefer the drier, more uncluttered, more positive approach of Mr. Aftalion; other find the philosophical underpinnings given to the writings of Mr. F. S. lend it a richer groundwork, and a deeper perspective" (Pirou 1932: 1267).

to scrutiny (1938). Guitton argued that Simiand did have a theory but thought the path taken by Moore in proposing to unite mathematical economics with statistical evidence to be a more promising one (Guitton 1938: 142, 146). Here Pirou contended that Simiand's position was more solidly based than that of Guitton:

> For my part, I see this triptych of methods and schools in a different light, and rank them very differently. The first element would come from abstract and rational economics: here I would place Moore alongside Walras. The second element would include the "historicist historians" and those descriptive or statistical economists, such as W. C. Mitchell in the second period of his work, who consider it imprudent or dangerous to leap from facts to general views. In the third element I would place those who wish to begin with facts and end up with theory: François Simiand would here be the central figure. (Pirou 1938: ix)

It is true that, unlike Simiand, Pirou did not decide between the first and the third element in this series, nor did he think that there was any way of choosing between the "Baconian inductivism, the position taken by E. Durkheim and F. Simiand" and "simplified models followed today by the adepts of mathematical economics and the majority of former students of the Ecole polytechnique who devote their time to economic studies" (ibid.).

That being said, there are many economists during this period who, prompted by Pirou (Guitton's book being a direct result of Pirou's seminar [ibid.: v]), draw upon the works of Simiand—for example, Henri Denis (1938) on money and method, Marjolin on cycles (1941), Jean-Louis Guglielmi on the theory of wages (1945), or Bernard Damalas on all of Simiand's writings (1947). It was a suggestion by Rist that led Jean-Marcel Jeanneney to attend Simiand's seminars and come under his influence. In sum, Simiand as a Durkheimian economic sociologist was no minor author during this period,[20] and those economists whose formation derives from the interwar period and who would reemerge after 1945 could not ignore his work.

This interwar period was decisive for those who would dominate political economy from the Liberation up to the shock of spring 1968. Some struck out on their own, such as François Perroux at the Institut de sciences économiques appliquées, while others, such as Jean and André Marchal, and Guitton, were primarily significant as teachers, their engagement turn-

---

[20] Simiand's writings all have no small echo in the work of contemporary theoreticians; in France this includes the Polytechniciens of the X-crise Circle (X being the symbol of the Ecole polytechnique) and Landry's papers on his theory of wages; and abroad, reviews by Edgar Jaffé and John Hicks, for example.

ing on the Paris Faculty of Law and various journals, chief among which was the *Revue d'économie politique*. Guitton was editor in chief of the *Revue* from 1965 to 1984, following Lutfalla, whom we have come across alongside Simiand in the *Annales sociologiques* and who had managed the *Revue* from 1949. But the educational landscape changed with the appearance of the *Revue économique*.[21]

The May 1950 editorial of the new journal announced its purpose as "the firm guidance of political economy in all social sciences and social research". Since "economic facts can only be detached from the mass of social facts through abstraction, by brute force, we [the editorial committee] would say, through mutilation". Consequently the managing committee had the clear intention of "devoting its main effort to organising the exchange of views between the various disciplines of the social sciences and political economy, furthering closer cooperation and joint investigations". The wish to put political economy in contact with other social sciences marked a clear distancing from orthodox economics. Such a position should not be seen as an aberration or as a strategy whose time had passed by 1950. In the later 1940s the rise to dominance of neoclassicism was not a foregone conclusion. Debate on the theory of the firm was as yet inconclusive, and Milton Friedman's methodological irrealism had not yet closed down the debate on entrepreneurial behaviour which had been opened up by the studies of Hall and Hitch.

The journal's founding editorial group laid emphasis on the importance of "systems and structures", through which they sought to integrate history, sociology and political economy. Here we find once more the methodological position outlined above, but it should also be said that this idea about the nature of political economy was given an institutional foundation thanks to significant developments in the teaching of political economy in France: in the mid-1950s a course on "systems and structures" was introduced as a central element in the university curriculum. Secondly, the *Revue*'s founders were very active in defence of economic sociology, even when French sociologists seemed to have lost interest in it.[22] They wrote the section "Economic Sociology" for Georges

[21] This was founded by nine scholars: Aftalion, Fernand Braudel, Emile James, Ernest Labrousse, Jean Lhomme, Jean Marchal, Jean Meynaud, Henri Noyelle and Jean Weiller. They were joined in 1956 by A. Marchal, following the death of Aftalion. Positive economics was present through Aftalion and Labrousse, who was personally and intellectually close to Aftalion (whose assistant he was) and to Simiand (Charle 1980).

[22] Lhomme published one, and Weiller four, articles related to economic sociology in *Cahiers internationaux de sociologie*, representing about one third of all its publications in economic sociology from 1946 to 1965. The case of *L'année sociologique* is even more interesting since Lhomme edited the section "Economic Sociology" from 1951 to 53, and again in 1960, while it was edited by A. Marchal from 1967 to 69.

Gurvitch's major *Traité de sociologie*[23], and some of them then contributed to the book published by Guy Palmade in 1967 as *L'économique et les sciences humaine.*[24] The economics series that they edited for Presses universitaires de France published, among other works, dissertations that they had supervised which revealed the structural dimensions of economic activity and the relations between economics and sociology. Apart from Guy Aimard's book on Durkheim and economic science (1962), André Nicolaï's book on economic behaviour (1960) is the most ambitious project of this kind, since Nicolaï seeks to articulate economic structures and individual behaviour on the basis of a critical reassessment of recent economic research, demonstrating the historical determination of structure and behaviour through a study of conflicts over scarce goods. The journal with which the *Revue* was in competition—the *Revue d'économie politique*—did not exclude economic sociology from its pages, and Lutfalla, one of its leading editors, planned to publish a book called *Sociologie et économie.*[25] Perroux, who had seen a number of these economists pass through his own turbulent Institut de sciences économiques appliquées, likewise followed these socioeconomic issues closely, which is evident in his publications on power and the gift arising from his teaching at the Collège de France (1960, 1973). The founders of the *Revue économique*, together with a number of important French economists of the period, were part of a movement that A. Marchal described as follows: "The reintegration of economic science within a sociological framework is without any doubt the leading characteristic of contemporary French economics—at least that represented by those currently active in French universities" (1953: 75). This shows that, beyond whatever relationships they had with Aftalion, such writers had absorbed a great deal from Simiand. The most sustained effort is quite plainly that of J. Marchal and Jacques Lecaillon, whose book on the distribution of incomes has an important sociological basis: "Our investigation begins with a reality reflected in statistics, surveys, and monographs. Basing our work on the information thus put together, we seek to distribute individuals and institutions into homogenous categories related to their behaviour in respect of distribution . . . and these are the participants that will be presented in the models which

---

[23] This text was published in 1958; the three articles in the section "Economic Sociology" ("Sociology of Economic Systems, Regimes and Structures"; "Sociology of Economic Cycles"; "Political Economy and Sociology") appeared as the work of Lhomme, A. Marchal and Weiller, respectively.

[24] A. Marchal contributed the article "Economic Dynamics and Sociology", and Meynaud the article "Pressure Groups and Economic Policy".

[25] The publication of this work was announced by A. Marchal in his text on method in political economy (1952–55, I: 160 n. 2).

seek to take account of these distributional processes" (1959 I: 34–35).[26] The final phrases here echo Simiand's own approach: he had sought to transform political economy by creating new analytical categories from sociological concepts.

There is, therefore, a strong connection between this new, postwar journal and French interwar positive economics. To be sure, these economists treated politics and the work of Marx[27] in a manner different from that of the regulation school. Nevertheless, the *Revue économique* stresses the importance to political economy of history and sociology in a way that would survive into the 1960s and 1970s. It is no accident that one of the first articles that Boyer published in *Revue économique* emphasised the built-in obsolescence of macroeconomic models, arguing that econometric modelling could not do away with a historical and sociological location of relevant social classes or social groups, the manner in which they related one with another, and the way in which the structure of these relationships was regulated (1976: 930–31). This emphasis upon the sociohistorical foundation of modelling recurred when he stressed that empirical data was needed to verify working hypotheses as much as the results one drew from them—dissociating himself therefore from Friedman's version of positivism (Boyer 1989: 1403)—but it was also important to have several logics of behaviour based upon empirical study rather than logical deduction, employing conceptions drawn from sociology, most notably that of *habitus*.

Boyer was writing at a time when the early dynamism of the *Revue économique*'s founders was spent; the approach which he took up breathed new life into Durkheimian positive economics, emphasising the importance of history and social institutions in renewing the set of tools that economists required to explain the workings of a sphere essential to modern life. It is for this reason that Durkheim's first research programme is of more than merely historical interest.

[26] A theoretical account of this approach was provided in a 1952 article by J. Marchal, in which he employed sociological arguments in explaining how he sought to reestablish that which Marxists had discredited in confronting the conceptual approach of classical economics (1952: 148).

[27] Marxism was not something outwith economics according to the founders of the *Revue économique*. Their interest in Marx relates as much to the importance he gave to structures as to the political situation of the later 1940s; thus they also contributed to the diffusion of Marxism in France during this period (Pouch 2001: chs. 1–2).

CHAPTER FIVE

Religion and Economy

MAUSS AND THE SECOND DURKHEIMIAN PROGRAMME

Durkheim provides two different paths by which the economic fact can be linked to religion: through the connection that goes from religion to law, then from the law to economy via the genesis of property rights or the formation of contracts; or through the theory of knowledge. As suggested above, the second Durkheimian research programme in economic sociology requires that we take into account the work and thought of Marcel Mauss in regard to the sociology of religion and, more generally, to anthropology.

The reorientation effected by Durkheim in this second programme was taken up and adopted by Mauss during the first series of the *Année sociologique*. There is, however, what might be thought of as a third path, the economic anthropology of primitive societies, a perspective attributable to Mauss's own interests and activity rather than those of Durkheim. Thus, in the conclusion to his essay *The Gift*, Mauss opened up an entirely new perspective by bringing religion and economy together, making use of an economic anthropology and at the same time successfully elaborating a genetic approach of some complexity. His use of the idea of "rock", the founding tension between altruism and selfishness, between exchange and the gift as a basic social element, enables him to telescope both distance and time in the use of ethnological and historical evidence, leading to the remarkable conclusions of this well-known work of 1925.

There is no radical division between economic anthropology and economic sociology. As Fournier has proposed (1994, 1997), we need to acknowledge Mauss's activism: he was the advocate of cooperation, the socialist wary of the modern world (who, however, never forgot that he was a sociologist), keenly interested in the transformations and crises of the first half of the 1920s, a sociological socialist who also published an "appreciation" of Bolshevism. His socialist allegiances made him conscious of very definite economic realities, leading to insights which he incorporated into his economic sociology,[1] a suggestive convergence be-

---

[1] It was certainly no accident that Mauss made himself the editor of his uncle's manuscripts on socialism (Durkheim 1895–96); the introduction that Mauss wrote is directed to the connection between Durkheim's sociological work and political action (Mauss 1928).

tween the realities with which he was all too familiar as a scholar and those with which "citizen Mauss" was familiar *hic et nunc*.

Mauss's intellectual endeavours are not to the liking of those who want to distance him from his uncle. He quite explicitly linked his work to the second Durkheimian programme and made it one of the prime axes of his studies; he also sketched out a convergence between exchange/gift-giving and the phenomena of the modern economy. It is for this reason that the arguments presented in *The Gift* could enter into contemporary debates turning on a perceived radical opposition between market order and gift-giving.[2]

RELIGION AND ECONOMY IN DURKHEIM

The proclamation of the second Durkheimian programme has been traced above to a passage at once suggestive and sibylline in content. It is easy to identify where this programme is set to work in Durkheim's writing in the manner envisaged in 1912. The first instance is the most complete and can be found in the lecture course, repeated several times, that he devoted to contract and property.[3] The second, more programmatic, instance is the conclusion of *Elementary Forms*, posing the problem of the religious origin of the categories of the economy. Durkheim never elaborated the second programme as extensively as he had the first; such elaboration is mainly to be found in the work of Mauss, and Durkheim drew directly upon this in developing some of the ideas contained in the programmatic note with which the *Elementary Forms* concludes.

---

[2] This explains why, in contrast to the previous chapter, which considered Simiand's economic sociology, it seem to me unproductive to seek here a direct connection between Mauss's work on the gift relationship and contemporary economic sociology, given that this connection is today a familiar one, thanks to a substantial body of writing and a review (La revue du *MAUSS*) sometimes linked to the work of Polanyi (and to the Polanyi centre of Montreal). One could also mention here the work of Jack T. Godbout and Alain Caillé (1992); Caillé 2000; Godbout 2000 and Marcel Hénaff (2002), as well as the greater part of Bourdieu's work on symbolic exchange, and also more directly on the gift relationship (1971b; 1972; 1994; 1997a).

[3] According to Hüseyin Naïl Kubali, a former student of Mauss and editor of a published version of this course, Durkheim delivered it several times in Bordeaux between 1890 and 1900, then in Paris in 1904 and 1912 (Kubali 1950: 5). Lukes is more precise: they were delivered from 1896 to 1900, during the academic years 1903–4 and 1904–5, then again between 1908 and 1911, and perhaps in 1914–15 (Lukes 1973: 618–20). Their editorial dating as 1898–1900 follows that proposed by Mauss, who noted that the subsequent versions were significantly revised (1937: 501, 504). Finally, Mauss extends the period beyond that presented by Lukes, declaring that he had heard the lectures in Bordeaux in 1890–92, and also that Durkheim had presented them again in 1915–16.

Property and Contract

Durkheim delivered his lecture course on the physiology of law and of *mores* many times. So what did this course deal with? Formally its object was stated to be "The study of moral and legal facts, rules of sanctioned conduct" (Durkheim 1898–1900: 41). Two approaches were to be employed: first, seeking the historical causes and the functions which made up these rules; second, examining the functioning of the rules themselves, that is, the way in which they were observed to a greater or lesser degree by the individual. In the first, the sociologist draws upon history and comparative ethnography; in the second, he works with comparative statistics (ibid.).

What is it about these moral and legal rules that might be of interest to a Durkheimian sociology of the economy? First of all, there is the fact that these lecture courses gave Durkheim the opportunity to develop his ideas on professional groups, a topic that we have already encountered in the first two chapters and of whose importance we are aware. Secondly, there is the fact that Durkheim explains the origin of property and employs it to extend the thinking on contracts which he had first elaborated in his criticism of Spencer in the *Division of Labour*. Exchange and the origin of property are treated as fundamental economic categories: appropriation is defined as the socially sanctioned acquisition of things by individuals; and transaction is the exchange of objects so defined between individuals. Appropriation and exchange are fundamental economic categories which Durkheim anchors in religion, so we are already at the heart of the second programme.

Having dismissed the theory that labour is the source of property, Durkheim characterises property as a relation of exclusion:

> We must not lose sight of the fact that simple enjoyment does not characterise property; it is instead exclusive enjoyment that is the mark of property—the ability to exclude all others from enjoyment of the object. The law of property consists essentially in the right to withdraw an object from common usage. The proprietor will use it, or will not use it—that is a secondary matter. But he has a legal footing in preventing others from using it, or even touching it. (ibid.: 171)

The definition of the religious fact as developed by Durkheim during the same period shows what he sought to achieve. The distinction of the sacred from the profane is effected by arguing that the first is elaborated socially, while the second is constructed by the individual through sensory givens and experience (1898a: 163). It follows from this distinction that the sacred is obligatory because it derives from society, to which the individual is subordinate. Once it is related to the sacred, property then draws its characteristics from it: its existence is of course social and as such almost the epitome of sacredness, but the function of exclusion echoes the conception of the profane, as well as the requirement that rites effect this exclusion and separation (1898–1900: 175–76). Durkheim illustrates his argument with reference to landed property.

He had good reason to do so. Of course, in the later nineteenth and early twentieth centuries property in land remained at the centre of economic, political and social thinking, but it was also an institution that one of Durkheim's teachers at the Ecole normale supérieure had studied in relation to religion. Numa Fustel de Coulanges, the great comparative historian with whom Durkheim discussed the relationship of sociology to history, built his *Ancient City* on the idea that the institutions of antiquity were related to contemporary beliefs (1864: 3). These beliefs are argued to derive from religion, themselves the outcome of beliefs regarding life and death (ch. 1), just as Spencer had suggested in his *Principles of Sociology*. Fustel de Coulanges drew simultaneously on Greek antiquity, Roman antiquity and India—showing that their institutions, especially property in land, could be clarified by relating them to religious beliefs (ch. 6). And so it is not surprising that Durkheim adopts the same argument and, following his teacher, uses examples from the Romans, Greeks and India to define the sacred character of landed property (1898–1900: 179–81). The difference between them turns on their respective understanding of religion and the sacred: Fustel de Coulanges relates this to the domestic cult of death, whereas what is important for Durkheim is the ubiquity of religious beings in nature. Consequently, rites are required so that agriculture, a profane activity, can be conducted on the land, which is in the possession of the gods; these rites create a sacred connection between the individual and the soil:

> When, in spite of everything, the agriculturalist has troubled the Gods, committed an offence which exposed him, redemption becomes necessary. A sacrifice resolves this: the victim takes the error on itself and expiates those who are culpable. And then (as a reflex) thanks to the sacrificial act, not only are the deities propitiated, but are transformed into protective powers. They watch over the field, they defend it, they assure its prosperity. . . . A moral connection is formed by the sacrifice between them [men] and the Gods of the field and, as this connection already existed between these deities and the field, the land was also connected to men by a sacred bond. And that is how property right comes about. The property rights of men are only a substitute for the property rights of the Gods. (ibid.: 184–85)

Durkheim does not seek to hide the fact that this explanation will require that the origin of religion be elucidated, and that this proliferation of gods be linked to the original sacred nature of the soil; a problem which remains unresolved, he states. (ibid.: 189). But he goes on all the same, and considers the problem of the individualisation of property; this arises from the emergence of patriarchal power and the development of personal property (ibid.: 193).

In this genetic investigation, contract follows on from individual property, and so the contract is no more a primitive fact than the connection between two individual wills. Introduced in this way, the contract is initially related either to the status of persons or to that of things. However, if one or the other of these is capable of binding the individual as such, this relates to "their sacred character, the moral prestige with which they are invested" (ibid.: 204). Durkheim alludes to the "blood covenant", a ritual procedure which through the ritual ingestion of food imparts a sacred character to the connection formed between the two contracting parties. The following stage is the solemn contract, in which the interpersonal connection is created by a formula stated according to a specific rite:

> It can now be seen how slowly the notion of the contract is created. The blood covenant, real contracts are not true contracts [in the sense of a contract formed between two individual wills]. The solemn contract comes closer to this. For here the wills involved are affirmed by words stated according to the consecrated formulae, the commitment is sacred. (ibid.: 209)

Emancipation from ritual and from formalism involves the second causal principle touched on above: the development of exchange. Durkheim is anxious that exchange should not be treated solely as utilitarian in aim. He takes into account an alteration in the representation of the solemn and binding contract, treating it as at once a pledge to the gods and an externalisation of this transaction that allows others to treat it as something to be retained (ibid.: 218). The consensual contract thus has its origin in an obligation of a sacred nature, although it binds by virtue of the rights of the individual, an individual who, as we saw above, first emerges in the form of the patriarchal head of household.

Durkheim states that the consensual contract effects a legal revolution since, once established, such a contract derives from the wills of the contracting parties—more precisely, from their intentions (ibid.: 225). The obligation is only legally binding inasmuch as it does not result from any constraint exercised over the individual. Hence the consensual contract is linked to the sacredness of the individual and the emergence of the idea of justice as an organising principle of the commerce—in the broadest sense—between human beings. Here labour intervenes as a legitimating principle of property and, as such, conflicts with the religious principle that had prevailed hitherto, as when property is transmitted by inheritance

(1969: 195; Fustel de Coulanges 1864: ch. 7). The latter mode of transfer, which as we have seen in chapter 2 was criticised by Durkheim, was especially linked to the sacred character of a good that could not be passed to anyone outside the family. This tension between inheritance and labour arises because because inheritance makes people rich or poor independently of the efforts made by the present generation, so that exchanges entered into are not made from a position of equality, and thus place in question the conception of liberty underpinning contractual relations.

The Formation of Economic Categories

Alongside this genetic exploration of the connections between religion and economy, the programmatic statement (1912/1995: 421 n. 4) in *Elementary Forms* suggests a linkage of the economy to religion by virtue of the categories within which the economic phenomenon is thought.

In the second and third parts of the *Elementary Forms*, Durkheim's leading idea is that, originally, religion brings together the cognitive and speculative functions, before the increasing autonomy of science monopolises the former. The religious foundation of all thought, including economic thought, is a given, a postulate, unless one supposes, as Durkheim does not, that there are two quite distinct domains of social life—the religious and the economic, or the integrative phases on the one hand and the disintegrative on the other, both phases lending social life its character.

But nothing precise is developed relating to what might be considered the origin of concepts and categories which, taken together, constitute the economic. He only deals with the origin of categories of time, space, effective force and totality, all of which are respectively related to the rhythm and to the space occupied on the land, to collective force and to society (ibid.: 441–44). But none of this can be related to the economic. Besides, it would be difficult to know to what Durkheim would here create a relationship: to scarcity? to need? to value? He never mentions the first. The second is there in his theory of anomie when he talks of the lack of any limit to desires, but it is never presented as a founding economic category. By contrast, the third is taken into account more frequently, since we have run across it in connection with the definition of the economic fact as a social fact and the role that representations play in this case; we have also encountered it in respect of the social evaluation which conditions the relation of contribution/retribution in the representations of a given society. It is also there in that very important footnote, where he alludes to the fact that value is a form of power, and that the origin of power is religious, as is the origin of the notion of efficacy (ibid.: 421 n. 4).

Nonetheless, one cannot avoid noting those allusions which, while being nothing more than allusions, are very suggestive when Durkheim characterises the social group in terms of its unity of perspective (the common goal) and its internal order which requires differentiation (the clans) and harmonisation:

> Society is possible only if the individuals and things that make it up are divided among different groups, which is to say genera, and if those groups themselves are classified in relation to one another. Thus, society presupposes a conscious organization of itself that is nothing other than a classification. That organization of society is naturally passed on to the space it occupies. To forestall conflict, a definite portion of space must be assigned to each individual group. In other words, the space must be divided, differentiated, and oriented, and those divisions and orientations must be known to all. In addition, every call to a feast, hunt, or military expedition implies that dates are fixed and agreed upon and, therefore, that a common time is established that everyone conceives in the same way. Finally, the collaboration of several in pursuit of a common goal is possible only if there is agreement on the relation between that goal and the means that makes its achievement possible—that is, if a single causal relation is accepted by all who are working together in the same enterprise. (ibid.: 444–45)

Here Durkheim presents a particular perspective upon social order, differentiated but also internally coordinated, within which the different parts are adjusted with respect to both time and to space, in striving for a common goal. Durkheim here raises the general problem of coordination, a question of direct interest to economists, since it is the market that is defined as an a posteriori form of coordination, as opposed to the conscious form of organisation of which Durkheim speaks here. This passage locates the original significance of the economy—a trope we can find from Aristotle and Xenophon right up to the mid-eighteenth century—in terms of a totality in which everything is so proportioned that there is neither superfluity nor want, and where the different parts contribute harmoniously to the goal of all. This is a definition of the economic that can be applied to animal economy, or to architecture, or to the work of God (divine economy, the economy guided by a divine plan).[4] It might also be noted that in this quotation Durkheim discreetly raises the ques-

---

[4] Here we are paraphrasing the definition given in the eighteenth century by the Abbé de Condillac, a major sensationist philosopher: "as *economy* requires order, this word is sometimes taken to be an order where nothing is wanting, or there is nothing in excess; and since all parties share amongst themselves a just proportion, they are completely subject to the same goal. Civil *economy*, military *economy*, the *economy* of the human body, the *economy* of the universe, or a building. In one word one can refer to everything where proportion is at issue" (Condillac, *Dictionnaire des synonymes*).

tion of means and ends, that is, instrumental action considered as at the heart of any description of rational economic activity.

But all of this remains somewhat sibylline, Durkheim having probably found here his limits in respect of economic knowledge.

Mauss and the Second Durkheimian Research Programme in Economic Sociology

Although close to his uncle when it was a matter of the relationship between economy and religion, Mauss never wrote any text devoted specifically to this question. Mauss pursued several paths of inquiry, as did those—primarily Davy and Maunier—who worked with him on the junction of economy, ethnology and religion. First of all some suggestive insights can be found in those texts devoted to the sociology of religion, as is the case with the studies on magic, sacrifice and prayer. It is also true of those texts devoted to money and archaic forms of exchange. Following this there can be found the kind of genetic approach followed by Durkheim when investigating property and contract: Davy, for example, took an interest in the way that potlatch formed a stage leading to the status of a contract. Mauss did not dismiss such studies, but while he embarked on occasional excursions of this kind, his prime interest lay elsewhere, as Bruno Karsenty in particular has noted (1994; 1998): with what we can call, taking up one of Mauss's own phrases, the "rock hypothesis". Here the gift is supposed to touch on a fundamental structure of human societies; consequently, the genetic method may be bypassed in order to compare different societies in respect of a structural tension traversing historical time: the tension between the gift and market exchange.

Religion and Ancient Economy

Mauss's writings on the relationship between religion, efficacity and economic activity, and also concerning the origins of money, are linked through the notion of *mana*; and here we intend to focus on these texts at the expense of those that accent social rhythms and the cleavage between economy and religion (Beuchat & Mauss 1906), an issue dealt with in chapter 2 above in respect of Durkheim's own writing.

The essay on magic highlights a phenomenon closely related to religion[5] and one dimension of the economic phenomenon, technology: "magic is

---

[5] Mauss and Hubert define the ritual of magic as "*any rite that is not part of an organised cult*, a private, secret rite, and at its limit tending towards the prohibited" (1904: 16). Later, Mauss thought that religion and magic should be related to the sacred, suggesting that religion represents a more restrained domain than magic (1947: 167), and that magic—excepting

truly born of religion on the one hand, and technique and science on the other" (Hubert & Mauss 1904: 134). Three constituent parts of magic are considered: the magician, magic rituals or actions, and social representations involving these actions (ibid.: 10, 17–83).

These representations are important because magic has an efficacity for those who make use of it. Hubert and Mauss emphasise this in a passage that recalls Durkheim's insight into the religious foundation of the contract: certainly, they say, legal actions have a ritualistic character that obligates the parties involved, but the magic ritual has something more:

> Ritual acts, by contrast [with legal acts], are in essence capable of producing something other than conventions; they are extremely effective; they are creative; they do things. Magical rites are even more specifically conceived in this way. . . . But techniques are themselves creative. The gestures from which they are formed are likewise reputed to be effective. From this point of view, the greater part of humanity has trouble telling them apart from rites. (ibid.: 11)

Mauss extended this idea in his unpublished thesis on prayer. Not only did this rite have an economic function by allowing the sacerdotal class to enrich themselves, but above all it is considered as one factor of production among others by a large part of humanity: "There are entire civilisations where they are taken for factors of production. The effectiveness attributed to them is analogous to that of labour, or mechanic arts" (Mauss 1909: 383; see also 1936: 371). He also proposed to distinguish the technique of magico-religious rites, not in terms of material efficacity, but in regard to what is at the root of this efficacity—here mechanical labour, and there the spirits which the rite is able to set going (Mauss 1909: 405–6).[6] Magic is a "gigantic variation on the theme: the principle of causality" (Hubert & Mauss 1904: 56), and in this respect it was part of the endeavour that ended up as science. But, according to Hubert and Mauss, it involves more the practical than the theoretical side of knowledge; it is not the abstract dimension which characterises magical thought but its pursuit of the concrete properties of things (ibid.: 69), and it is here that it rejoins the economic dimension, which in Mauss's understanding is closely related to technique:

---

black magic—makes use of few sacred objects, which brings it close to the notion of *mana*, of power (1947: 207). Notwithstanding that, Mauss did not seek to deny the fact that the relations between magic and religion vary across societies (ibid.: 208).

[6] "Techniques will define themselves as traditional acts grouped in regard to mechanical, physical or chemical effect, acts known as such. It will be rather difficult to distinguish between the techniques (1) of the arts and fine arts . . . (2) of a religious efficacity" (Mauss 1947: 22).

The inventor has his theoretical logic, which is his own; but it is this notion of a practical solution to a problem which is the trademark of the technician. Very often it is run together with administration, the economical and the technical. No doubt, for many techniques to converge on the same end, all of them must be adapted; thus there exists a category of administration of movements, a co-ordinate of the administration of movements; there is an administration of the totality of techniques of one individual, the one related to others. But a man is not solely economic, *homo œconomicus*; he is also a technician. A large part of the time of French peasants is devoted to *bricolage*, in other words, to technique. (Mauss 1947: 41)[7]

Where does the effectiveness of magic come from? According to Hubert and Mauss,[8] magic entails an important dimension of belief, of collective faith, which they set out to study by making use of a "non-intellectualist psychology" (Hubert & Mauss 1904: 101). We can understand this to be a psychology which, without treating individuals whose intellectual humanity would be different from our own, does however consider their reason in terms that are not ours.

This non-intellectualist psychology turns on the notion of *mana*. Hubert and Mauss state that its primitive nature evades logical analysis, for mana groups together a very heterogeneous complex of phenomena, mixing magic and religion, things and individuals, within the same rites. Of the same order as the sacred, mana has two characteristics which secure the linkage of religion and the economic. First of all, mana is the origin of the social hierarchy, in its political, symbolic and economic dimensions. It can be found in that which has become a sign and a symbol—money:

> *Mana* is strictly that which lends value to things and to people, magical value, religious value, and even social value. The social position of individuals is directly related to the importance of their *mana*, especially the positions in secret societies; the importance and the inviolability of property taboos derives from the *mana* of the person imposing them. Wealth is supposed to be the effect of *mana*; on some islands the word *mana* is even used to designate money. (ibid.: 102)

[7] The importance of this technical dimension must not be underestimated in Mauss, for he considered Marx to be wrong in thinking that "economy determines technique—it is rather the reverse" (Mauss 1947: 22).

[8] On this point they differ from the interpretation that Boudon (1999) has put forward in respect of Durkheim's theory of magic: Boudon deploys (extended) principles of rationality, whereas Hubert and Mauss lay emphasis upon the dimension of illusion and mystification—even self-mystification—for belief in the effectiveness of magic. Nonetheless, while magic did coincide with the formative period of science, one does not have to think that Hubert and Mauss ignore the rational dimension which lends credibility to magic.

Secondly, mana involves the idea of mechanical force, the physical effect produced and sought by the magician and the "magic effect" strictly speaking, that which calls up another level of reality superimposed on the existing level without eliminating it, a spiritual action at a distance between phenomena set to work by the magician. Whence the relation of magic to the economic along the dimension of technology: "*mana* is force *par excellence*, the true efficacity of things, corroborating their mechanical action without annihilating it. It is this which makes the thread hold, the house secure, the canoe seaworthy. In the field, it is fertility; in medicine, it is the healthy and the fatal virtue" (ibid.: 104).[9]

It is plain that Durkheim would have been able to refer to the economic value and to mana as the principle creating the connection between the religious and the economic domains. This connection is clearer in Mauss's text on the origin of money. Noting that he had already been concerned with the definition of economic phenomena, value and money, Mauss shows how a reading of documents from central Africa on *dzó*, a category close to that of mana, leads into a generalisation of earlier remarks regarding the relation of magic and money. Mauss brings together the power that money can have on individual action and the power that the talisman holds over the same individuals, on account of its magical and religious power. Mana designates the magical power accruing to particular things and individuals, and also designates their authority:

Is not the purchasing power of money natural when attached to the talisman which, to some extent, can compel the subordinates of the chiefs, the magicians' clients, to the prestations that are demanded of them? And, conversely, is it not necessity, as soon as the conception of wealth arises, however indistinctly, that the wealth of the chief and of the magician is located above all in the emblems that embody their magical powers, in a word, their authority, or which symbolise the power of the clan? . . . We consider the power of primitive money to make purchases derives, above all, from the prestige conferred by the talisman upon he who possesses it and which allows him to dictate to others. But isn't there something with which we ourselves are familiar? (Mauss 1914: 107)

---

[9] This aspect will be followed up by Maunier in the sociological studies he undertook in Kabylia, in particular the rites involved in the construction of a house: "I want to examine [the construction of a house, that is, the form of cooperation through which the formation of a family is realised] in respect of one of its aspects, describing the religious rites which it occasions. For two series of actions are at work here that are generally barely separate: technical or economic acts; ritual or liturgical acts. The house has to be built; it also has to be consecrated. Both are necessary. From whence emerge two parallel movements: for material effect, and for spiritual effect" (1930: 154).

The question is neither purely formal nor without importance for the concerns of Durkheimian economic sociology insofar as it takes a direct interest in money. On the one hand, as we shall see in the following chapter, Mauss anticipates in an important respect the analysis of money that Simiand advanced in his important 1934 article—"La monnaie, réalité sociale" ["Money as a Social Fact"]—in making money, or gold, an article of faith, of confidence expressed in the social.[10] On the other hand, Mauss places himself directly in relation to Durkheim's second programme when he declares: "we are talking about the origin of a conception, of an institution, of a faith" (1914: 106).

From Gift to Contract

The relationship between Mauss and those of his students with whom he worked on the gift relationship has been well covered in recent research.[11] Davy's 1922 dissertation was directed to this topic, making use of a wide range of material—mostly on societies in Northwest Canada, so that he could focus on *potlatch*—which Mauss had already begun to consider. Maunier's research was more fieldwork-based, dealing with the *twassa* in Kabylia, and considered the strategies employed by agents, an approach which, as has been emphasised by Mahé (1998), would later be adopted by Bourdieu (1972, 1980).

Among the second generation of Durkheimians, Maunier was the first to take up the second research programme in economic sociology, publishing a series of articles in the *Revue internationale de sociologie*. Maunier sought to found the principles of the division of labour on ancient religion, starting out from the sexual division of labour, which he linked to religion, that is, to sexual taboos, not to the physiological characteristics of the sexes.[12] Maunier follows Durkheim's interpretation of

[10] The following two passages, from the opening and closing parts of this short article, are very clear on this point—and in any case, in the debate that followed the publication of Simiand's essay, Mauss immediately referred to it: "Money is by no means a material and physical fact, it is essentially a social fact; its value is its purchasing power, and the measure of the confidence placed in it" (1914: 106). "Is the essence of faith in the value of gold not based upon the belief that, thanks to its possession, we can obtain from our contemporaries whatever prestations—in kind, or as services—which the state of the market will allow us to demand?" (ibid.: 112).

[11] The sole exception is without doubt René Lenoir, whose role remains obscure. But Mauss mentions him twice in his essay on the gift, citing an article in the *Revue philosophique* which presents Davy's argument and an article on *potlatch* in South America published the same year in *Anthropologie* (Mauss 1954: 83–85).

[12] "This social separation is clearly religious in nature. It is merely the outcome of religious prohibitions, taboos. Apart from their distinct and obligatory character, this is shown by the physical or even penal consequences which sanction them, a fact that goes

the profusion of totemic animals (1902b: 319, 349–50), suggesting that this rite is first and foremost a religious phenomenon which only much later assumed a utilitarian dimension (Maunier 1908: 43–45). Maunier suggests that a totemic division of labour finally established itself, moving then from specialised clans to castes, equivalent to nascent professional groups, and from which formed in particular the caste of magician-priests, who quite explicitly brought together the economic and religious dimensions (1908: 51–52). Maunier's publication coincided with the publication of a work on Indian castes by Bouglé (1908a), although some of this had been published the year before in a series of articles in the *Revue d'économie politique* (Bouglé 1907). Bouglé shared the view that the religious base of social life was a determining factor and treated the caste system as expressing the social hierarchy in India; he rejected "materialist" interpretations of castes in favour of an explanation based upon religion.[13] He implied that taboos are certainly at the origin of the system of "repulsion, hierarchy and hereditary specialisation" through which he defined the caste system (1908a: 4, 32). However, he did not go much beyond this point.[14]

Davy's approach can also be aligned with the second Durkheimian research programme. He does not take up the connection made by Durkheim between religion and contract. Instead, he places emphasis upon

---

unchallenged. The sexual division of labour is therefore itself the outcome of prohibitions. And so it is above all a religious institution, *a particular case of taboo between the sexes*" (Maunier 1908: 31).

[13] Bouglé involved himself in criticism of historical materialism to a greater extent than all other Durkheimians (1908a: 45, 50, 82ff.; 1908b; 1934). This is related to the fact that he edited the rubric "General Sociology" in the *Année sociologique*, and that he had a strong interest in doctrinal disputes and their political dimensions (1899).

[14] "If one is able discover the taboos which are the origin of repugnance, one will perhaps capture the underlying reason for clan specialisation, which hardens into castes. . . . But even if this detail escapes us, what we clearly see, beyond the reasons for specialisation of each class, are the broad lines of the hierarchical system which, overriding everything else, orders these closed groups, sustaining a general parallel with the distinction between noble and ignoble races, and that of pure or impure trades and professions" (Bouglé 1908a: 220). In a letter dated July 1907, Mauss criticised Bouglé for remaining so vague on the central point, the religious dimension of caste: "In my opinion, the most serious lacuna is the impact of your point of view, which is always legal, political, general. You deal at great length with the religious character of caste. But you do not give what you call a fundamental phenomenon the individual chapter that it merits. You dissipate your observations and would certainly profit from pulling them together. Caste is religious by definition. It is composed of groups of men who are ritually separated, through prohibitions of varying intensity and of variable quality. The investigation of this is, in my opinion, merely sketched out" (Mauss 1930: 46). Weber's work on the relation between the caste system and the theodicy specific to India is conducted in terms entirely at one with Mauss's sentiments here (Weber 1916–17: 225–233).

kinship relations.[15] Davy seeks to demonstrate that family status, and especially the change of status involved in marriage, represents an origin for contract of greater significance than religion; he suggests that marriage and kinship relations are at the origin of property, which is modelled on kinship relations (1922: 42). He therefore understands the blood covenant in a manner different from that of Durkheim, since instead of a religious formalism he sees this as a formalism in which kinship can be represented as the manner in which individuals are connected one with another (1922: 49). Only much later is religion able to create a contractual relationship:

> As far as the evolution of the notion of contract is concerned, one sure conclusion follows from the preceding analyses: before one can talk of contract in a strict sense, it can be seen that under particular circumstances religion and magic produce general connections analogous to those of kinship and friendship, as comprehensive as the second and having the same legal precision as the first. (ibid.: 81; see also 373)

He treats these ethnographic facts as an experience that cannot be found in historical societies. In so doing, he isolates a problem that Durkheim stumbles upon when seeking to explain how economic facts become attached to religious facts: should the aim of the investigation be to place methodically successive elements in a continuous chain leading from ancient to modern societies? Davy rejects the evolutionary implications of such an approach.

What then becomes of Mauss's attempt to place his linkage of economic activity to its magico-religious basis within such an evolutionary strategy? We have seen above in respect of the role of money that Mauss did not distance himself from such an approach (1914); it is the same in the *The Gift*, where many passages suggest that Mauss had nothing against the work of Davy, even if one knows that Mauss had "serious reservations" and was no doubt relieved that he did not have to become involved in the doctoral examination. Nonetheless, Mauss often cites Davy's work (Mauss 1925a/1954: 3, 5, 8, 35–37, 82, 84–85), joining with him in criticising the way in which legal and economic historians with an a priori evolutionary mindset contrast ancient and modern economies through the construction of a "myth of barter", supposing rational agents who, starting out from an exchange economy without money,

---

[15] "Contract emerges therefore at the crossroad of two paths, one leading to the domain of family relations, the other to that of kinship groups" (Davy 1922: 6). In a later passage he elaborates on this comment: "We will thus see that the contractual function arises before the contract itself in alliances based upon blood and upon marriage, creating a true communion of nature between those who are mutually bound" (ibid.: 31).

finally discover the benefits of a universal equivalent and so enter economic modernity. Here, as Mauss points out, there is a fictional history running from primitive societies that know only barter, to sale and purchase on a cash-only basis, to the extension of credit, which at first combines cash sales and loans (ibid.: 33). Mauss argues that this story is quite erroneous, since the starting point is quite different—the gift:

> Now a gift necessarily implies the notion of credit. Economic evolution has not gone from barter to sale and from cash to credit. Barter arose from the system of gifts given and received on credit, simplified by drawing together the moments of time which had previously been distinct. Likewise purchase and sale—both direct sale and credit sale— and the loan, derive from the same source. (ibid.: 34)

At the beginning of chapter 3 of *The Gift*, where he moves from ethnography to history, Mauss adopts an evolutionary approach as a means of linking his argument to developed European societies. Greek, Roman and Semitic societies, he suggests, had the capacity to distinguish forms of law under circumstances where there was at first a lack of distinction between persons and things, between interest and rites:

> For it was precisely these Greeks and Romans who, possibly following the Northern and Western Semites, invented the distinction of personal from real rights, separated sale from contract, and above all formulated the difference between ritual, law and economic interest. (ibid.: 52 [trans. revised KT])

Mauss recognized that this was little more than a "likely hypothesis" (ibid.: 53), but its likelihood was supported by the existence of other relevant Indo-European laws. We can also introduce here Maunier's work on the *twassa* of Kabylia, which adds a cultural gloss that we do not find in Mauss, but which can be placed in the chain of phenomena linking ancient to modern facts (1927a, 1933). By contrast with Mauss, Maunier studied a contemporary phenomenon of which he had direct knowledge, since he worked in Algeria, specialising in colonial sociology, and primarily that of North Africa.

However, the greater weight of Mauss's work can be explained by the existence of another research strategy in the same text: the hypothesis of the "rock".

The Hypothesis of the "Rock"

There is another possible reading of *The Gift* when placed in the context of the second Durkheimian programme of economic sociology. This reading is closely associated with the preceding one and is exposed by Mauss when outlining his project:

> *In primitive or archaic types of society, what is the legal or interest rule that renders a counter gift obligatory? What force is there in the thing given which compels the recipient to return it?* That is the problem with which we are here especially concerned, while outlining others. We hope, by presenting sufficient facts, to be able to answer this question precisely, and also to indicate the direction in which answers to cognate questions might be sought. We shall also be led to pose new problems. Of these, some concern the permanent morality of the contract: that is, the manner in which even today the law of things remains bound up with the law of persons; and some refer to the forms and ideas which have always been at least partially present in exchange and which even now make up the idea of individual interest. (1925a/1954: 1–2 [trans. revised KT])

He goes on to explain that he anticipates a dual aim:

> We shall arrive at a set of more or less archaeological conclusions on the nature of human transactions in societies which surround us, and in those which have immediately preceded ours. . . . We will find markets before the development of merchants, and before their most important innovation, currency as we know it. We shall also see how they functioned before assuming what we might call modern forms (Semitic, Hellenic, Hellenistic, and Roman) of contract, and of sale on the one hand and legal tender on the other. We shall encounter the moral and economic features of these institutions.
>
> We contend that the same morality and economy are at work, albeit less noticeably, in our own societies, and we believe that in them we have discovered one of the human bedrocks upon which our societies are built. We believe that we may draw conclusions of a moral nature from this concerning some of the problems confronting us in our present legal and economic crisis. (ibid.: 2 [trans. revised KT])

The first point to which we can draw attention here is the reference to established societies with a clear distinction between real and personal rights; this allusion to legal and economic modernity betrays an evolutionary perspective that it would be vain to deny. This is an element of the second Durkheimian programme and so there is no surprise in finding it here.

Secondly, while Mauss goes on to state that he will deal with *one* problem, he asks *two* questions: the first regarding the rule of law and interest, and the second concerning the force embodied in the object given as a gift. This second question raises the (controversial) theory of *hau* which Mauss outlines in respect of Maori mythology, an idea that Levi-Strauss later suggested most likely reflected misinformation. This question is of no concern to us here; we can instead focus upon the first question, which is a decisive one from the perspective of economic sociology since it involves the rule followed in exchange/gift giving, provided that this is interpreted as a sociological rather than a legal rule.

"What is the legal or interest rule that renders a counter gift obligatory? What force is there in the thing given which compels the recipient to return it?" This question bears comparison with the way that Adam Smith presented his own programme in the opening chapters of *Wealth of Nations*. Having presented the different aspects of the society he seeks to describe—commercial society, in which all individuals are traders—Smith states:

> What are the rules which men naturally observe in exchanging them [goods] either for money or for one another, I shall now proceed to examine. These rules determine what may be called the relative or exchangeable value of goods. (1776 I.iv.12)

The parallel is a suggestive one.[16] Both Mauss and Smith pose the problem in terms of the rules for the circulation of goods—the gift for the former, commodity exchange for the latter—in such a way as to determine the functioning of two types of society structured around distinct social mechanisms. Gifts involve three obligations—giving, receiving and giving in turn—while commodity exchange involves an equality of *do ut des* and monetary equivalence between the things exchanged. Around this distinction two quite different societies are formed. This helps us understand that Mauss had absolutely no intention of describing a system of low-intensity exchange:

> These people [the Melanesians] have an extra-domestic economy and a highly developed exchange system, and are busier commercially than French peasants and fishermen have been for the past hundred years. They have an extensive economic life and a considerable inter-island trade that ignores geographical and linguistic boundaries. They replace the system of sale and purchase with one of gifts and return gifts. (Mauss 1925a/1954: 30 [trans. revised KT])

---

[16] It is possible that this parallel is a conscious one, since Mauss was familiar with *The Wealth of Nations*, alluding to the so-called "natural propensity to truck and barter", a notion which can be traced to a misinterpretation of the natives encountered by Captain Cook; this was not exchange in the trading sense but rather exchange of presents, hence of gifts prompting counter-gifts (Mauss 1947: 104).

Mauss isolates the "rock" upon which a significant section of humanity have taken up a position before we grasp that we also are standing upon it:

> Thus we see that a part of mankind, relatively wealthy, hard-working and creating significant surpluses, exchanges vast amounts in ways and for reasons other than those with which we are familiar from our own societies. (ibid.: 31 [trans. revised KT])

The gift is therefore a specific social form, distinct from exchange, thanks to which things can change hands. The circulation of things is as necessary to societies as nourishment is to an individual, but the manner in which this is done is a work of society on itself; it is a mode of being which lends one society its character relative to others where the rule is not the same.

The work of Maunier supports this. Following a line of argument all his own which, notably, leaves entirely to one side the hypothesis regarding *hau*, he draws attention to the numerous associations between economic phenomena (the interest payable when wealth is transferred during the festivals that he studies) and religious phenomena (benediction and good fortune for those astute enough to be liberal when responding in turn to the *twassa* received) and social (since what is at stake is the extension of association within the group and its hierarchy, for *twassa* is a "matter of pride"). Maunier emphasised the fact that gifts offered have to be returned augmented, sometimes by as much as twice the original amount (1927a: 93). Is this not simply a form of (temporary) capital accumulation, permitting economic ventures to be realised that would otherwise be hard to initiate? Maunier denies this, noting that in the first place the *twassa* takes place at the end of summer when the economic cycle is at a low point, and that secondly there is uncertainty regarding the date when the reciprocal repayment will be made, so that the sums involved can only with difficulty be treated as capital since their receipt cannot be linked to any clearly delimited period. *Twassa* destabilises the equilibrium of patrimony (one has to give, so that one can receive a larger amount in return at some future, but uncertain, date), and this fluctuation directly nurtures the association between individuals in the group, as can likewise be seen in contemporary systems of local exchange (Servet et al. 1999: 19).[17]

---

[17] "The advantage created by the gift must therefore be sought elsewhere [than in economic advantage]. It is above all an agent of translation, or a cause of circulation. It motivates the connection of transactions one with another. It prompts an indefinite movement of goods. It multiplies and renews the transmission of values. It ensures that patrimony will constantly be in flux. At each feast it is necessary to give *or* to receive, and sometimes also to give *and* to receive. But this is a form of circulation *sui generis.* . . . The gift is not thought of as an isolated gesture. It arises in the context of a feast, but also has a purpose in itself.

But beyond this opposition of commercial economy and the logic of symbolic exchange, what is the "rock" to which Mauss alludes? It is that alloy of interest and disinterest, of egoism and altruism; it is that which directly brings together the man from ancient society and the contemporary modern man:

> There is no need to wish that the citizen be neither too good nor too subjective, neither too insensitive nor too realistic. He should be vividly aware of himself, but also of others and of the social reality (and what other reality is there in these moral matters?). He must act with full realization of himself, of society and its sub-groups. *The basis of moral action is eternal; it is common to societies of the highest degree of evolution, to those of the near future and to societies of the least advancement. Here we touch bedrock [roc].* (1925a/1954: 67–68, my emphasis [trans. revised KT])

Hence Mauss uses the idea which we have already seen at work in Durkheim's *Elementary Forms*, where the manner in which the sacred arises and functions among the Arunta is used to directly clarify what is sacred, its formation and transformation in modern society. Mauss takes up the idea that man is, and has always been, a dual person, and he inscribes this duality in the fact that the two systems of circulation of goods are likewise at work within modern societies.

The importance of this idea in sociology goes back to Comte, who in his *Cours de philosophie positive* emphasises the importance of behaviour oriented toward others, to the detriment of selfish behaviour (1830–42 II: 180–82). In his *Système de politique positive*, Comte goes further, considering four forms of circulation or wealth within society:

> According to their dignity and decreasing efficacy, our four general modes of material transmission have to be arranged in the normal order, which is also the order in which they were historically introduced: the gift, exchange, inheritance, and conquest. The second and third modes have become the usual ones among modern populations, the forms best adapted to the industrial existence that had to prevail. But the first and the last do contribute to the initial formation of big capital. While the last must finally fall into total disuse, this will never happen to the first, whose importance, as much as purity, is today obscured from us by our industrial egoism. (1851–54 II: 155)

The place given to the gift and to inheritance reveals how important the opposition between egoism and altruism is in Comte's thinking, since he

---

Circulation, obligation, benediction are run together. Profit is not distinct from duty and thoughtfulness. Honour and purity mingle with self-interest" (Maunier 1927a: 94–95).

considers that the prime problem of humanity is the way that the latter prevails over the former. (ibid.: 173). With economic modernity, exchange and inheritance definitively take over violent forms of the appropriation of goods, but this is not the same for the gift. Comte hardly went any further; he did not even draw attention to the proximity between inheritance and the gift, a proximity which is also apparent in the Civil Code.[18]

Mauss lends an empirical content to this form of circulation of wealth (Caillé 2000). This does not involve a vestige destined sooner or later to be forgotten; it is by contrast a principle of the actual life which should have a larger part in contemporary society (Godbout & Caillé 1992).[19]

The Conclusions of *The Gift*

"Let us extend our observations to the present day"—this is how Mauss opens the concluding chapter of his essay *The Gift*. Here once again we will be primarily interested in how the argument which he constructs can be related to the second Durkheimian research programme, where religion and economy come together, as sketched out in *Elementary Forms*. Let us examine the three concluding points that Mauss presents in this chapters, relating to morality, economic sociology and political economy, and finally to morality and general sociology.

The Moral Ideal

In his moral conclusions, Mauss makes the point that social behaviour is not entirely dominated by an economic vision of the world relating everything to commercial transactions:

> Much of our morality and of our everyday life itself is situated within the ambiance of the gift, mingling obligation and liberty. It is our good fortune that all is not yet couched in terms of purchase and sale. Things still have a sentimental value greater than their venal value, and indeed

[18] Part 3 of the Code deals with "Different Ways in which Property is Acquired." Having quickly reviewed the different contractual forms, Title 2 of this third part examines conjointly gifts made among the living and wills. This convergence between gift and inheritance is something one frequently encounters in French nineteenth-century political economy (Steiner 2008).

[19] Moreover, and in spite of the strong interpretative difference between Caillé and Bourdieu (see Caillé 1986: 109–15), we might add Bourdieu's generalisation of the gift in terms of the symbolic exchange typical of the economy of honour, domestic economy, etc., which is then opposed to what he calls the "economic economy," for which calculation and interest are taboo (Bourdieu 1994: 175ff.).

in some cases the value is entirely sentimental. We do not only have a shopkeeper morality. (1925a/1954: 63 [trans. revised KT])

But for Mauss the point is not simply to praise this vestige of ancient morality; here he makes a move characteristic of theories of socioeconomic action (Gislain and Steiner 1995: 89–104) and underscores the axiological dimension of modern action. He lends this claim regarding the place of the gift in modern social life a specific orientation, suggesting a strong interconnection between personal and collective interest,[20] an interconnection that is linked to the freedom and the obligation of exchange/gift and that poses a major sociological problem, the problem of "social deception" touched on in the introduction (Mauss 1925a/1954: 1). This section of Mauss's conclusion deals with motivations to action, motivations which play a decisive role in all sociological understanding of social reality, whether of ancient societies or of ours today, directly echoing Durkheim's thinking on egoism and altruism in his discussion of the manner in which education effected the attachment of children to a group.[21]

The leading ideal among Mauss's moral conclusions concerns the important question of the relation to the economic, dealing with the social transactions through which human beings circulate goods, what is "so badly termed" exchange (ibid.: 70), barter, the *permutatio* of useful things. At issue is the moral or political decision to which Mauss alluded in the closing passage of the essay,[22] leading societies to provide a place for commercial exchange or contract:

---

[20] "However, it is necessary for the individual to work. He has to be compelled to rely upon himself more than upon others. On the other hand, he has to defend his interests, personally and in a group. Excessive generosity and communism will be of equally little use, and will also be of as little use to society as the selfishness of our contemporaries and the individualism of our laws" (Mauss 1925a: 262–63; passage missing 1954: 66–67).

[21] In *Moral Education*, Durkheim examines the opposition between egoism and altruism. He argues that two motivations are combined within the same behaviour: "Thus, we have egoism embedded in altruism; conversely, there is altruism in egoism. . . . We feel that in the activity deployed to reach these diverse but internalized objectives, there is something other than pure egoism. There is a certain gift of ourselves, a certain aptitude in giving ourselves and spreading ourselves and not turning in on ourselves" (1902–3/1961: 215–16).

[22] The final paragraph runs as follows: "We can see how one can, in particular cases, study the totality of human behaviour, the entirety of social life; and we can also see how such concrete study leads not only to a science of manners [mœurs], to the beginnings of a social science, but even to ethical conclusions—'civility', to use an old word, or 'civics', as we say today. Through studies of this kind we can gain insight, measure and assess various aesthetic, moral, religious and economic motivations, and the material and demographic factors which, taken together, form the basis of society and constitutes communal life, and whose conscious direction is the supreme art—politics in the Socratic sense of the word" (Mauss 1925a/1954: 81 [trans. revised KT]).

Even in these societies the individual and the group, or rather the sub-group, have always sensed a sovereign right to refuse the contract, and it is this which lends the circulation of goods its aspect of generosity. But on the other hand, they never usually had either the right of, nor interest in, such a refusal; and this renders such distant societies similar to our own. (ibid.: 71 [trans. revised KT])

Without forcing the text, one can read here the idea that beyond the formalism and social deception of free but obligatory circulation, the gift is of significance as much for its disavowal of utility as for the way it is deployed in social relations. This has been extensively discussed by those (Godbout & Caillé 1992; Caillé 2000) who see in Mauss's work the founding programme of an anti-utilitarian social science, or even by those, like Bourdieu (1994: 174–79), who see in the denigration of calculation within the "non-economic economy" of symbolic exchange an essential element of the self-deception of modern society. There is also an empirical sense to this when, following Gøsta Esping-Andersen (1990), modern welfare states are classed according to the degree to which they eschew commercial calculation with respect to particular goods. Political and moral ideas combine in a way that coincides with Mauss's own views when Richard Titmuss (1970) argues passionately against the sale of blood. This was in order to sustain the obligation of a gift in such a way that the gift, or altruism, became obligatory, given that our societies had decided that the *permutatio* of this vital organ (one dare not say "useful") should be effected without contract or market intervening between donor and recipient.[23]

We need, then, to pay attention to the series of examples with which Mauss illustrates this idea: artistic and literary property, and by way of consequence, their inheritance; scientific property in technical and industrial matters; and finally, above all, social insurance. Mauss thought that this last instance meant that the employer—whether private enterprise or government—could not simply pay the worker, that he was owed "a certain security in his life against unemployment, sickness, old age and death" (1925a/1954: 65), security to which, however, the worker had to contribute. Here Mauss again goes back to Durkheim, to the first programme that had been abandoned after the "revelation":

We are seeing the dawn and realization of professional morality and corporate law. The compensation funds and mutual societies which industrial groups are forming in favour of this or that corporate task have, in the eyes of pure morality, only one flaw: their administration

---

[23] I have elaborated this issue in a study of the sociology of organ transplantation (Steiner 2010).

is in the hands of the bosses. Furthermore, groups are acting. . . . We are therefore returning to a group morality. (ibid.: 66 [trans. revised KT])

And to be certain of being properly understood, two pages further on Mauss made clear this direct connection to the work of his uncle, referring directly to his discussion of professional morality:

> For honour, disinterestedness and corporative solidarity are not vain words, nor do they deny the necessity for work. We should humanize the other professional groups and make all of them more perfect. That would be a great deed, and one which Durkheim already had in view. (ibid.: 67)

Mauss attributed great importance to the lecture course that Durkheim had given on the physiology of mores. He kept the manuscript, and gave a copy to one of his students, who edited and published it (Kubali 1950). The first three lectures, devoted to professional morality, were edited separately by Mauss and published in the *Revue de métaphysique et de morale* in 1937;[24] he also drew from them for his lectures at the Collège de France during 1931–32. So it is not pure chance that he drew on these ideas in the closing pages of *The Gift*. But, it could be said, here Mauss creates a connection with the first Durkheimian programme, and there appears to be no linkage between religion and economy. The answer to this problem lies in the second part of his conclusions, which are the most decisive for the argument advanced here.

An Improved Analysis of Economic Facts

The conclusions of economic sociology and of political economy seek in general "an improved analysis of the most general economic facts" so that one might create "insight into the best procedures of management applicable to our societies" (Mauss 1925a: 266).[25] It is here that Mauss

---

[24] "The philosophical public, sociologists, and even men of politics will perhaps be pleased to find expressed here the principle of professional morality in a form which while clearly provisional and schematic, at least deals directly with this issue in its own terms. In these times of soviets, corporations of every sort, all kinds of corporatism, in these times of clashes, tactics, of systematically confrontational politics, of radical institutions, of savage revolution and reaction, we must not keep knowledge of Durkheim's thought on these problems to ourselves; problems which, in our opinion, he already knew how to pose a long time ago, and perhaps better than anyone since, proposing by simple intuition the good and practical solution: morally, legally, economically" (Mauss 1937: 504).

[25] The relevant passage in the existing English translation runs: "Our facts do more than illumine our morality and point out our ideal; for they help us to analyse economic facts of a more general nature, and our analysis might suggest the way to better administrative procedures for our societies" (1925a/1954: 69) [KT].

comes back to the ideas sketched by Durkheim in *Elementary Forms*, making reference to the very specific note which has been cited above in chapter 2. And so Mauss here has in mind the second Durkheimian programme. What arguments does he advance?[26]

Mauss's essay presents a wide range of facts relating to societies diverse both geographically and historically, providing him with a "very solid sequence of facts" of the kind quite typical of the Durkheimian school. To this can be added the nature of these facts. Firstly, they underscore the idea that primitive economies are not societies in penury; rather, that they accumulate significant surpluses, which are conspicuously consumed or destroyed as a pure loss. This, therefore, establishes an empirical equivalence between primitive societies and societies of abundance (Sahlins 1972). Secondly, Mauss draws attention to the fact that situations in which *permutatio* of useful things is set to work, or again, their ritual and ceremonial destruction, sets up forms of social relation which differ from those found in commercial societies:

> It is something other than utility which circulates in these multifarious societies, which are for the most part fairly enlightened. Clans, age groups and sexes, in view of the many relationships to which contacts between them give rise, are in a state of perpetual economic effervescence which has little about it that is materialistic; it is much less prosaic than our buying and selling, hire of services and speculation on the stock exchange. (1925a/1954: 70 [trans. revised KT])

The reintroduction here of the idea of social effervescence is linked to Mauss's own work on Inuit societies, but it also of course makes a link back to the arguments made by Durkheim in *Suicide* and in *Elementary Forms*, where it is used in a neutral sense, not seeking to emphasise the harmful aspect of such aggravated social relations but rather to highlight their contribution to socialisation and the pleasure of common action.[27] In other words, effervescence is associated by Mauss with the multidimensionality of social action, underpinned by the methodology of the total social fact. This provides the means for conceiving an economy—or even a managerial team, a practical application from which Mauss would

---

[26] It has to be said that these pages present a very dense argument open to a number of different readings. Here we deal with them in terms of the second Durkheimian programme of economic sociology, but they can also be read in terms of a critique of economic categories (i.e., the Durkheimian sociology of economic knowledge), or in terms of the constitution of an economic ethos, the last being an issue that we deal with in relation to the work of Weber in ch. 8 below.

[27] Mauss does not, however, ignore the existence of a harmful side to "effervescence", as can be seen in his writings on Bolshevism, in which he presents the Bolshevik revolution as moral effervescence and political and economic chaos (1925c: 709).

not have recoiled—quite explicitly in terms of the relation of gift and exchange, altruism and egoism. Here he sees the possibility of new forms of wage relations:

> There is the feeling that there is no better way of making men work than by reassuring them of being paid loyally all their lives for labour which they give loyally not only for their own sakes but for that of others. The transacting producer feels now—as he has always felt, but this time he feels it more acutely—that he is giving something of himself, his time and his life. Thus he wants recompense, however modest, for this gift. And to refuse him this recompense is to incite him to laziness and less effort. (ibid.: 75 [trans. revised KT])

The final step in his conclusions completes the emplacement of the second programme of Durkheimian economic sociology. Examination of the economic functioning of primitive societies shows up their religious dimension:

> But all this very rich economy is nevertheless replete with religious elements; money still has its magical power and is still linked to clan and individual. Diverse economic activities—for example, the market—are impregnated with ritual and myth; they retain a ceremonial character, obligatory and efficacious; they are imbued with ritual and rights. From this perspective we are already answering the question raised by Durkheim regarding the religious origin of the notion of economic value. (ibid.: 70 [trans. revised KT])

This is a very significant passage, for the final sentence has a footnote which refers directly to the passage in the conclusion to *Elementary Forms* in which Durkheim identifies the connection between economic and religious value, but states that "the nature of these relationships has not yet been studied" (Durkheim 1912/1995: 421 n. 4). *And so Mauss's conclusion can be read as taking up this agenda, seeking to link in an explicit way economic sociology to the sociology of religion.* It can also be observed that here Mauss sheds the rather awkward aspect of Durkheim's argument that sought to insert religion in the place of economy in historical materialism. The conception of the total social fact expresses, above all, the idea, trivialized since Montesquieu's "general spirit" or Comte's notion of the consensus, of a unity between the different dimensions of social life. Seen in this light the concept of the total social fact is hardly original, nor more useful for empirical research than the other two ideas; but this concept has an essential function in the way that Mauss distances himself from the work of his uncle. The total social fact expresses the sense that no sphere of social life is more fundamental than any other (the religious no more than the economic); each sphere has a different functional mode, but they interact and the sociologist finds their joint impact mingled in social facts (the gift, wages, etc.). But there is a difference: some spheres are more central than others, here religion, there economy, depending on the type of society concerned (Mauss 1947: 102, 164).[28]

Having noted this, Mauss passes over the problem to be resolved in the various remarks he scatters in conclusion. He only throws out some incomplete hints. Firstly, we need to examine what is involved in the two Durkheimian programmes of economic sociology, an issue which concerned Simiand during the same period. Secondly, Mauss's conclusions contain a number of points where he discusses the concepts (the gift, exchange, interest) with which modern societies think; this is closely bound up with the second Durkheimian programme and the sociology of knowledge. Thirdly, having reintroduced the sociology of religion and the sociology of knowledge with the second Durkheimian programme, Mauss asks us to consider the process by which we have become what we are, that is, the fact that "It is only our Western societies that quite recently turned man into an economic animal" (1925a/1954: 74). Mauss here invites examination of the process through which rational self-interested behaviour was created, and how self-interested behaviour was modified in such a way that commercial behaviour appears to be the essence of rationality. The slow development of self-interest, linked to the "victory of rationalism and mercantilism" (ibid.), calls for the extension of Durkheimian economic sociology to Weberian economic sociology as laid out in the *Protestant Ethic*, in the light of the work and ideas of Durkheim, Mauss, Simiand. Each will be dealt with in turn in the three following chapters.

---

[28] Commenting on the Russian Revolution, Mauss wrote: "Few doctrines ended up more shaken by the terrible events of the past ten years than that of 'historical materialism'. But what marks it out from other political doctrines is its founding defect. The sophistry of the claim that this or that sequence of social events is primary must always be challenged. Neither political entities, nor moral entities, nor economic entities dominate any society, even less so the arts applied to them" (1924b: 555; see also 1947: 21, 41, 69, 111).

CHAPTER SIX

The Encounter between Two Programmes

So far we have followed the unfolding of Durkheim's two programmes in the sociology of the economy. Simiand and Mauss explored their potential during Durkheim's own lifetime, and then on through the 1920s and 1930s after his death.

But while Durkheim moved from the first to the second, Mauss and Simiand draw upon both programmes, facilitating their convergence. When in 1934 Mauss attended Simiand's lectures on money, he first praised the way that Simiand highlighted the social dimensions of money—faith, social expectation—and thus its status as a "total social fact"—and then noted:

> But you have been able to do this because you have an idea that you share in common with me—and I must say that here it is more an encounter than a joint venture—that expectations, emotions, wills are quantifiable. A panic on the stock exchange can be quantified, and the proof is the difference in prices. (Mauss, in Simiand 1934b: 61)

This encounter is an important stage in the work of the Durkheimians and prompts some of their most powerful writing.

MAUSS AND SIMIAND DURING THE INTERWAR PERIOD

Mauss occupied a central position among the group of researchers associated with the first series of the *Année sociologique*, partly because he was Durkheim's nephew and partly because of the importance that Durkheim attributed to the sociology of religion. But Simiand was no less important, establishing and directing a subsection of the *Année* devoted to economic sociology (Besnard 1979; Steiner 1994: 11). From this period of the first series, relations between Simiand and Mauss were close, not least because Durkheim was in Bordeaux and it was Mauss, in Paris, who was able to maintain personal contact with contributors to the periodical and hence form them into a collaborative group (Fournier 1994: 144). Mauss contributed in turn to Simiand's own periodical, *Notes critiques—Sciences sociales*, writing fifteen reviews for it (Fournier 1997: 16). Moreover, their common socialist engagement led to their creation of courses run by the *Bourse du travail* between 1898 and 1910, as well as their participation in the socialist investigations initiated by Robert Hertz, another contributor to the *Année sociologique*, in 1908 (Fournier 1994: 276). This set of relationships took on a new form after the death of Durkheim.

During the interwar period, Durkheimians clearly belonged to one of two groupings: on the one side, researchers such as Marcel Granet, Halbwachs, Mauss and Simiand, and on the other, university teachers such as Bouglé, Fauconnet, Lapie and Davy. The first group was associated with socialism, had gained new specialist skills—in Mauss's case, in languages and the science of religions, in economic sciences and statistics for Simiand and Halbwachs—published original work and did not hesitate to criticise Durkheim's findings, reevaluating them and shifting their emphases, as Halbwachs did in the case of suicide, for example (1930). The second group was more closely associated with the Parti radical, they added no skills to those they had first acquired (mostly in philosophy) and their publications mostly took the form of professorial expositions and popularization that tended on the whole to defend the work of their founding father.

Mauss and Simiand played a leading role among the researchers, while Halbwachs tended to defer to Simiand (Heilbron 1985: 222; Marcel 2001: 89). These three wrote the majority of the single volume in the second series of the *Année sociologique*, edited by Mauss, and they played a major part in the direction taken by the five series of the *Annales sociologiques*, editing three of them.

These factors in social morphology, to apply a Durkheimian category to the Durkheimians, translated into intellectual cohesion. Mauss very much admired Simiand's work in political economy, citing him before all others when asked who best embodied French sociology (Marcel 2001: 89), and he was very flattering in reviewing Simiand's *Le salaire, l'évolution sociale et la monnaie* (Mauss 1933: 143).

When writing his articles on "the franc and foreign exchange" (1924c; 1924d), Mauss first discussed them with Simiand (Fournier 1994: 451; 1997: 42). Mauss likewise attended Simiand's lecture on money as a social reality, and in his comments referred to his own work on primitive money and his concept of the total social fact. Simiand was also one of those whom Mauss consulted in connection with his work on the gift relationship (Fournier 1994: 518; Mauss 1954: 34, 93), and it is no surprise that Mauss adhered to Simiand's definition of the economy in his teaching at the Institut d'ethnologie between 1926 and 1939 (Mauss 1947: 101). Finally, one should not ignore the growing importance that Mauss attributed to statistics in his work on social morphology (Marcel 2001: 31), an importance also relevant to Simiand, who had devoted himself to the construction of a positive economics founded upon quantitative data.

MAUSS AND CONTEMPORARY ECONOMIC LIFE

There were no limits to Mauss's scholarly curiosity; he remained undaunted by the sheer extent of ethnographic material. He was the despair of his uncle, who would have preferred that he complete work that had been started but which was only rarely, if ever, finished; sometimes a project remained just a few sketched pages, organised as the chapter headings of a book to be written.[1] Mauss would quickly shift his attention; he lived in the modern world, and consciously so. Two studies related to this interest in the contemporary world are of especial interest here. The first deals with the question of Bolshevism: as a socialist, Mauss was extremely interested in the turmoil that was contemporary Russia, and he had an active interest in the Bolshevik experience of social transformation. The second study concerned the phenomenon of exchange rates at a time when, following the First World War, foreign exchange was under intense speculative pressure as a consequence of the political and social disruption of war. The place of the market in a socialist society and that of money in a liberal economic order—these are the two domains into which we shall follow Mauss, marking his concrete interest in the economic sociology of the contemporary world. Here we can gain insight into some of his principal reference points: first in some of his introductory comments, then in the closing pages of *The Gift*, written around the same time as his lesser-known works on Bolshevism and foreign exchange.

Bolshevism, Planning and the Market in the Modern Economy

Mauss took a very close interest in political developments in Russia at least as early as the 1905 revolution, travelling there in 1906 at the instigation of Jean Jaurès and *L'humanité*. This visit left a lasting impression upon him, as can be seen from the many articles he published in *La vie socialiste* and *Le populaire* on cooperatives in Russia, on the relations between Bolshevism and the cooperative movement, and on political violence, whether arising from Bolshevik power or Italian fascism. His thoughts on economic organisation warrant reconsideration, which does

---

[1] Mauss's essays, including *The Gift* and a number of other pieces (1924b, 1925c, 1936, 1938), were divided into chapters, even if each chapter contained no more than a few paragraphs.

mean, however, that we will leave to one side, despite its importance, the overtly political dimension of Mauss's understanding of the Soviet experience in the mid-1920s.

Mauss considered the socialist nature of the Soviet experience and drew negative conclusions. If socialism meant the conscious organisation of economic activity, as Durkheim himself thought, then Bolshevism was not a form of socialism. In the countryside, Mauss wrote, Bolshevism was no more than an individualistic revolution, running its course in a way very similar to rural France in 1789, when peasants had seized the land; and it was an individualism to which was added state communism, whose requisitions and exactions had brought about an abrupt decline in agricultural output (1924b: 540). Mauss had a better opinion of industrial legislation (ibid.; also 1925c: 707), in that he saw in Soviet legislation the beginnings of an attempt to create professional groups as understood by Durkheim.[2] But this phase passed by very quickly, giving way to a statism which stifled and blocked new initiatives. Mauss argued that the requirement to work combined with the military organisation of economic activity could have no other result than the diminution of such activity (ibid.: 548).

Mauss was extremely critical of the attempt to collectivise economic activity, and this led him to formulate a series of forceful theses concerning the place of the market in the modern economic world:

> we can understand that production will be regulated until goods come to market, including in this the regulation of stocks; and we can also understand that there could well be an interest in setting limits to consumption, while neither abuse nor avarice is permitted. But a society without a market is inconceivable. In using the term "market" we are not talking about marketplaces, stock exchanges or any like locations, for these are merely the external aspects of a market; rather, we simply note the economic fact that, publicly, through the alternatives presented by prices "supplied and demanded", the price sets itself; or rather through the legal fact that anyone "on the spot" has the right to buy in peace, with secure title, whatever he wants. And that he is also not compelled to buy what he does not want. (ibid.: 541)

[2] "The Bolshevik Revolution—inventive as are all popular and workers' movements—had created not only an idea but a form of organisation: the soviet, a professional organisation which was at the same time the manager of the national property entrusted to the workers' councils and the 'cell', the elementary political 'nucleus' of the whole administrative and legislative life of the state. This was the first attempt at a simultaneously national and professional organisation both of property and of the state. The idea and the realisation of the soviet corresponded—to the very image—with two of the few moral, political and economic conclusions that Durkheim had always advocated and that death had prevented him seeing actually materialised" (Mauss 1924b/1992: 172).

Understood as a price-setting system or as a body of legal rules facilitating transactions, the market is an *institution* inseparable from modern society. Mauss emphasises this point:

> This market system, slowly developed through the economic history of humanity, today regulates the greatest part of production and consumption. Of course, other systems of social facts carry out the same function, and one could imagine other systems that could effectively do so, but the liberty of the market is the absolutely necessary condition for economic life. It has to be said that, whatever doctrinaire socialists, communists, or even distinguished economists like Thorstein Veblen might claim, the Soviets have not been able to "evade the price system". It is therefore by no means certain that any known society is capable of such experimentation. For the moment, and as far as one can foresee, *socialism, communism, must seek its path through the organisation of the market, not through its suppression.* (ibid.: 541–52)[3]

Mauss therefore regards the market to be indispensable for modern societies inasmuch as it secures freedom of exchange. The rock hypothesis that we encountered in the previous chapter implies that the circulation of goods can be effected according to rules arising out of work that societies do on themselves, commercial exchange being only one of the possible ways to do this work and one which requires that altruism surrender to egoism. It is not, therefore, that Mauss denies the possibility of a transformation of the market, but he instead defines what can, and what cannot, be modified. In short, what he calls the "transacting nature" of "the man of *today*" (ibid.: 543, my emphasis) has to be taken into account—how the individual behaves as an *homo œconomicus*, who "only works and transacts so that he might have the best product and service at the best price, or to sell his good or labour at the highest price" (ibid.: 543).

Mauss also objected to the idea that a society could do without money, or gold, as the Bolsheviks sought to do:

> The equally striking examples of Mexico, of Austria, then of Germany and soon Poland, do prove and will prove that modern societies, which might themselves be backward, like Mexico or Russia, or highly civilised, like Germany, have faith only in gold, or in credits which represent gold, or in commodities tradable in gold. Gold and the various securities that represent it are the sole guarantees an individual has for the freedom of purchase. Are the people who think this way right or wrong? That is a different question. For our part, we do not believe we will see purely rational societies for a very long time. . . . Why would

---

[3] Mauss refers here to Veblen's *The Engineers and the Price System*, published in 1921.

one wish that the domain of the economy, a domain of needs and tastes, be ruled by pure reason? (ibid.: 542)

Of course, money is a rational medium, but its rationality includes those times when practical reason feels the ground shifting under its feet, since this standard of values places at the same level all human productions—Mauss takes as examples the tomfoolery of a clown and patents for the best inventions—with no concern other than the monetary uniformity between relative scarcities. Money is also the object of social belief, of a faith, and it would be vain to think that only its functional element, rational calculation, explains its existence.[4]

Exchange: Money, Politics and Trust

Between December 1922 and May 1924, Mauss wrote a number of articles for *Le populaire*, a journal on whose editorial board he sat, dealing with the situation in Russia in general and on cooperatives in particular. He also wrote three series of articles (thirty-five in all) devoted to the problem of foreign exchange and the status of the franc, that is, the value of French money from the international perspective. Mauss did not, of course, consider these writings to be of a scholarly nature, but his approach to money in an international context is of interest—partly because it demonstrates so clearly his degree of engagement with the modern economy, and also because of the way he deals with the social impact of foreign exchange. His treatment of its fiscal and inflationary impact is not without interest for the economic sociology of the time.

These three series of articles are built around a clear plan: the fall in the value of the franc is due to the excessive printing of money, falling exports and the loss of confidence in paper money in general. The war had had a damaging impact on the finances of the belligerent countries, and the return to a peacetime economy dictated some drastic changes. At the same time the political situation was dominated by radicalisation, whether tending to fascism (Italy) or to socialism (Russia, of course, but also Germany). We should also recall that the value of the franc had not been a problem for more than a century, and that the now familiar phenomenon of inflation was then a novelty. What are the main features of Mauss's analysis?

---

[4] The first would correspond to methodical confidence (founded upon routine and repetition) and the last to ethical confidence (which bears the power of political authority in the name of the value accorded to the individual), in the distinction made by Aglietta and Orléan (2002: 104–6); but hierarchical confidence is absent (depending on the religious or political authority which legitimates the monetary authority).

First of all, there is the argument that the market is an institution with its own rules, rules that could not simply be by-passed in the name of political voluntarism—the current example being the revanchist formula "Germany will pay". The way in which one currency had an international value expressed in other currencies meant that a country was unable to isolate itself from the rest of the world, in this case the sequence of devaluations that affected European currencies (Mauss 1922: 477). In addition, France had moved from being a creditor to a debtor country, dependent upon loans from other countries or on the fluctuating returns on capital invested, long or short term, in other countries. These facts, Mauss argued, meant that France was now subject to the imperatives of the international market:

> So that is the situation. Not only the French state, but French credit and the French nation, depend upon foreign countries. The cry goes up: speculation! There is a wish to regulate the Parisian market. All this is in vain. The gold market is not here, but in New York, Geneva, Amsterdam; it is slowly returning to London. You would have to go there to stop speculation. (ibid.: 483)

The same argument is repeated in the second series of articles, this time laying emphasis on the way that the value of money is determined by supply and demand in the markets, and that there is no future in the belief that this value follows from political decisions. This does not, however, exonerate politics from mistakes which have had an effect on the conditions according to which market agents behave:

> [D]ebtors—we are the playthings not only of our present foreign creditors, but even of their bankers, together with their associated financial institutions. The French state has no power over them. . . . Nothing can be done in such situations, nor against the evasive power of capital. Money is no more containable, or rather potential money is no more containable, than power is subject to conservation. It is best to let nature take its course. Let liquidations take place, the rates adjust themselves. Politicians, the bureaucrats of the central bank, are even more incapable than bourgeois financiers, and it is best to leave the latter their responsibility. (ibid.: 486)

Secondly, Mauss sometimes appeals to the idea of confidence and of faith in money, above all in national money, that is to say, money in relation to a space of political decision. First of all, Mauss equates confidence and faith when talking of what economists call the flight from money (ibid.: 485; 1924d: 678).[5] Confidence and faith are mingled even though

---

[5] The flight from money means that agents are seeking to rid themselves of their monetary balances by buying goods in proportion to their lack of confidence in the money that

the two phenomena cannot be reduced to the same sociological explanation. Confidence can be based upon personal relations or, as is the case for money, whose collective and institutional nature is evident, upon a rational appreciation of the continuity inherent in the immense social framework of the nation and its institutions. Faith is something different: it evokes religion and does not call for explanation in terms of instrumental rationality. But the imbrication of the two ideas is not treated theoretically by Mauss, and there are instances where his use of the term "faith" would have been better served by "confidence". Mauss emphasises the fact that confidence is not a phenomenon that politics can easily pigeonhole, inasmuch as a lack of confidence can ruin policy: "The Bourse, international stock exchanges, are extremely anxious moral persons" (1924c: 644), and he echoes this in a statement one month later: "The confidence of all anonymous and unknown creditors [the holders of short-term assets approaching maturity] has to be anticipated from day to day. One is never certain about tomorrow. One thing is certain: consequent upon the trust or mistrust of the holders of these treasury bills, the Bank of France will have to consent to their issue and to supply a more or less large amount of notes" (ibid.: 667). Here one finds once more the idea that the economy cannot be subject to political decisions. Moreover, as Frédéric Lordon has shown (1997) in regard to the policy of a strong franc, decisions regarding economic policy are subject to an evaluation by economic agents, who allow the said policy to run its course if they consider it to be credible or, by contrast, intervene to bring it to a halt before it has been able to show any results. Finally, Mauss takes care to relate money, and confidence in money, to something other than beliefs and representations. His argument refers to the "real economy", that is, to work, the soil, human capital and the effort that individuals have to make, since there is no alternative—all of which lies behind confidence in money, behind the confidence that the country itself has in it. These are the macrosocial foundations which provide a rational basis for confidence in an institution:

> Happily, a country, a nation, is more than money. It is its human capital, its soil, its labour which, despite all the faults of the state or of capitalists, underwrite its credit, and recreate even if it has been extinguished, as one can see with Austria, in Germany, in bolshevised Russia itself. (1924d: 668)

As *The Gift* was gestating, Mauss was a very long way from burying himself in ancient societies. No doubt this explains the sometimes surprising conclusions of this famous essay, conclusions sometimes dismissed in

---

they hold. This money can no longer play the role of a reserve of value; it no longer can be believed in as a current value representing future wealth.

later commentary as too far removed from the central issue of the three obligations: to give, to receive, and to reciprocate.[6]

CONVERGENCE IN METHOD

In their article "Sociologie" in the *Grande encyclopédie*, Mauss and Fauconnet characterised sociological method as having four aspects: definition, observation, the systematisation of facts and the scientific nature of sociological hypotheses. The material that Durkheim had assembled in the last chapter of the *Rules of Sociological Method* belongs to the third and fourth of these, but with some significant differences. Mauss and Fauconnet maintained that it was important to bring together only facts of the same order, arranging them in a well-constituted series and forming sociological hypotheses in respect of a grouping of such series. These hypotheses derived from a methodological process of induction and had the character of necessity and of generality; they spoke to the "why and the how of things" (Mauss & Fauconnet 2005: 26). It is never a question of concomitant variations; this expression cannot be found in the article. As has already been noted (Lukes 1968: 80; Dubar 1969: 518), the article draws attention to the provisional, contentious character of sociological hypotheses rather than emphasising the production of a proof and some of the more rigid formulations of Durkheim in *Rules*. All the same, statistical method is not neglected, since Mauss and Fauconnet argue that sociology and ethnography are two parallel sociological methods, which differ only over their point of application: modern life in respect of sociology and so-called primitive nations in ethnography. There are, therefore, some real differences with Durkheim's *Rules of Sociological Method*, even though he had been closely involved in the formulation of the *Encyclopédie* article.[7] If we extend the field of investigation, these differences become more clearly apparent.

Mauss came back to questions of method in his unpublished thesis on prayer. For the investigation of those social facts that were brought together by the concept of prayer, Mauss thought that two approaches would be of use: the construction of generic concepts and a genetic method. The first is defined in the following manner:

> In the first place, by analysing phenomena which are more or less abundant but suitably selected, a generic notion is constituted. This is ex-

---

[6] See the different comments to be found in Lévi-Strauss (1950), Claude Lefort (1951), Caillé (2000) and Hénaff (2002).

[7] Durkheim took a close interest in the writing of the article; there are several letters from him to Mauss between April and May 1900 which touch on it, two of them containing a plan for one part of it (Durkheim 1998: 257–66).

pressed in a formula schematising the fact to be explained, whether concerning prayer, sacrifice, suffering, or the family. One can then explain the very general characteristics of the facts in question. Having done this, one examines the way in which this schematic formula varies when one interposes this or that cause in response to which the institution must vary. This creates a system of concepts ranging from the very general to the most particular, from which one can see how and why the genre, enriched by specific differences, gives rise to the diversity of species. (Mauss 1909: 394)

Mauss immediately made clear that he had used exactly this method in his essay on sacrifice. Having first defined sacrifice, having selected some interesting experiences, notably because the critical review of the documents yielded relatively complete information on the cases studied, Mauss and Hubert constructed the sacrificial scheme by breaking it down into its elements: the admission to sacrifice, the sacrificial personnel (the sacrifice, the person making the sacrifice, the locations concerned, the instruments) and the exit from sacrifice. Once this schema had been realised, the second part of the essay directed its efforts to an explanation of the variety in the forms of sacrifice: "Since the aim of sacrifice is to alter the religious state of the person making the sacrifice, it is possible to anticipate a priori that the general lines of our framework must vary according to the state prevailing at the beginning of the ceremony" (Hubert & Mauss 1899: 256); in the same way, the scheme varies with the function of the sacrifice, which may focus on the sacrificer himself or an object to which the sacrificer attaches interest (ibid.: 266).

Mauss and Hubert emphasise that, while they seek an abstract schema of sacrifice so that they might not be diverted by the infinite variety of sacrifice as reported in ethnology and history, "this schema differs from a simple abstraction. We have seen it *in concreto* in the case of Hindu animal sacrifice; moreover, in connection with this rite we have been able to group a collection of sacrificial rites which can be linked to Semitic, Greek and Latin rituals" (ibid.: 255–56). The abstract schema provides insight into the structure of the social phenomenon being studied, but it is not an arbitrary abstraction created by the sociologist. Moreover, they stress that bringing the diversity of phenomena into a unity in no respect implies that this diversity is neglected, for in the second phase of this approach rigorous comparison emphasises the deformation introduced by the schema, enabling this diversity to be dealt with in terms of a generic structure.

The second, genetic method is defined by the study of the evolution in social facts associated with successive historical periods:

Instead of starting with the genus and arriving at the species, one begins with the most rudimentary forms presenting the fact in question, passing then to forms which are more and more recent, and it can be shown how the second derive from the first. One then has, as in the first case, a series of hierarchised notions. However, the schema takes no account of time and space, since it considers the genus and all species as if they occurred all at the same logical moment. Here in the genetic approach, by contrast, one deals with types which actually succeed each other historically, the one created out of the other, and the intention is to retrace the order of their genesis. (Mauss 1909: 394)

The genetic method begins from a genealogical classification which "constitutes types by ordering them according to their evolution" (ibid.: 396). This involves the methodical construction of a series of historical facts. Once this has been accomplished, the series has to be explained; that is, one must discover the determining factors, which, Mauss maintained, were to be found through comparison:

As concerns the instrument of genetic explanation, it is the same as that at work in genealogical classification, or the determination of causes. This instrument is the comparative method. For, where social phenomena are concerned, one can only arrive at any kind of explanation by way of comparison. (ibid.: 397–98)

Mauss advances three arguments in favour of this method:

It follows the order of facts and so leaves less room for error. This also makes it more difficult to omit anything, since a gap in the evolutionary sequence will create a problem of continuity that will be quickly detected. In addition, one is better able to take account of the nature of the facts when one attends to their genesis. Finally, this method serves to prepare a schematic explanation which will be much more complete coming after methodical review and an initial systematisation of facts. (ibid.: 395)

During the 1920s Mauss does not endorse this genetic method with the same force; indeed, in his essay *The Gift* he foregoes all historical research[8] and instead adheres to the generic method (examining the rules of circulation of goods in terms of the three obligations of giving, receiving and reciprocating) and the comparative method. The genetic method definitively yields to the hypothesis of the "rock".

If we turn to consider Simiand's work during the same period, the difference of his choices from those of Mauss is quite striking. So far as sociological method is concerned, Simiand employed several arguments

---

[8] Implicitly criticising the approach of diffusionists, Mauss rejects any attempt to write a history of the phenomenon: "Let us then for the moment content ourselves with demonstrating the nature and wide distribution of a theme in law. It is for others to reconstruct its history if they can" (1925a/1954: 17).

drawn from Durkheim, as evidenced by the series of polemics with historians (1903; 1906), but while he dealt at length with the notion of causality, he did not deal with the question of the production of a proof. It cannot be said that he lacked interest in this—quite the opposite in fact (Damalas 1943: 195)—but his principal thinking is to be found in his studies of positive economics. In the essay on the price of coal in France, his first work and one with which Durkheim was very happy (Letter to Simiand, 18 December 1901, in Durkheim 1975 I: 441), Simiand was meticulous in his treatment of method. He defined the object (price) as a social fact (1902: 1), detailed the conditions of observation and emphasised that the purpose was explanation, that is, the determinations of causes (ibid.: 3). He devoted no less than sixteen pages to an examination of the legitimacy of his approach, and he took great care to review his statistical sources[9] as a way of explaining why it was the variations that interested him, and not absolute values. He then examined the "persuasiveness of such a study" (ibid.: 11) so that he might forestall those who would criticise his study (one price in one country) and draw attention to the importance of price interdependence, the internationalisation of markets, or the dependence of the price of coal on the general price level.

His argument was taken to a higher level in his book of 1907. First of all, what had in 1902 been no more than a sketch of the structure-type now took a central role. From all the statistical evidence, Simiand extracted a sequence which he treated as the structure of the phenomenon to be explained (involving a cycle composed from variable prices, labour productivity, daily money wage and the cost of labour per unit generated, as already examined above in chapter 4), so that his approach here conformed with what Mauss called the generic concept. Once this sequence was fixed, Simiand proceeds to pose the problem of causality and explanation, since concomitance or succession does not arise mechanically. In particular, a rise in price is insufficient explanation of this cycle-type, being only a necessary condition (Simiand 1907: 103). Based on his theory of self-interested action, Simiand puts forward his causal explanation. To motivational conditions (price variations) or permissive conditions (variations in the quantities produced) had to be added the cause properly speaking, what he later will call "the dependence which is closest and least capable of substitution" (1932a I: 23). The argument is made in the following terms: if some conditions (price and production) emerge, then the representations of management and labour that set these variables to work result in human actions determined such that productivity and

---

[9] This side of things is always well developed in Simiand, as in Halbwachs (1912, 1930) and Mauss (1927: 226). Simiand did not hesitate to criticise *Suicide* on this point (Simiand 1898: 650; see also Halbwachs 1930).

monetary income evolve in a manner that takes account of other magnitudes involved in the definition of the cycle-type.

Positive Durkheimian economics involves causal investigation, but Simiand also quite forcefully emphasises the role of quantitative data.[10] This is the theme of his presidential address to the Statistical Society of Paris in 1921, whose title is revealing: "Statistics as a Means of Experimentation and of Proof", published under a slightly altered title the following year. The importance that Simiand attributed to statistics marked a clear difference with Mauss, for while the identification of the cycle-type is not different from the construction of a generic concept, Simiand ascribed to this method of statistical investigation a role in the determination of proof.

It is here that there is a methodological hiatus between the Durkheimians—hiatus, because it is like a tipping point between the first and the second of Durkheim's research programmes in economic sociology. Mauss raised this point in an article printed in the second series of *L'année sociologique*, expressing his regret:

Here, for example, in the science of religions, we concentrate, perhaps too much, on the "primitives" and neglect our own major religions, and the movements of feelings and ideas which agitate them. There, in economic science or politics, we perhaps give too little attention to ethnography and ancient history. In addition, we make too little use of quantitative methods, even though one can measure attendance at churches and cinemas, as well as the totals of working hours, errors in the postal service, or the ages of those who committed suicide. . . . Whether rightly or wrongly, the history of religion is completely oriented towards the past and is not accustomed to calculation, whereas political economy is a science of numbers, entirely oriented towards the present—indeed, towards the future—and forgetting perhaps too much the past or the societies which surround us. (1927a/2005: 51. [trans. revised KT])

This cleavage recapitulated the divide which Simiand traced between economic sociology and other sociological fields,[11] while making clear that

---

[10] This is also true of Halbwachs, whose work is in this regard of the same nature as that of Simiand. Halbwachs was, in addition, particularly interested in the work of Adolphe Quetelet (1835), and his theory of the *homme moyen* (Halbwachs 1913), a theory which Durkheim had examined in *Suicide* (Durkheim 1897a/2006: 332ff.)

[11] "Just like money, a factor in which prices are expressed as magnitudes, positive research seeks first of all to attain the phenomenon not by qualitative observation, vague and sometimes personal, but above all by quantitative determination, precise and objective, that is, through monetary measures" (Simiand 1902: 2). He emphasised this in 1932: "But we note that, in our case, the phenomenon that we wish to consider, as in general with all phenomena of economic value, possesses, as much in itself as in the characteristics through

he dreaded the piling up of facts without any kind of theoretical frame-work (facts without theory). Furthermore, Simiand was very critical of those who chose the easy way out by studying origins, instead of studying the way the institutions and representations of the modern economic world function. This was an error, he said, since

> *the economic fact in its strict sense* had a quite distinct existence and quite varied characteristics, and *is, as such, a relatively recent fact* in human societies, different from other categories of social phenomena, which, by contrast, present themselves in all their plenitude right back to primitive societies, or even primarily among them. (1932a: 582)

There are, however, differences in the methods employed by Mauss and Simiand, differences that can in part be attributed to the work that they did. But is that all that can be said about the issue?

Mauss had no aversion to the use of statistics in sociology; he made use of them on occasion in the course of his writing, as he did, for instance, in his essay on the morphology of Inuit societies. The principal shift in Mauss's thinking fell between 1927 and 1934. Taking up the distinction Durkheim made between morphology and social physiology, Mauss argued in 1927 that the first was the most developed element of sociology, since social morphology was "the group qua material phenomenon", and "this very large base, of masses and numbers, can be graphically depicted, and at the same time mathematically measured" (1927a/2005: 56, 57). When it came to social physiology (the physiology of practices and representations), Mauss stressed the material aspect of physiology, since its omission

> would be letting slip from consideration the *two characteristics* by which every social fact is distinguished from facts of individual psychology: (1) *it is statistical and can be counted* (we repeat this observation and will return to it again), being common to definite numbers of humans during specific periods; and (2) (which is included) *it is historical*. (ibid.: 57–58 [trans. revised KT])

A little further on, concluding his discussion of the various parts of sociology, Mauss came back to the question of statistics, insisting upon their importance:

> The principal interest of these observations is that they permit us to expound, to systematise, and to demand the use of quantitative methods. To refer to material and social structures and the movements of

---

which one can in fact grasp it, a property which necessarily lends it, from the point of view of the observer, the quality of objectivity: this is the *property of being quantitative*" (1932a II: 576).

these structures is to refer to things which can be measured. The link between the morphological and physiological allows one to estimate the considerable place which should be occupied by statistical research in all studies of social physiology. (ibid.: 69)

Mauss went further in declaring that "Basically, every social problem is a statistical problem" (ibid.: 69), and here he found himself in agreement with Simiand, seeing in statistics a means for grasping the group in motion.[12] Nonetheless, Mauss emphasised the importance of the quantitative character that descriptive sociology must have even when dealing primarily with ancient societies (1934: 305, 313) or with matters that did not fit naturally into the framework of quantitative sociology: "At every point the power, and absence of power, of every tradition must be measured. That will lead us to a description, almost a measurement, of the quantity of tyranny, the scale of the mechanical force of the collective tradition" (ibid.: 334). This dimension is likewise to the fore in the lectures that Mauss gave at the Institute of Ethnology from 1926 to 1939, instructing his auditors on techniques of investigation in the field, including philological, historical, phonographic and photographic methods, while not neglecting the attention due to statistics (1947: 5, 7, 13, 15, 18ff.).

This evolution in method is also apparent in the work of Simiand, especially in regard to money. Here Simiand approaches his study of money on the basis of the work of the Durkheimians on the sociology of religion. He states, resuming a line of thought that clearly runs back to Comte, that there are three broad ways of dealing with religious phenomena: uncritical belief, the Voltairean view that religion is nothing but superstition, and the sociological approach, which raises religion to the status of a social fact to be studied as such (1934a: 18). The sociological approach proceeds: "by positive recognition of this fact. . . . And so contemporary interpretation achieves recognition and understanding of this religious fact. . . . Is it not the same process, and the same stages, that we today notice and distinguish in respect of the monetary phenomenon?" (ibid.: 18–19). It is also no surprise to see that Simiand defines money as a "belief and social faith" (ibid.: 38, 39, 44ff.), attributing to money, as Durkheim had done to religion, an essential motivating character: "money here

[12] "The strength of a church is measured by the number and the wealth of its temples, by the number of its believers and the magnitude of their sacrifices and, though it is always necessary to consider also the imponderables in them, to consider only faith and theology is a no less serious error than to forget them. Managed with prudence and intelligence, statistical procedure is not only the means of measuring but the means of analyzing every social fact, because it forces us to perceive the acting group" (1927a/2005: 69–70). This is a leitmotiv in Simiand, who considers the statistical method capable of grasping "*the emergent phenomenon*, that is, able to follow the variation in how prices form by date, scale, tendency, and how the variation of wages arises" (1922: 43; see also 1932a I: xii).

performs the function of anticipation in regard to future values which will be produced, and even functions as the anticipated realisation of these values, a function that actually enables one to acquire in advance what is needed for the realisation of these extra goods" (ibid.: 51).[13]

Mauss approaches this from the religious dimension, but so that he might accentuate the evolution towards the calculative and quantitative side of money, which allowed it to be added, subtracted and divided, and this emphasis on the process of rationalisation lent his triptych more a Weberian than a Comtean dimension:

> We hold that mankind has made a number of tentative steps. At first it was found that certain things, most of them magical and precious, were not destroyed by use, and these were endowed with purchasing power. . . . In the second stage, mankind, having succeeded in circulating these things within the tribe and far outside of it, found that these purchasing instruments could serve as a means of numerically tallying up and circulating wealth. This is the stage we are describing at present [in ch. 2 of *The Gift*]. The third stage began in ancient Semitic societies, but possibly also in other ancient societies, which invented the means of detaching these precious things from groups and individuals and of making them permanent instruments of value measurement, even of universal measurement—universal, if not rational—for want of any better system. (1925a/1954: 94 [trans. revised KT])

There is, therefore, something of a to and fro between Mauss and Simiand. Each, in fact, chose a path from the two that were open to Durkheim, but in spite of the distance that existed between these two paths, as much for Durkheim himself as for the Durkheimians, this divergence did not lead to any antagonism between the two—in fact, quite the opposite. Of course, Simiand and Mauss accented that which attracted them in their respective research, but they recognised the importance of those dimensions which they left to one side, taking them up again when the opportunity to do so arose.

SIMIAND, MONEY AND THE SOCIOLOGY OF THE RELIGIOUS FACT

As a member of the Durkheimian group, Simiand could not ignore the importance that Durkheim and Mauss attributed to the religious fact, as

---

[13] "The believer is not only a man who sees, who knows things ignored by the unbeliever; he is a man *who can do more*" (Durkheim 1913: 23). "This [religion] is, above all, a form of action. Beliefs are not at root knowledge that enriches our mind; their prime function is to support action" (ibid.: 26–27).

can be seen in the conclusions to the book that would establish the principles of the positive method in economics:

> The decisive, key argument seems to be that *in fact* all these phenomena—religious, legal, moral, economic—have, in the reality presented for our study, the essential character first and foremost of social phenomena, and that the positive method used in approaching knowledge and explanation will be for each and every one necessarily a sociological method. (Simiand 1912: 206)

Simiand's parallels between the approach to the religious fact and the approach to the fact of money were far-reaching.

All the same, it has to be conceded that Simiand took little account of the religious fact in his writing on economic sociology. But does that mean that the methodological remarks that we have just noted are empty phrases? Not at all. An examination of his body of work shows that social interdependence—Simiand does not use the Comtean concept of *consensus*, but rather the term *Zusammenhang*—is always taken into account when seeking to account for this or that economic phenomenon. Further, all of his major publications from the 1930s give a place to the religious factor so that he might account rationally for economic phenomena. This is true of his study of long-run economic cycles (1930–32: 429–30, 510) and his study of wages (1932a II: 24–26). These two texts provide insight into why the connection between economy and religion does not play a significant role in Simiand's economic sociology.

In his investigation into long-run cycles in the general price level, the starting point is in the early sixteenth century. This, of course, coincides with the Reformation, so he does note the relationship that Max Weber had identified between economic activity and religious belief.[14] The temporal frame, however large it might be, focussed on "economically developed societies" such as were to be found in Western Europe (1930–32: 406). Might the religious fact contribute some relevant explanation of cyclical price movements? Simiand has a dual response. The relationship is clear, but not pertinent to the problem he studies:

> It is possible, therefore, in the process of economic evolution to note factors of this [religious] kind as perhaps related to a transformation in men's minds, contributing a certain spirit of initiative, of free inquiry, of renewal; but in such instances these factors neither brought about the initial price movement nor sustained it. (ibid.: 510)

[14] "[A]t the same time, especially among those of Protestant confession, Puritan sects emerged; and possibly therefore a development of that spirit and morality for which Max Weber and other theorists have established a close relationship with the thinking of those in charge of enterprises, and new economic men" (1930–32: 510).

Seeking a cause for the rise and fall of prices, the religious fact did not provide Simiand with an explanation of an order where a series of religious changes, generalised among different countries, could explain changes in prices. That settles the matter, but all the same one should not neglect the place given to the impact of the Reformation, which Simiand associated with "intellectual facts" that, from the sixteenth century, contributed to the laicisation of the economy.[15]

The same line of argument becomes more marked when dealing with wages, prices and money in his book of 1932, since the series used in the study go no further than 1790. Once again, Simiand mentions that the religious fact can have an impact through doctrine of the just price, although this is not solely a matter of religion (1932a II: 24), but throughout the nineteenth century there is no religious phenomenon capable of explaining the variations of wages and of living conditions even of one section of the population. Quite the reverse: the pressure of secularisation upon Catholicism, especially in France, meant that the Church progressively withdrew from social life, and Simiand concluded that if it still existed, this relationship between religion and wages "was neither immediate nor topical" (ibid.: 26).

Things altered dramatically in the lecture on money, when the monetary social fact is put at the centre of the analysis, something Simiand never did in the texts cited above, for all the importance he granted the monetary factor, what has been called his "social monetarism". Taking as his point of departure some major contemporary theorists (Menger, Hawtrey, Maynard Keynes), he delighted in pointing out the hesitations and contradictions (between theory and policy recommendations) that characterised the subject (1934a: 1–5). In addition, he retracted what he had written in his book on method,[16] arguing now that money is the least satisfactory province of economic theory, a judgement in which he agreed

---

[15] "It is very obvious that economic values in what we might call a medieval economic system are mingled with ethical or religious values; while from the beginning of the sixteenth century and on through the seventeenth, gaining momentum right up to the present day, it is very notable that economic value became increasingly separated from ethical and religious values, and that it is marked by a characteristic possessed by no other kind of value, that is, its quantitative character." (1930–32: 430).

[16] Simiand explained the success in monetary matters as follows: "It will hardly be contested that of the theories presented by economic doctrine, the most well founded is the theory of money; is this not because in the use of money the psychological attitude of men is relatively simple and more or less uniform across both individuals and societies?" (1912: 36) Immediately following this he added a second argument linked to the impact of theory upon something that will be dealt with at length in the following chapter: "It is also freely acknowledged that the theory of banking and credit is more advanced than many other theories: is this not because, among other reasons, the phenomena of credit and of the bank depend above all on a class of specialised men, and that this class, carrying out its specialised

with Menger, who is cited from the first few lines of the lecture. How can we account for this?

Economic theory first appeared in the sixteenth and seventeenth centuries in the form of discussions of money (Simiand 1934a: 5–6), and up to the first classical economists—Smith and Say—it had remained a source of interesting ideas, because economic theory had not yet succumbed to the "conceptual constriction of the Ricardian construction" (ibid.: 12) nor to the "rational arguments of the Austrian [marginal utility school"] (ibid.: 16); it retained contact with social realities. According to the methodological triptych outlined above, this represented a turning point for economic thought, a point where one left the vision of the world bequeathed by the Middle Ages, according to which economic value and "ethico-religious values had . . . been freely mingled—just as the economic aspects of social life were mingled and subordinated to the ethico-religious aspects which ruled and regulated all social life" (ibid.: 9) This vision of the world, dominated by religion, was left behind in a process by which social life was "secularised", separating out the different elements and passing into the so-called Voltairean phase of economic theory. With Ricardo, Marx and the marginalists, it was now a matter of finding something real that money hid: here, social labour; there, the individual preferences of agents. In short, this is the period when theories of value were compelled to take account of money, which is no more than a phenomenon floating on the surface of social life and which is explicable in terms of realities which lie deeper. But money resists this treatment, and theorists recognised this yesterday as much as they do today.[17] What does Simiand make of this?

Conforming to his methodological principles, Simiand here sees the elimination of the social when the attempt is made to take account of economic reality. The formulation that he uses to assess physiocratic theory—today we would could it holistic—represents a striking encounter between the first and the second Durkheimian programmes, turning on the religious dimension of the social:

> Let us transpose the divine hypostasis which contemporary sociology, in many other areas, has rendered manifest: this explanation [of the physiocrats] expresses, with penetration and weight, that the creation

---

functions, is no doubt following a psychology of an equally specialised kind, that [economic] analysis can master and in which induction can be secured?" (ibid.: 37).

[17] From this perspective a parallel can be drawn between Simiand's approach and that of Orléan (1998). The latter takes the most recent results of monetary theory (models of overlapping generations, search models) and shows how unsatisfactory they are. Moreover, it is recognised (by Frank Hahn, among others) that economic theory is incapable of integrating money into a theory of value based upon utility.

of an economic value is not the work of men *ut singuli* (because it imposes itself upon them, and sometimes exists outside or in advance of any act expressed on their part, and when outside, differing or even contrary to their own estimation): it proceeds from a power superior to individuals who also create other social values: the creation of economic value arises out of society. (ibid.: 9)

The positive study of money as a social reality borrows from the way in which sociologists had dealt with the religious fact, for in the economic domain money is a hypostatisation of society. And in that Simiand recognises what Durkheim never tired of repeating, that society is increasingly secular, leading to an inevitable detachment of its religious dimension.

Following up the logic of his methodological critique, Simiand contrasts his own approach, based upon the social aspect of money, to those accounts of money which treated it as a convention agreed between individuals seeking to deal with their reciprocal needs, or the effort on the part of those in an exchange relation to reduce their transaction costs. This latter account is seriously defective, apart from the fact that it provides a finalist explanation of money—money exists because it serves the purposes which modern men find for it (ibid.: 20)—it leaves out precisely the social dimension that is at the heart of Simiand's thinking.

Having got to this point, Simiand makes a quick incursion into the domain of economic anthropology (ibid.: 23–25), from which he draws the conclusion that, originally, money was an adornment, an ornament, directly linked to the sacred, to magic. And, here opposing Keynes's *Treatise on Money*, he took seriously superstitions regarding gold, or, more precisely, he raised as a question that which this use of "superstition" pushed back into the past, as a residue of magical thinking relocated in the modern world. Is superstition only a "sociological curiosity", which runs back to ancient societies? "Would it not be surprising to find, as the essential and ultimate basis of references for the entire price system of the most advanced economy, a residue of magico-religious superstition now alien to the beliefs and practices of the most advanced type of religions?" (ibid.: 31).

Simiand sets out to entirely reverse this perspective. What theoreticians casually treat as superstition, a relic of long-superseded past, is nothing other than the social connection at the heart of money. How can we be sure of this, according to the principles of the positive method? By examining the functioning of the modern monetary system of a "secular" society which functions with paper, not gold or silver. How do we know? Money is inscribed into the commercial practices of agents through routines (agents treat the accounting unit in which money is held to be fixed) and a political authority which places them in circulation in a given economic space. But beyond that, Simiand places the emphasis on indeterminacy: money represents a purchasing power assigned to values, present and future. The quantitative determination of present values is difficult, if not impossible, and this indeterminacy is all the greater when it concerns future values over which money has purchasing power. As a result, fiduciary money is a "matter of appreciation, estimation, opinion and, therefore, and in particular regarding the future, we can use just one word—it is a *matter of 'trust'* (or of distrust)" (ibid.: 35). But what sort of trust is this? It could be a methodical confidence in the sense of Michel Aglietta and André Orléan, founded upon routine; it is more than this as soon as the future intervenes—since money can be "assigned" to future values, this necessarily happens—but the relation is something else, because of the fundamental indeterminacy with which it is freighted. Considering the case of hyperinflation, Simiand sees a discontinuity in the relationship between the quantity of money issued and its function as a reserve of value (ibid.: 38). This discontinuity gives rise to the true basis of what money is, and allows Simiand to state that gold is a fiduciary money like any other (ibid.: 46)

> Gold is made up of appreciation, of estimation, of belief, of confidence, products of sentiment as much as of reason, which cannot be distinctly separated one from the other into the two orders that we seek to distinguish here; it is simply and together a belief and a faith. . . . This representation, at once intellectual and affective, which is a money of this kind, is not made from competent and informed individuals, but rather by groups, by collectivities, by a nation; it is social. It has a character and a role manifestly objective, because it is a *belief and a social faith*, and, as such, *a social reality*. (ibid.: 38–39)

This passage, like many others in the book, presupposes a rigorous opposition between what is quantifiable and the instrument of such quantification in economics. Money is certainly of decisive importance in Simiand's eyes, since it makes possible the quantification of social and economic relationships, a quality which marks it out in that sector of the social that interests him. He links the emergence of quantification of this kind to the "secularisation" of social relations which brings to light the unfolding of economic activity, especially since the sixteenth century. But the operator of quantification and of secularisation remains charged with previous significations: money remains a matter of confidence and of social faith; it is therefore freighted with "religion and with magic", for it is through this that it is able, in the form of gold, to have this heightened effect upon ancient societies (ibid.: 44)

The discussion with Mauss took a quite exceptional turn. Mauss immediately referred to his 1914 article on the magical and religious origin of ancient money, making two points related to the difference between ancient money and modern money that he had made in a footnote, added to *The Gift*, on the definition of money, contra Simiand and Malinowski. Then he passed to the overall agreement that he saw between his work and that of Simiand:

> Because what you and I basically agree about is the importance of the idea of expectation, taking account of the future, which is exactly one of the forms of collective thought. We are ourselves, in society, anticipating this or that outcome; that is the essential form of communality. Expressions such as constraint, force, authority—we have been able to use them in the past, and they have their value; but this idea of collective expectation is in my opinion one of the fundamental ideas with which we have to work. I know of no other such productive ideas in law and economics: "I expect"—this is the very definition of every collective act. It is at the origin of theology: God will hear—I do not say, will grant—my prayer. (Mauss in Simiand 1934a: 60–61)

Expectation is here made into a central concept of sociology, as much religious as legal and economic. Durkheim's two heirs are on the way to understanding, each in their own way, that they are converging upon common problems in the understanding of social life: one in respect of the lack of distinction between the religious, magical, aesthetic, legal and economic freighting of the gift; the other in the rational, secularised and quantified world that symbolises the extended use of a money founded in confidence and faith. And since Mauss is not lacking in brio in this encounter, he goes a step further and argues that money, as in Simiand's own study, joins the set of facts that he calls total.

The support of Mauss reassures Simiand, as he acknowledges (1934a: 78); the generalisation which is sketched by the sequence *money, mana, manitou, Mawu* gives him more than he had hoped as regards the connection between magic, religion and money. He adopts the notion of expectation when prompted by a member of the assembled audience, who relates his notion of the power of anticipation in money (the purchasing power assigned to future values) to the concept that Mauss supplies, and in so doing clarifies a social characteristic which expectation renders actual: "expectation can only be social. One has to expect something that depends upon others" (ibid.: 80). And he links, more so than previously, money with liquidity:

> That which endures socially, which responds best to collective expectation, is that which is capable of transformation into the most varied possibilities; and it is this power of transformation, into who knows what, which is something specific, and in this respect marks the

superiority of societies in which a monetary economy functions over those where it does not. (ibid.: 82)

Subsequently this concept of expectation, already present in his major book on wages (1932 II: 513–14), is systematically employed in his writings on the economic development of the United States (1934a: 219ff.) and in his final lecture course at the Collège de France dedicated to the psychology of crises (1937: 9–11), where he reformulated the problem of market coordination in terms of a "coordination of impressions".

The convergence of the two programmes calls for a closer examination of a central element common to both programmes. The sociology of knowledge is an important part of the programme announced in Durkheim's last major work, but is also present in the early writings in which he criticised economic knowledge. The sociology of knowledge is also something that Mauss, Simiand and Halbwachs dealt with, whether in their critique of economic categories (*homo œconomicus*, interest, money) and the theoretical practice of economists (scholarly argument) or in respect of the way in which the economic view of the world diffused through the scholarly system.

The two following chapters, exploring the sociology of knowledge in the writings of Durkheim, but also of Mauss, Simiand and Halbwachs, seek to demonstrate the relevance and fruitfulness of the two programmes, relating the sociology of knowledge to religious sociology, and this will provide an opportunity to introduce a parallel between their work and that of Max Weber on the religious origin of the spirit of capitalism.

CHAPTER SEVEN

Sociology of Economic Knowledge and the Critique of Political Economy

> You will there see a sample . . . of the works of the French school of sociology. We are especially attached to the social history of categories of the human mind.
>
> (*Mauss 1938: 333*)

So far we have shed light on the nature and content of the sociology of the economy advanced by Durkheim and the members of his group. We have followed the elaboration of Durkheim's two successive research programmes—at different rates and to varying degrees—in the writings of Halbwachs, Mauss and Simiand. Economic sociology was clearly established by Simiand and Halbwachs as a domain extending from the behaviour of an actor (representative of a class) to the transformations of the modern economic system in respect of distribution, consumption and the monetisation of wealth. Mauss developed the sociology of religion as a far-reaching comparison between two frameworks securing the circulation of goods. And finally, the two programmes converged in a way that permanently linked economic sociology, the sociology of religion and the sociology of knowledge.

The last of these will now be explored. In the process, it will be of help to compare Durkheim's approach with that of Comte, especially in regard to Comte's critique of political economy. It will then become plain that Durkheim and Simiand followed him when they directed themselves to representations allied to the diffusion of economic knowledge and the social processes which this engendered.

COMTE AND POLITICAL ECONOMY

The first name that comes to mind when the critique of political economy is mentioned is Karl Marx, who published in 1859 a book carrying this title, and who then used the phrase in 1867 as the subtitle of the first volume of *Capital*. But in respect of Durkheim and the Durkheimians, the importance of Comte should not be forgotten, for Comte was a writer with whose work they were certainly familiar, even if they did seek to distance themselves from it (Heilbron 1993; Petit 1994). Comte was secretary to Saint-Simon when the latter was seeking a way of understanding the conditions for the emergence and stabilisation of an industrial society, and it was he who in August 1817 gave Comte the task of reforming political economy (Gouhier 1970 III: 167, 189–98).

Comte and the Reform of Political Economy

It was not sheer chance that directed the work of the young Comte. Having had a keen interest in biology, Saint-Simon had then discovered in the political economy taught by Say the means for creating a social science of a kind he had sought since 1802. Still very much in awe of his "master", Comte was set to work on this, first sketching his critique of political economy in the pages of two short-lived journals and then developing these arguments in a number of pamphlets which he later reprinted as appendices to his *Système de politique positive* (1851–54 IV). In the meantime, his thinking on the subject had also been set forth in the harsh critique we find in his *Cours de philosophie positive*.

Adopting Saint-Simon's view that political economy is rational politics, Comte argued that property was the most fundamental institution and had to be organised in the manner most favourable to industry (1818: 447). In the article that he wrote on the budget the following year, Comte then adopted Say's position, arguing that a scientific politics forsook constitutional problems in favour of the fiscal balance—the "major political question," for it sought "the most modest taxation possible, assessed and devised in the least onerous manner, employed in a way the most profitable to the public" (1819: 115). But it is here that the question of the organic character of positive social science first emerges in Comte's thinking. Wishing to found politics upon political economy, Comte envisages adding positive moral science to it, which likewise "has to be grafted onto political economy, for I consider that moral rules, like political institutions, should be judged according to the influence that they exert, or can exert, upon *production*" (1818: 448). This makes it clear what is at stake: while Say sought to make political economy positive by linking it up with utilitarianism, Comte saw things differently.

Comte's thought is post-Revolutionary, dominated by an emergent conception of society as *industrial society*. He was dissatisfied with contemporary conditions, in which the prevailing regulatory mechanisms of civil society were being destroyed and, at the political level, the *légistes* were dominant—a class of individuals whose action and thinking were heavily marked by their legal training. From this he developed a critique of the liberal understanding of the economy, in which the state was thought of as an adversary at the heart of society (Comte 1822: 52). Comte rejected this idea, since it clashed with his organic view of society as "une action générale combine," a coordinated collective action (ibid.: 63). He argued that it was necessary to take politics out of the hands of *légistes* and metaphysicians, for whom politics was a matter of rhetoric and political practice the domain of men of routine, so redefining politics as a demonstrative science, policy then being grounded in this political science.

Where does political economy fit into this vision of a scientific and industrial society? Initially Comte had believed that, once reformed, political economy would be able to contribute to rational politics, economists accordingly taking their place in the scientocracy that he sought. But when, in the following decade, Comte proposed that the three fundamental classes (scholars and scientists, artists and the industrial class) cooperate in setting up the new social state, he mistrusted the industrial class and, consequently, economists.

His mistrust of the industrial class derived from the rivalry that economic activity always stirred up within this class. Firstly, the progressive movement of society towards the scientific and industrial state was pan-European, and it had to be conducted at this level. But the industrial class was far too nationalistic to take a primarily European political role (ibid.: 74–75). In addition, Comte took note of an unsocial hostility within the industrial class of any given nation, linked to enmity between industrial bosses and workers. A final argument came from his examination of the problems posed by mechanisation, problems vigorously debated by the best economists of the day. Comte conceded that those economists favourable to mechanisation were right in the long run—that mechanisation was generally advantageous to society as a whole, as well as to the working class in particular (1828a: 171–72)—but he maintained that in the short run the fact could not be ignored that mechanisation brought about mass unemployment on a scale that no promise of future advantage could offset. "From a particular point of view all social questions are only questions of time; and that is especially true for classes who live only by their daily labour" (ibid.: 173).

Industry led entrepreneurs into disputes (crises), to the use of specious and unpromising means for industrial development (protectionism) and to the exacerbation of class differences (the hostility between proletarians and industrial bosses)—and so there could be no question of giving the industrial class a major role in the creation of a rational politics for the industrial and scientific state. That sealed the fate of economists who theorised about the workings of the industrial system without any concern for its regulation.

The reform of political economy was outlined in the forty-seventh lecture of the *Cours de philosophie positive*:"Philosophical Reflections on the Nature and Object of Political Economy". Comte first of all criticised the tendency to isolate political economy from social science in general (1830–42 II: 92). According to the principle of sociological statics or *consensus*, society is an organic whole in which the parts are in a system of interdependence; hence, the isolation which political economy assumed with respect to other moral and political sciences is methodologically inappropriate, promoting the illusion that political economy can deal with an order of fact independent of others. Furthermore, this supposed autonomy transmuted into the erroneous belief that political economy might provide a model for the whole of social science. Comte added to this general criticism some remarks about method and its metaphysical characteristics, which ran counter to the canons of scientific reasoning:

> The entire dogmatic element of their supposed science is, in a manner at once direct and profound, quite simply metaphysical, despite the illusory affectation of the particular forms and habitual protocol of scientific language, already unsuccessfully mimicked on many other prior philosophical occasions, as, for example, in the theological-metaphysical compositions of the celebrated Spinoza. (ibid.: 93)

Comte has here in mind the intellectualist and rationalist tendency that can be found in the introduction to Destutt de Tracy's *Traité d'économie politique* (1823: 1–64), where Tracy systematically relates Say's political economy to the analysis of sensations upon which the philosophical project of the Idéologues was founded. Comte rejected this perspective, which would later become known as that of *homo œconomicus*, an indefatigable, consistent and perfect calculator of his own utility:

> Even when one allows these demonstrations [of the spontaneous order of economic life] all the (much exaggerated) logical latitude which economists attribute to them, it will remain certain that man is not guided uniquely, or even primarily, by calculation; and secondly, that it is not always possible, nor even sometimes possible, to calculate accurately. The physiology of the nineteenth century, confirming or indeed explaining universal experience, has shown up definitively the frivolity of these metaphysical theories which represent man as essentially a calculating being, impelled by the sole motivation of personal interest. (1826: 209; see also 1830–42 I: 856, 862; II: 447, 455)

This argument has become commonplace, but here Comte presents it with a precision all the more remarkable for the fact that, when formulated in this way, political economy was at a very early stage of its development.[1] The source of this acuity comes from the centrality of such

---

[1] The period 1838–44—with the publication of work by John Stuart Mill, Pellegrino Rossi and William Nassau Senior—saw the emergence of a political economy based explicitly on axiomatic general principles which were then employed deductively, and this was,

problems to his work, combined with his scientific training. To create industrial society, individuals have to become impassioned in pursuit of their own interests; it is not enough merely to show individuals the true or the useful to motivate them to action. Reason alone is insufficient; the affective side of human action must be engaged as well. This idea was developed into a systematic anthropology in his *Cours de philosophie positive*, where he distinguished between the affective and the rational in man, so that he might emphasise the importance of affective impulses in human action (1830–42 I: 856, 866). Egoism allowed the individual to render himself autonomous in determining his own aims, taking account of instincts of sociability and reason which bound the individual to the collectivity (ibid.: 180–82). In the *Système de politique positive*, Comte laid emphasis upon the contrast of egoism and altruism, with the elevation of the latter motivation being "the great human problem" (1851–54 II: 173).

Comte's quite virulent criticism of political economy did have its positive side, however. Comte considered that the interest of political economy derived from the manner in which it showed the solidarity between producers, in which each one received a part of the product of all, since each provided the other with what he needed. Comte did in this way acknowledge the existence of a "spontaneous order" (his own term) in economic affairs, coordinating the interest of parties to the division of labour, but for him this was purely a "local" matter and should not be generalised to society as a whole. A generalisation of this kind was proof that the economist was a theorist of commercial anarchy, as could be seen in the case of machinery:

> Instead of seeing, in the just and urgent complaints which this fundamental lacuna in our social order frequently raises, an indication of one of the most important and pressing applications of true political science, our economists can do no more than repeat, with pitiless pedantry, their sterile aphorism regarding absolute industrial freedom. (1830–42 II: 96)

Comte was far from believing that social facts were infinitely malleable; quite the contrary, he thought such an idea to be simply a sign of immaturity (ibid.: 105). Such malleability is limited by the laws of social life, laws which it is the task of sociology to discover. Remaining at the same level of generality as Comte, we can say that when the political system is adequate to the social state there is a spontaneous order which the legislator can neither create nor modify at will. This idea comes from

---

above all, a political economy based upon optimising economic behaviour, formalised as such by Antoine-Augustin Cournot (Steiner 1998: 187–88).

political economy, and the contribution of political economy ends there too. The existence of this spontaneous order does not imply that the outcome is satisfactory. The hierarchy that Comte elaborates supposes that social facts are the most complex, but also the most susceptible to modification, since complexity is associated with imperfection.

This fundamental relationship, linking on the one hand the relative simplicity of facts (of astronomy, for instance) to that of the laws which regulate their functioning, and on the other the complexity of social facts to the variety of natural laws upon which social facts depend, is thus completed by the idea of the perfectibility of complex facts.[2] This leads Comte to give a major role to education: the first task of positive philosophy is to promote rational education (1830–42 I: 61). The very great plasticity of social facts allows, even demands, the imposition of education upon individuals, in the knowledge, however, that education is a social process subject itself to natural laws, and that it would be a great error to accord it infinite power in its work on humanity (ibid.: 870).

Comte therefore makes two arguments in favour of sociology. On the one hand, statics demonstrates the existence of a consensus relating the different parts of the social whole to each other. Comte's critique of political economy derives from this thought, arguing that political economy isolates its object of study from the rest of social life, aping the methods of the inorganic sciences: by isolating the economic domain from the remainder of social life, the economist is well on the way to forgetting that human action is not only economic, rational and conscious but also contains moral and affective dimensions (1830–42 II: 117). The functioning of social order cannot be understood without due regard to these features, and by "the functioning of social order" we here also include the economic dimension, which cannot be abstracted from the combination of egoistic and altruistic motives.

On the other hand, the source of the sociologist can be discovered in the dynamic approach, the only element that Comte developed. According to him, history is the "ensemble of the social past" (ibid.: 97) once this has gained "a truly scientific nature, finally establishing a true rational linkage between the sequence of social events, in such a way as to allow, as for all other phenomenal orders, and within the limits imposed by a superior complexity, some systematic foresight regarding their subsequent succession" (ibid.: 97). For Comte, there is no serious method-

---

[2] This relationship explains why Comte rejected the idea of the mathematisation of the social sciences, as well as that of the life sciences: mathematics can intervene in simple phenomena that follow set rules, but it is less suited to complex phenomena—phenomena that are determined by an increasing number of important laws of nature, whose variable combinations allow for large variations in possible social behaviour.

ological alternative to this use of history; he never ceased to criticise the supposed method of introspection, according to which the brain was divided into two parts, one part reasoning and the other observing this process of ratiocination (1830–42 I: 32, 853). Beginning with the "reform of political economy", Comte ended up developing a vigorous critique of a science which he thought to be the premature beginnings of a social science, leading him to propose a new science: sociology, capable of grasping consensus and evolution in determining the ruling laws of social life, of which the economy was only one small part.

Beyond its methodological aspect, the critique of political economy had two sides to it. On the one hand, it sought to take account of the plurality of human action, in contrast to economists who saw human action only as the individual prompted by selfish interest, just as Mill described the ideal type of economic behaviour in his *System of Logic* (1973/4: bk. 6 ch. 9 §3). On the other hand, Comte attributed great practical weight to his critique, for in opposition to some economists, who thought that rational economic behaviour was increasingly the norm,[3] he considered that the progressive diffusion of positivist education lent support to the practice and ascendancy of altruistic behaviour over egoistic behaviour.[4] In short, not only does theory have a legitimating impact upon practices, but Comte also identifies the principle Bourdieu called the "theory effect", the inscription of theory in practice through the legitimation of the one by the other, and hence the production of the behaviours posited in theory.

History, the Social and Representations

The similarities between the sociologies of Comte and Durkheim and the Durkheimians have been known for a long time, including their critical approach to political economy (Aron 1967: 89; Boudon 1991: 130–32). The distance between the Durkheimians and Marx—with whose work they, like Durkheim, were not that familiar (Llobera 1980)—is likewise well known, especially in respect of their treatment of politics and conflict in social life (Giddens 1971: 199–204).[5] Comparison of the three

---

[3] This relates to Cournot (1838: 48), who relied on this line of argument; it has recurred from the mid-nineteenth century to the present.

[4] "Since [on account of the division of labour] each in effect works for others, this truth will necessarily end in being generally felt, when positivism has finally succeeded in effecting the prevalence everywhere of an exact apprehension of reality. However, such a habit will prompt all the more profound a reaction if its development should coincide with the spread of new religious convictions regarding the natural existence of purely benevolent inclinations" (Comte 1851–54 II: 159).

[5] But we should not overemphasise this. It has been shown in ch. 4 how sensitive Simiand was to the conflictual aspect of wage determination. Moreover, as Cherkaoui (1998) has

critiques of political economy will make things a little less complex than would normally be expected from lining Comte and Durkheim up against Marx.

Despite the changes in economic activity occurring from 1830 to 1870 and then from 1870 to 1900, the similarities between Comte, Marx and Durkheim are clear: they all face a social formation in which the importance of economic activity has become incontestable. First of all, they agree on the importance given to history. This is a procedure for presenting the subject of study, or grasping it intellectually, since the social is a complex fact (Comte and Durkheim) or a fact manifesting itself mysteriously (Marx). History is above all a methodologically central element, in the absence of which one risks failing to understand both the functioning of economic life and its social dimension. This agreement among the three writers exists even though Comte's sociology is oriented to the social dynamic—the law of the three states—and there is no treatment of statics or consensus in the *Cours de philosophie positive* apart from one lecture, the fiftieth. By contrast, Marx and Durkheim develop a fine-grained analysis of socioeconomic mechanisms, which enables the precise functioning of particular domains of modern society to be identified.

Secondly, there is the impossibility of separating the economic from the social framework. Here the three writers agree, but they do not share a fixed procedure. Comte emphasises the methodological angle, denouncing the separation made by economists between economic facts and all other kinds of social fact. Here Durkheim follows Comte entirely, as does Simiand. Their agreement can be seen when discussing the impoverishment of a conception of humanity reduced to the rational behaviour of an egoistic calculator. This is not the approach that Marx takes, and he does not consider this assumption about human behaviour to be methodologically wrong; on the contrary, such an assumption represents the behaviour of the economic agent in his own critique of political economy. Simiand himself ended up making allowance for this form of social reality, accepting that the social groups set to work in his economic sociology of wages were in fact made up of just such actors.

What now of the differences? These are no less marked than the similarities. Comte and Durkheim adopted the sociological approach so that they might trace the outlines of science and the significance of sociopolitical factors, and there is a perceptible difference between them as regards politics, which plays a part in Comte's work but almost none in Durkheim's. There are some remarks relevant to this in the most scientistic

---

very rightly insisted, Durkheim's *L'évolution pédagogique en France* is a text in which great weight is given to political and ideological struggle in explaining the turning points in the French educational system.

sections of *Rules*,[6] and some remarks in his lecture course of 1898–1900, but this does not make politics central to Durkheimian sociology. Both Comte and Durkheim put sociology above economics, Comte excluding economics from the positive sciences, Durkheim reconstructing it as an economic sociology. The Comtean and Durkheimian critique is primarily directed to the method and place of political economy within the social sciences. Marx does not share this approach: sociology plays no part at all as a form of knowledge specific to modern society. His critique of political economy is an economic sociology that does not acknowledge itself as one (Steiner 2000b).

The differences bear, secondly, on the place of religion in the understanding of modern society. At first glance, the stance taken by Comte and Durkheim on religion—a stance related to their search for a secular substitute for the religion and morality of the past—is quite different from that of Marx, who hardly touches on this form of ideology. Nonetheless, there is a strong connection when it comes to the role of the sociology of religion in understanding some aspects of economic activity, such as money and the gift relationship. There is a firm link between Marx, Durkheim and the Durkheimians when it comes to the understanding of monetary phenomena; the centrality of such phenomena to modern economic life requires that their religious dimension be taken fully into account. Of course, for Comte fetishism is an essential form of industrial thought and action during the early stages of human history. He goes on endlessly about the prodigies that this representation of the world made possible before gods in the proper sense of the term had appeared and argues that fetishism did not imply the emergence of a sacerdotal class with a strong influence on social organisation (1830–42 II: Lecture 52). But fetishism is not a category relevant to social life in the industrial and the positive age. Comte at first places fetishism firmly in the past, emergent only on the occasion of accident or shortcoming in the "disenchanted" life of modern positive society. Later, he places this stage in human thought closer to positivity than the theological and metaphysical age, because of the importance given to the subjective and the affective. But even in this second take on fetishism, Comte does not consider that it can play a part at the core of industrial societies. Furthermore, he never touches very deeply on the problems presented by the functioning of money; the comments made in *Système de politique positive* remain at the anecdotal level by comparison with the importance attributed to it in Marx's conception of the fetishism of commodities, of money and of finance capital, or in the work of Simiand and Mauss, where money is

[6] In ch. 3, devoted to the normal and the pathological, and the bearing of the legislator's action on the pathological.

studied in the light of the sociology of religion. Money is an operator of commercial socialisation, creating a stabilised form in which systemic confidence and belief in the future is objectified. This social construction, in which individuals agree to relate to one another, generates the collective through a mechanism which Marx finds analogous to "the cloudy region of the religious world", and which Simiand seeks to understand sociologically through the introduction of both reason and faith. In this respect their positions on fetishism are quite different from Comte's.

There is another point on which Durkheim and Marx converge in relation to this question. Fetishism is distinct from ideology in an especially important way: fetishism is not a class of representations imposed by one class on another so as to assure the legitimacy of domination; it is a representation which arises from the work of the social itself, inverting real relations. Marx and Durkheim converge: both seek to decipher the enigma constituted by a common perception inadequate to its real object by studying the social process which founds it, without relating it to the "objective interests" of those served by the dissemination of such a representation.

Thirdly, there is an evident cleavage over education. For both Comte and Durkheim, this aspect of social life is of major importance, but it plays no great role in Marx. Comte and Durkheim conceive education to be an essential instrument for the dissemination of knowledge and representations capable of providing a common intellectual glue among members of industrial society. If one treats political economy as a social fact, as a way of doing, thinking and feeling through which the individual forms a conception of the social world and acts upon it, then education becomes essential for understanding forms of social organisation and the representations spontaneously formed by socioeconomic relationships.

Comte sees in education a way of counterbalancing the effects of economic discourse in respect of the opposition between egoism and altruism. For their part, Durkheim and the Durkheimians agree in giving an important place to immanent representations—social value in Durkheim, Simiand's representations of the nominal wage or the representations of different kinds of commerce in Halbwachs—and in taking a great interest in social representations constructed via the diffusion of economic knowledge.

In respect of methodology and the place of political economy in the social sciences, Durkheim clearly assumes a position similar to Comte's, but in marked contrast to Marx's. However, the relationship between the three writers is more complex as soon as one turns to examine the way in which they conduct their critique. They all agree on a due regard for history, the social and politics in making their critique, with the sole exception of Durkheim in respect of politics. While Comte treats science

TABLE 7.1
Comparison of Critiques of Political Economy: Comte, Marx and Durkheim

Critique	Comte	Marx	Durkheim
Bearing on			
Abstract method	Yes	No	Yes
Place of political economy in social sciences	Yes	No	Yes
Taking into account			
History	Yes	Yes	Yes
The social	Yes	Yes	Yes
Politics	Yes	Yes	No
Representations			
Immanent	No	Yes	Yes
Constructed	Yes	No	Yes

as continuous with common sense, both Marx and Durkheim make a strong distinction between common sense and science as an essential criterion of criticism. What is more, both Marx and Durkheim are led to draw a parallel between economics and religion when it is a matter of understanding particular economic representations linked to money. But when it is a matter of representations constructed via the diffusion of economic knowledge, there is again convergence between Comte and Durkheim, where the accent is placed upon education and common values.

The importance that Durkheim and the Durkheimians attribute to *two* types of representation merits further attention if we are to fully grasp the originality of the Durkheimian critique of political economy.

ECONOMIC KNOWLEDGE AS A SOCIAL FACT

In the first volume of the second series of the *Année sociologique*, Simiand introduced a new rubric devoted to economic policy. He considered that domain relevant to a positive study of social realities of which the books reviewed were an indicator, defining the categories through which economic policy is conceived (*AS* II 1925: 723). This approach conforms entirely to that of Durkheim in his lectures on socialism and in his comments on the work of Bouglé that was eventually published as *Les idées égalitaires* (Bouglé 1899). It was not a matter of philosophical discussion of these doctrines, an examination of them as concepts (Durkheim 1895–96: 39–40; Letter to Bouglé, 25 July 1897, in Durkheim 1975 II: 404); they had instead to be dealt with as things, as expressions, indicators of social reality. It is possible to transpose this idea to economic knowledge:

> If it [socialism] is not a scientific expression of social facts, it is itself a social fact, and of the greatest importance. If it is not a work of science, it is certainly an object of science. (Durkheim 1895–96: 38)

Durkheim was never interested in the history of ideas. He had little time for a genre to which he turned only at times of discouragement, as a stopgap suitable to "fill the void of professional existence".[7] This amounts to a powerful methodological statement that doctrines and theories are, from a sociological point of view, a social fact, a "thing" of no greater importance than any other social practice, to be studied as part of the sociology of knowledge. Such an approach leads to a sociological orientation that distances itself from either condemnation or praise of the discourse that economists elaborate as their own science.

Durkheim as a sociologist of knowledge thought about the relation of ideas to action, of the ideal to the transformation of the real; he laid emphasis upon the essential role played by ideas in the orientation of individual behaviour in society.[8] Together with pragmatist writers, Durkheim argued that beliefs held to be true were part of the social construction of future reality, so that in this sense ideas and the ideal create reality; but unlike pragmatists, he did not link this process of reality creation to utility. Durkheim did reject the idea that knowledge could have only action as its purpose; knowledge also involved idle speculation, a form of thinking without practical end or immediate utility. He considered it important to recognise this level of the functioning of knowledge, since it highlights more clearly than elsewhere in his writings the fact that consciousness also has the "role of producing beings" (1913–14: 170), individuals capable

---

[7] There is nonetheless an exception when it is a matter of pedagogic doctrines: because of the marked historical nature of pedagogical practice, he thought it useful and necessary to study the doctrines of the past so that one might properly appreciate those of the present (Durkheim 1902e: 85–87).

[8] Contrary to received opinion, Durkheim was no stranger to the definition of human acts in terms of intended ends, even if he did not wish to base his sociology on such a "finalist" foundation, and even if he only used this approach in a limited way, for example, in opposing egoism and altruism in the manner of Comte: "Human behavior can be distinguished in terms of the ends toward which it is directed. Now, all the objectives sought by men may be classified into the following two categories. First, there are those concerning only the individual himself who pursues them; we shall therefore call them personal. Second, there are those acts concerning something other than the individual who is acting; in this case, we shall call them impersonal" (Durkheim 1902–3/1961: 55–56).

of consciously evaluating actions, whether completed or to be completed, individuals who are therefore capable of reflexivity:

> A conscious being, a being who knows himself, cannot act just like a being who ignores his own existence; his activity will be of a new type. No doubt this activity will give rise to movements, but these will be movements directed by ideas: in other words, this will be *psychological* activity. (ibid.: 171)

When he applies this reasoning to the notion of truth, a notion he considers central to pragmatism, he defends the idea that truth, in the sense of conformity to reality, is not simply a matter of "reflecting" the real but also of creating the real:

> Mythological ideas have not been treated as real because they are based upon an objective reality. It is rather our ideas, our beliefs, which lend objects of thought their reality. And so an idea is real, not on account of its conformity with the real, but on account of its creative power. But these ideas do not have an individual origin: they are collective representations. (ibid.: 173)

And he is able to conclude with a strong affirmation:

> In the final analysis it is thought that creates the real, and the prominent role of collective representations is to "make" a superior reality, which is society itself. (ibid.: 174)[9]

This thesis allows us to give a precise content to Durkheim's remarks on the complexity with which classical rationalism cannot deal. The social as described here by Durkheim includes an element of self-realisation in which belief founds belief by virtue of social processes (in Durkheim, the schooling system; in Mauss and Simiand, the system of reciprocal expectations) through which belief assumes its place in social life. Durkheim does not, of course, think for one moment that societies are free to create any and every reality; there are social conditions for this process to occur. Where mythologies or religions are concerned, collective representations make and express social reality in one move, and do so through the intermediary of symbols that unite different individual consciousnesses so that they might communicate and feel things in unison. And of

---

[9] A little further on he adds: "It can finally be seen that the function of speculative truth is to sustain the collective consciousness. And this permits us to respond to the pragmatist objection that, if truth only expresses the real, it is purely redundant; it is necessary that it be *added* to the real—but if it adds something, it is no longer a true copy. In fact, this 'copy' of the real, which is truth, is not mere redundance, a simple pleonasm. It 'adds' to the real a new world, more complex than all others: the human world, the social world. Through this a new order of things becomes possible: nothing less than *civilisation*" (1913–14: 187).

course, Durkheim adds, these collective representations "are false in rela-tion to things, but true in relation to the subjects who think them" (ibid.: 177). Scientific truths, being as such true in relation to things, also have the status of collective representations, performing the same function of uniting consciousnesses and symbols, with the difference that this form of unification allows intellectual autonomy to individuals (ibid.: 179) and requires that the plurality of perspectives be respected, since it is only this that permits the complexity of the real to be faced (ibid.: 187). Nonethe-less, Durkheim never passes up an opportunity of accusing the prag-matists of sharing with economists the method that he criticised:[10] both neglected to seek in history concrete answers to their questions (ibid.: 150, 179) through appropriate treatment of empirical material (ideas and doctrines understood as social facts). Instead of presenting their ideal conceptions of the fact under study, these writers would do better to di-rect themselves to the study of social facts, that which could be taken for a truth or that which could be elaborated as an economic science.

For these relations to assume their sociological meaning, it is necessary to isolate the mechanisms and institutions through which ideas find their way into society, making possible an escape from the illusions of idealism so that one may understand how "the [social] value of thoughts [are re-alised] in spite of the powerlessness of discourse" (Comte 1851–54 II: 124). This institution is no mystery to Durkheim: it is the schooling sys-tem. His study of the history of the educational system contains insights useful for understanding its role in forming the modern world, insights which can then be extended to political economy.

The schooling system is the institution through which a system of ideas, a belief, is materially inscribed within social functioning, mediated by continuous and reflexive action on the part of adults trained specifically for the task of the "methodical socialisation" (Durkheim 1902d: 51) of new generations: "A person is not only a being who disciplines himself; he is also a system of ideas, of feelings, of habits and tendencies, a con-sciousness that has a content" (1902–3/1961: 73).

As "methodical socialisation", education has two objectives: firstly, it provides a uniform education to all members of the new generation, giv-ing substance to the collective consciousness. Secondly, in a society char-acterised by the division of labour, education also seeks to provide a training specialised according to the nature of the activity, an essentially economic activity to which individuals devote themselves. This is the ar-gument elaborated in the first few pages of the *Division of Labour*, when

---

[10] Durkheim did not hesitate to call pragmatism "logical utilitarianism" (1913–14: 151, 153), hence the convergence here between pragmatism and the critique of political economy as an exaggerated form of utilitarianism.

Durkheim contrasts the dilettante to the competent person, competent in that he usefully fulfils a precise function (1893/1984: 4). The duality of social ideals discussed in chapter 2 above is closely related to these two tasks, which, according to Durkheim, define modern education:

> Each society forms for itself a certain human ideal, whether from the intellectual, physical or moral perspective; this ideal is to some extent the same for all citizens; while at a certain point they begin to diverge under the influence of the particular milieus which all societies contain. It is this ideal, at once unique and diverse, which is the lodestone of education. It thus seeks to nurture in the child (1) a number of physical and mental states which the society, to which the child belongs, considers that no member of that society should be without; (2) some physical and mental states which the particular social group (caste, class, family, profession) likewise wish to be shared by all those whom they educate. It is therefore society, as a whole, and every particular social milieu, which determines the ideal which education realises. (1902d: 50)

Required to provide lectures on education, Durkheim was led to a close study of the history of the schooling system in France. What Durkheim has to say about the nature of Jesuit education in seventeenth-century France is of interest (1904–5: 313–17). Closely connected with the Counterreformation, and so with the way in which religion was related to social life, the Society of Jesus considered education to be a more suitable means for the ideological struggle than prayers and catechism (ibid.: 269).

The Jesuits had little interest in Erasmian humanism or Rabelaisean erudition and considered these to be hotbeds of heresy; instead, they turned to the classical literature of Greece and Rome (ibid.: 280, 287). Durkheim drew attention to the ingenuity of using pagan texts as a way to both maintain the ascendancy of the Catholic religion and prevent the Jesuits' subject populations from turning to reformed religion. In the process of becoming the substance of a modernised religious schooling, this literature was stripped of all historical content and presented as an abstract model of virtue, illustrative of Christian morality:

> And so the Romano-Greek milieu which the children inhabited was one empty of anything Greek or Roman, becoming a kind of unreal, ideal milieu, populated, of course, by persons who had historically existed but who, as presented, had nothing historical about them at all. They were henceforth no more than emblematic figures of virtues, vices, of all the great passions of humanity. Achilles stood for courage; Ulysses for prudent foresight; Numa is the pious king par excellence; Caesar stands for ambition; Augustus is the powerful monarch and man of letters; and so forth. (ibid.: 287)

The Jesuit school produced individuals whose training led them to see men of their time as continuous with those of the past:

> Is it not obvious that minds which have absorbed this culture and, consequently, have achieved a state of blissful ignorance in which they are unaware of change and variation in history, can do no other than portray man in the way they have learned to see him, at his most general, most abstract, most impersonal. (ibid.: 313)

This in turn explains the characteristic generally known as Cartesianism, with its "excessive simplicity, its mathematical spirit" (ibid.: 316), its disembodied abstraction, its desire that theory trace phenomena back to their most simple elements, including in this the domains of morality and politics. This way of conceiving the human being lent classical rationalism its power—its self-certainty—and its weakness—its inability to think about complexity:

> One can now see the extent of the influence which this system of education has had upon our national temperament and, consequently, upon our history. For a cast of mind which makes us see things from a definite perspective strikes us as a kind of intellectual blindness to a whole side of reality which, of course, is not without its impact upon action. This is in particular the source of eighteenth-century abstract individualism, with its atomistic conception of society and its misconception of history. Does that mean that the harm went uncompensated? No, of course not. Rationalism was almost necessarily a consequence of simplicity, and the power of reason is itself a power. But this supreme rationalism, a rationalism which related only to an illusion—the illusion that complexity is mere appearance—this is an inferior form of rationalism. Reason has to acquire sufficient force for it not to doubt itself, all the while sensing that things are complex and part of a complex reality. (ibid.: 316–17)

In *Moral Education*, written during the same period, Durkheim related Cartesianism to a particular way of thinking, mathematics. This supplied the clearest example of classical rationalism, deductive in nature, contrary to physical and natural science, experimental in nature (1902–3/ 1961: 250, 252, 254–55, 260):

> Simplism, therefore, is an act of faith in abstract reasoning. The belief at the basis of it is that the mind can draw knowledge out of itself, if only it has constructed the initial concepts that contain that knowledge implicitly. There is no need for any laborious and complicated methods in order to get at the secrets of nature. There is nothing so mysterious in nature, nothing to disconcert our understanding, since it is as simple

as that understanding itself. Once we rend the veil that masks this simplicity, everything stands brightly revealed. This tendency is so inherent in the simplistic mind that Cartesianism is, in essence, nothing but the attempt to reduce knowledge of the world to universal mathematics; when the philosophers of the eighteenth century applied Cartesian principles to social phenomena, they imagined that the new science could be conceived and constructed at a single stroke, by way of definitions and deductions, with no need to resort to observation—in other words, to history. (ibid.: 261–62)

Of course, Durkheim does not fail to indicate that a phenomenon which is so general has many causes other than the one he is examining. All the same, he highlights what is at stake in this approach to the sociology of knowledge: to move beyond the conceptual history of doctrines, the social mediations through which they disseminate must be isolated—here, the schooling system.

By treating Descartes as a social fact, Durkheim shows the importance of the schooling system in the organisation of the categories central to classical rationalism. Durkheim's chain of thought can be schematised following James Coleman (1990) (see figure 7.1).

Among economists this form of rationalism assumed the guise of *homo œconomicus*, which Durkheim argued was superseded so far as the social was concerned, for the social was of such complexity that classical rationalism, reducing elements to their simplest form by its analytical and mathematical method, had no purchase upon it. Nonetheless, instead of abandoning rationalism on the grounds of its inadequacy, he called for a sophisticated rationalism capable of taking account of the complexity of the real, the historicity and sociality of the human being (ibid.: 262–63).

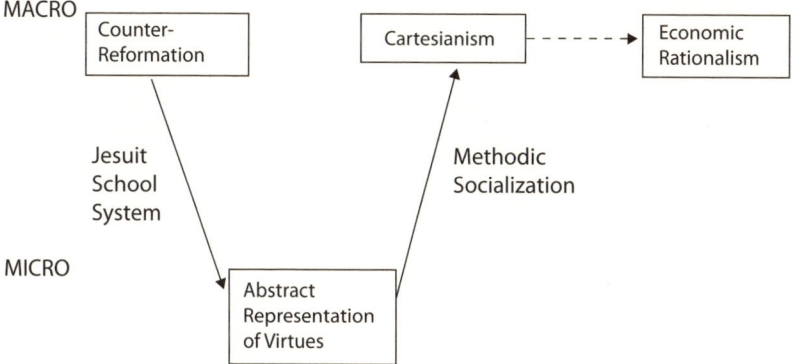

FIGURE 7.1 Counterreformation, schooling system and classical rationalism

From the criticisms he made of economists during the years 1885–93 to the critique of pragmatism in 1913–14, via the *Rules of Sociological Method* and the *Elementary Forms*, Durkheim always sought to elaborate the principles of a sophisticated rationalism, capable of approaching social realities by a route other than the reductionism of classical rationalism, which was incapable of giving a proper account of them. The cognitive dimension of social reality, whether as immanent representations, as socially constructed representations (deriving from the schooling system) or in respect of the reciprocal effects generated by such representations in social life ("ideas make reality")—all of these lie at the heart of a sophisticated rationalism. In this respect Durkheim did not alter his position from his earliest writings to those of his maturity, even after the "revelation" of 1895.

Towards a Sociology of Economic Knowledge

How important were such ideas to the Durkheimians when it came to their critique of political economy? This question applies in particular to Halbwachs, since he was the editor of Durkheim's lecture course on the evolution of educational ideas; but we shall also see that this orientation toward a sociology of economic knowledge can also be found in Simiand's writing.

A Never-Ending Project . . .

Halbwachs first developed his ideas in this regard when reviewing Pareto's *Trattato di sociologia generale*, arguing that Pareto had explored affective logic, or the logic of sentiment and of belief, through his analysis of the logical and nonlogical elements of action (1938b: 132–34). He argued that Pareto was interested in a modality of nonlogical action where a subjective end exists but not an objective one, the logic of such action being recognised within the group so engaged but not by a wider group. The nature of the action and rhetoric related to this is consequently linked to the existence of a social group that is engaged in such actions and that treats the justifications of such actions as valid. Halbwachs maintained that the same argument could be applied to scientific thought. Formal logic is presented as the result of a historical and institutional process within which European scientific thought had developed, from Greek classicism to the scholastic universities of the Middle Ages; mathematicians' rules of demonstration and the experimental science of physicists are as such logics associated with social groups which have made themselves autonomous with the development of the sciences. There were, of course, other collective logics, such as those shared by priests and those shared by lawyers, and the way in which he elaborated this idea is suggestive:

> Let us rather say that these are logics of values, of social values, distinct from the logic of sentiment which (in part) rests on judgements of individual value, employing, of course, particular real, psychological, moral and physical data but which, here differing from subjective logic, subordinating them to collective preferences, and hence in this respect drawing upon the principle of finality. (ibid.: 149–50)

This axiological rationality, to adopt a term used by Boudon (1998) in respect of Max Weber, is an original way of characterising how individuals enter into contact with one another and interact within a given group. It is also quite original to link this approach to that of Pareto in seeking to understand the behaviour of the specific kind of actors that scientists, lawyers or priests are.[11] One could well be surprised that Halbwachs did not seek to apply this line of thinking about logic, values and institutions to economists.

Here, once again, it is Simiand who comes to the fore. First of all, his critique of political economy is oriented to the theory effect; secondly, he lends much more importance to a new category of actors, those who could be called "experts", whether this expertise was legitimated institutionally, by economic practices or by the command of rational economic knowledge.

Simiand's critique of political economy assumes the form of a sociology of knowledge when he denounces academic economists as "scholastics". He is especially irritated by the manner in which economists study facts in terms of an externally defined norm (rationality), and that they then devote themselves to deducing consequences from this ideal norm instead of studying social facts for themselves, in a positive manner (1912: 97–98). Simiand finds the archetype for this approach among marginalist theorists:

> The psychological school, or more exactly the various psychological schools, turn away from this alleged sought-after objectivity, disappointing and misleading as it is, and instead develop an internal analysis of behaviour in respect of the needs and satisfactions of individuals; they

---

[11] Here is a passage from the conclusion of Halbwachs's text on the psychology of social classes, based on a series of lectures given at the Solvay Institute the same year (1938): "But those scientists from whom all public thinking, public opinion on matters of science, appears to flow have not arrived at their views all by themselves. They have come from colleges, worked in laboratories, in libraries, lived in scientific milieux, profited from an entire range of institutions whose purpose is to form and preserve a distinction from all other institutions, creating through their own language, convention and tradition what can be called 'scientific society'" (1955: 230–31).

think instead to discover there an irrefutable origin of economic value in a seductive theory that opens the way to all manner of ingenious introspective analysis and dialectical construction. In ever more esoteric combinations and complications—above all when matched with a mathematical apparatus designed to impress the amateur—this line of work gives its adepts the kind of satisfaction that erudite minds have most avidly sought . . . : that of an Aristotelian science that flourished for centuries with the blooming of scholasticism, and which has held out for a long time after the onset of modern science; a pursuit of the human mind concerned above all, not with a positive reality to be known and explained (which itself is not without trouble and difficulty), but with an internal analysis and conceptual construction which, at the risk of becoming purely verbal, simply but surely satisfies this mind through the agreement of this thought or that expression with itself—readily adding to it by a form of hermeticism the merit of conferring upon the initiate a sense of his superiority to the uninitiated. (1934b: 15–16)

In other words, "scholasticism" designates those who believe the reasoning of pure reason to be the reason of daily practice, for both are only the two faces of instrumental rationality, whether in the form of a theoretical rationality by means of which the theoretician reasons and provides his peers with proofs, or in the form of a practical rationality with which the concrete economic agent acts or would act if possessed of well-founded information and high cognitive competence.[12] This is also the reason why Simiand considers, quite correctly, that political economy is essentially normative, in the sense that it defines what will be rational behaviour for an individual instead of studying, as does positive economics, what individuals do so that one might understand what motivates them and why.

How is one to deal, in the twentieth century, with the existence and, above all, the perpetuation of such scholasticism? Simiand poses this question in a chapter of his essay on method. Confronted with what seems to him to be a veritable monstrosity, he sees two issues. Because orthodox economics is incapable of dealing with the facts of the real world, political economy has either to turn itself into an experimental science or declare that reality does not conform to theory and set out to create a world in which individuals do that which is rational according to theory. In the first case, Simiand's scientific strategy will come into its own; in the second, he does not hesitate to state that a political economy of this sort will lose all scientific status and become no more than an art (1912: 78–79).

---

[12] This is close to the way that Bourdieu defined the "scholastic fallacy" as "making meta-discourse the principle of all discourse, meta-practice the principle of all practice" (1994: 219); in economics the theory of rational choice is a good example of this scholastic fallacy (ibid.: 222).

Having come to this conclusion, he then considers the social consequences of such an art by sketching an argument regarding the effects that theory produces upon actors' behaviour, a performative effect which takes up the claim, often made by economists since the nineteenth century, that while theory might at present be inadequate, this was only a temporary state of affairs and matters would improve in the future:

> But, it is said, having admitted this normative character, is it not only a legitimate mental exercise, like any other mental exercise, but also a theoretically and practically a useful speculation to analyse, assuming such an ideal of economic life, the differences between present reality and this ideal? It would only remain to be shown that, since a theorist had formulated a particular economic ideal for society, and because the individuals of this society would be able to direct their reason by this ideal, this ideal would thereby be capable of realisation, or have some chance of realisation. (ibid.: 100)

Simiand rejects this proposal by invoking the viscosity of the social, where laws cannot be modified at the behest of the will of an isolated individual, or even at the behest of a collection of individuals believing in the same ideas. There is only one case in which such a process of autorealisation of theory might be possible: when the theoretical ideal is in conformity with the ideal towards which society is moving by itself (ibid.: 133). During this period Simiand's positive polemic put him alongside Durkheim: Simiand does not take up the idea of a social reality constructed by the ideas and ideals of actors. To see him put into practice ideas which he explicitly rejected in his methodology, one has to study his more technical works on money and finance (1934b, 1937).

Questioned on the relevance of nominal variables—upon which he had depended in his book on wages—in comparison to real variables, Simiand allowed that it would be conceivable that workers would no longer seek to maintain the nominal amount of their wage if a fall in wages was accompanied by a fall in prices which left their purchasing power unaltered. The possibility of such a textbook case derives from a modification of economic representations:

> If this [effort on the part of workers to maintain their purchasing power and not the nominal wage] comes about to a certain extent, that is probably where economists or oversimplistic thinkers have clouded the spontaneous ideas of people, and made them believe in the justice and the virtue of wage tariffs that are adjusted according to the price of consumption goods. (1934b: 83)

Taking account of the rather awkward character of the argument, burdened with normative terminology, it is worth noticing that Simiand introduces the position taken by economists and confers upon them the power to modify actors' representations and behaviour. The example that Simiand selects demonstrates that theories come into play which define that which is just and that which is not just, and that theories of economic justice define positions which can be considered legitimate because they are thought to be just. One can isolate a "theory effect" in the sense of an economic theory that modifies individual behaviour because, having changed the framework in whose terms people view the economic world, they modify their behaviour to achieve a new regime of action, satisfying the adopted criterion of economic justice.

Simiand poses the question: what is the "just wage"? (1932a II: 534) His response runs as follows: the just wage is the wage that conforms to economic law and to a morality, and social art seeks to realise this convergence:

> Hence, in our contemporary occidental economic societies, the just wage, like the just price, will be that which follows from the comprehensive application of the adopted principles of economic law: the designated principles of freedom of production, freedom of consumption, freedom to work or not to work, to enter into contracts or not to enter into contracts, free competition; and hence we consider that one does not have to make any complex and far-reaching effort to prove that under this regime, assuming it to be consistently enough applied, the payment made to the worker is exactly that which is his due, and that the price of a product is exactly that which flows to the producer. (1932a II: 535)

Simiand's terminology here seems very cluttered; behind this collection of freedoms there lies no more than the precepts of liberal economic theory translated into norms of economic justice. The justice here at issue derives from the dissemination and acceptance of this very theory, which is exactly the point that Simiand sought to discard by alluding to the desires and ideals of the scholastic economist. At the point where he touches upon the definition of the theory effect, without fully realising it, Simiand introduced something new into the argument by involving economic law. He takes account of a sociological phenomenon critical for any economic sociology by *socially inscribing theory in an institution (the law)* and, implicitly, in *the economic knowledge of persons* in charge of the elaboration, and the application, of law. This sets up the question of the economic knowledge of experts and of the social effects of such knowledge.

This issue surfaces on several occasions in the works that Simiand published during the 1930s. The first instance is to be found in the lectures which he gave on Taylorism in the *Cours d'économie politique*: he notes the role of efficiency engineers who calculate wages and the level of the bonus intended to provide an incentive for increased effort on the part of workers (1929–31 II: Lecture 7). Through the intermediation of the economic expert and the rationalising engineer, the institutions and behaviours capable of establishing a theory effect are established, not because of some miraculous coincidence of the ideal of an isolated theorist and the society's law of progress, but rather through the social inscription of theory in institutions in whose terms individuals are led to act in the economic world. This takes place, on the one hand, in the enterprise, since it is here that the productive effort occurs which provides a right to remuneration calculated according to the given wage formula; and, on the other, in the market, since it is here that the wage is bargained for before being spent on consumption goods. This cognitive aspect of economic activity is introduced again when Simiand, giving his last course at the Collège de France, turns his attention to the financial market. Economic agents are here directly confronted with shifting opinions regarding the future, and their decisions reflect their beliefs relating to the future. Such beliefs are socially circumscribed: the beliefs of a few agents in a single location are imposed upon all economic agents via the value of money and securities objectifying social belief respecting the future (1937: 6). He emphasises that the social mechanism realised through a very large number of economic transactions is not based upon observation, but instead partly upon estimations and partly upon incentives (ibid.: 27–28). Because of the cognitive dimension assumed by economic activity, the role of economic expertise becomes decisive inasmuch as it creates a point of reference around which agents are able to coordinate themselves in respect of a common belief, which, as a result, becomes self-fulfilling according to the terms of contemporary economic analysis (Aglietta & Orléan 2002; Orléan 1992b). Simiand stops at that point, noting how experts were mistaken about the onset of the 1929 crisis (Simiand 1937: 5; see also 1934a: 173, 246). But the idea remains that economic knowledge, in its different forms, on the one hand, through its dissemination by the schooling system and on the other through its social inscription in economic law and commercial or industrial expertise, plays a central role in the functioning of an economy.

. . . Which Always Relates to the Present

Durkheimian teaching has not been lost. One can find it developed by Polanyi in the mid-twentieth century (1944: chs. 12–13), when he maintains that the social inscription of theory is a fact of major social importance for the understanding of contemporary modern society. It can also be found in contemporary French economic sociology, which retains a special place for the sociology of economic knowledge (Heilbron 2001).

There are, nevertheless, some marked differences on this point, and we can approach this problem from three directions.

First of all, there is the path taken by Lebaron (2000, 2003), following Bourdieu: the convergence here of a symbolic domain with the schooling system secures a real continuity with the Durkheimian approach and that of Bourdieu. The radical nature of the critique of political economy also sets up a continuum of sorts between Comte, Simiand and Bourdieu; each treats political economy as a false science, while Simiand and Bourdieu give preference to an economic sociology which, in the case of Bourdieu, is buttressed by the theory of fields and of habitus (Bourdieu 1997, 2000; Lebaron 2000: 245). The relationship of economy to religion is justified by the similarity of the economic field to the religious field: they are both social spaces, whether autonomous or relatively autonomous; that is, each involves a specific issue around which agents struggle for domination. The economy is therefore treated as a "belief", of a kind analogous to a religious belief, and the status of the producer of economic belief, in other words, the status of an economist, depends on the authority conferred in the economic field, this field being based upon the nature and volume of scientific and symbolic capital held by the agent. Just as the economy has a major political role, this belief is raised to the status of a "secular substitute for religious faith" (Lebaron 2000: 7, 244), since it is the foundation of the symbolic order justifying essential institutions, such as, for example, central banks, through the competence or neutrality of the personnel and experts who work in them (ibid.: ch. 6).

But for this role of symbolic legitimation to work, it is necessary that economic belief be broadly diffused. Lebaron examines at length the economic education provided by the National School of Statistics and Economic Administration (ENSAE) (ibid.: ch. 3), as well as the effort made during the immediate postwar period to disseminate an economic culture among a public which lacked such a culture—a programme with a definite technocratic perspective closely related to the French style of reconstruction and planning (ibid.: ch. 5; see also Duval 2000). This places us in a structure of thinking and reasoning which amounts to a concrete extension of the work of Durkheim and Simiand: first, orthodox political economy is a belief lacking a genuine scientific foundation and, as such, has to be superseded by a scientific economic sociology. Second, the knowledge so disqualified is not, however, regarded as consequently harmless; it retains significant and real social effects through the spread of economic categories as means of apprehending the social world and as a symbolic system justifying domination in the established social order.

Michel Callon takes a quite different approach: he disregards this symbolic level in favour of the objective forms through which economic belief is inscribed in contemporary society. Instead of seeking to compensate for the defects or methodological errors of a political economy incapable of studying the market because of the level of abstraction at which it functions, and its inability to deal with social relations in the marketplace, he takes it as a cognitive social fact whose prime function is to "perform, configure, and format the economy, rather than to study its working" (1998: 2). The social inscription of economic theory is effected by its inscription in frameworks of technique, such as the accounting techniques employed by firms and public administration, the computerised setting of prices in electronic financial trading or the establishment of competition law according to the game-theoretic modelling of behaviour (Steiner 2001b).

Both of these approaches make similar claims regarding the inability of political economy to account for the organisation and working of economic life, whether because it denies the truth of social relations (of exploitation), or because its object is performative—that it is an art, not a science, as Simiand said—and it succeeds in including individuals who do not know this but put it into practice through its material inscription. One can also understand why, in both cases, one finds conceptions which locate the sociology of scientific knowledge as a zone of conflict, the pure struggle for influence and power. This conflict-oriented dimension has, of course, been a part of all forms of the sociology of science since the classical work of Robert Merton on a "scientific community" which is at once cooperative and competitive. Here, however, something different is at stake: it is not simply the recognition of the scientist and his discoveries which is of interest but the production of knowledge itself. In short, it concerns the symbolic or performative dimension, the two approaches agreeing in not allowing any rational and practical foundation to economic rationality.

These two approaches are not contradictory, although they do operate along two distinct paths; they do not deal with the same objects, nor do they consider them from the same angle. They differ here from a third approach—one related to an important, yet open, question—that can be isolated in the work of the Durkheimians. Once it is admitted that political economy provides a framework of categories by means of which actors can match their behaviour and expectations to those of others, it is still important to know the reasons for the social inscription of these categories. In spite of what it clarifies in respect of the effects produced by economic education, the research strategy which places almost exclusive emphasis upon the symbolic order seems to me too reductionist; we cannot see how it is possible, without further examination, to reject the effectiveness of theorised instrumental economic rationality, as abstract as one likes, by economists. The approach which places the emphasis upon the material inscription of economic theory seems to be preferable, since it does not discard or ignore the technical dimension of economic activity, a dimension which is certainly as essential as the symbolic dimension. But in so doing this approach also ignores the question of whether economic rationality has a consistency of its own before which the performance, or the "economic construction of economic reality", has to yield, as Hacking states with regard to the social construction of facts (1999). Once the question of economic rationality has been posed as it has been, can one escape from the responses that have been made?

CHAPTER EIGHT

From Religious Rationalisation to Rational Education

The second Durkheimian programme, in linking the sociology of religion and the sociology of the economy, invites comparison with the work of Max Weber. The question upon which we seek to shed some light is the following: starting out from the well-known thesis of Weber's *Protestant Ethic*, what might there be in Durkheimian economic sociology that would make it possible to extend Weber's argument beyond the period upon which he focuses, primarily the seventeenth century?

We begin with a brief reminder of the thesis that Weber developed in *Protestant Ethic* and a consideration of his essay *Confucianism and Taoism*, which contains some very suggestive remarks on the role of education in the creation of an ethos specific to an elite of literate officials. We will then come back to the manner in which Durkheim dealt with the seventeenth century in his own lecture course on the development of teaching in France, in which he examined the formation of elites and of the schooling system. It will be shown in conclusion that there is a convergence in the social mechanisms identified by Weber and Durkheim in which the ideas involved in religious or secular doctrines become social forces orienting interests in specific directions.

We will also deal with the way in which the sociology of economic knowledge developed by Durkheim and Simiand sheds light on the formation of the modern individual at the point where the spirit of capitalism, having discarded the crutches initially supplied by Puritanism, begins to draw upon modern utilitarianism and supply both a pragmatic legitimation and a rhetoric adequate to this new form of rationality which constrains us, as if it were an "iron cage", to use Weber's expression.

RELIGION AND THE RATIONALISATION OF SOCIAL LIFE

Weber begins by posing a very precise, if broad, question: that of the origin of one particular form of capitalism, that characterised by the bourgeois enterprise based upon the rational organisation of free labour (1920–21: 10, 11). He emphasises the religious dimension of social life to draw attention to the originality in world-historical terms of the Protestant

Reformation, from Luther to Calvin and on throughout Europe, starting in the early sixteenth century. What is so special about this reformed religion?

Weber's central argument rests on *the social mechanism of proving oneself (Bewährung)*. What animates the Puritan in the practical conduct of life, what impels him to rationalise his work on earth systematically and methodically, is the search for renewed confirmation of grace through physical work. Weber's own summary of this argument in *Protestant Ethic* is easily understood:

> what has been crucial for our consideration was always the view (which recurs in all denominations) of the religious "state of grace" as a status that separates man from the depravity of the creaturely and from the "world". Possession of this status, however—no matter how the dogmas of the different denominations might teach their followers to acquire it—could only be guaranteed by *proving oneself* [*Bewährung*] in a specific form of conduct unambiguously distinct from the style of life of the "natural" man. The consequence for the individual was the drive to *keep a methodical check* on his state of grace as shown in how he conducted his life and thus to ensure that his life was imbued with *asceticism*. This ascetic style of life, however, as we have seen, meant a *rational* shaping of one's whole existence in obedience to God's will. And this asceticism was no longer an *opus supererogationis*, but could be expected of everyone wanting to be sure of salvation. This *rationalization* of the conduct of life in the world with a view to the beyond is the *idea of the calling* characteristic of ascetic Protestantism. (2002: 104)

Having arrived at this point, Weber shows that this conception of inner-worldly asceticism has an "elective affinity" with the spirit of capitalism, which is Weber's provisional designation of "that attitude which, *in the pursuit of a calling*, strives systematically for profit for its own sake" (ibid.: 19). The outcome is a "specifically *middle-class ethic of the calling*" (ibid.: 118), which Weber illustrates with passages from Benjamin Franklin's "Advice to a Young Tradesman" and "Hints for Those That Would Be Rich".

The mechanism of proving oneself translates the religious dogma to which the believer adheres into a way of leading a life, a practical orientation of life determined by religious values. This is made possible by the lack of a clear break between religion and the world, a result of the religious valorisation of life on earth and the imperative to forgo enjoyment of wealth and instead seek through the acquisition of wealth the signs of a state of grace. The mechanism is, therefore, at the core of the Protestant ethic, and, as an unanticipated outcome, this is what lends work its specifically bourgeois ethos.

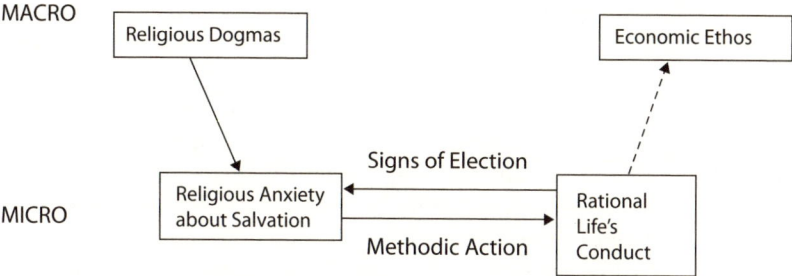

FIGURE 8.1 Religious dogmas, confirmation and economic ethos

This mechanism is a key component of Weber's sociology. Adherence to religious values lends meaning to the world of the believer and to his actions in the world: adding to the glory of God by methodical, unrelenting labour. The believer profits from such labour, for he is able to read the signs of his election in the success of his professional life, finding in it the means of alleviating his religious anxiety as well as the means of pursuing his asceticism. But such alleviation does not exempt the believer from continuing in his exertions, since the mechanism of proving oneself cannot provide any certainty, leaving the believer in a state of constant tension that enforces the religious rationalisation of inner-worldly behaviour. And that is in itself a perfect example of rational, value-oriented action of the type dealt with by Weber in *Economy and Society*. This is a rational, value-oriented action and not an action oriented to an end, for both the point of departure and the point of arrival are religious; the coherence of the action is assessed in respect of religious values and not in respect of a relation of means to ends according to a criterion of optimality. This point is important for Weber since it leads into the idea of the unanticipated consequences of Puritan behaviour in connection with economic activity. Rational action so pursued leads to an outcome which is the reverse of that which had initially been sought: worldly goods result from a religious imperative which, for Luther and for Calvin, values material wealth as little as did Catholicism. In short, the economic consequences of the capitalist spirit, and by extension of the capitalist system, are unanticipated at the macrosocial level; they are the unsought outcomes of religious ascetic behaviour deriving from the mechanism of proving oneself, of confirmation.

Proving oneself assumes a different form when emphasis is placed upon the social aspect of human behaviour, rather than on the interiorised psychological anxiety of the believer. As every reader of the *Protestant Ethic* knows, Weber also makes use of the mechanism of confirmation in his essay on American Protestant sects, which was based on his observations during a visit to the United States in 1904. Proving oneself no longer operates here on a psychological level, as a relationship between the believer and his God, as an interiorised dialogue in which the believer weighs his actions in respect of what he considers to be the accomplishment of the task imposed upon him by God. In the American sects, this mechanism assumes a social dimension, for proving oneself is now linked to the group of believers. There is, of course, considerable sociological significance in the opposition between a sect as a community of the elect who choose and mutually recognise one another and the Church as an institution dispensing grace, for in the second instance proving oneself before a group of believers does not entail the rationalisation of life as a whole.[1]

Economic relationships are very much facilitated when the individual is able to become a member of an association rigorous in regard to individual morality, since adherence to the religious sect is subject to verification (only the pure are admitted) and the member "had to *prove* [*bewähren*] repeatedly that he was endowed with these qualities" (Weber 1948: 320):

> Furthermore—and this is the main point in this instance—membership was again acquired through balloting after investigation and a determination of moral worth. And hence the badge in the buttonhole meant, "I am a gentleman patented after investigation and probation [*Bewährung*] and guaranteed by my membership". Again, this meant, in business life above all, tested *credit worthiness*. (1948: 308)

Proving oneself is closely and universally supervised by the community of believers. Weber does not conceal the fact that some of those assisting at the ceremony he witnessed in the United States attached little credence to it as a purely religious event and considered it primarily in terms of the direct economic benefits sought. By the beginning of the twentieth century, the economic effect was no longer involuntary or unanticipated; it was rather the goal of a rational action taken in order to arrive at given ends, although initially the action had been value oriented. Puritanism had become purely utilitarian.

It is useful to draw attention to this configuration so that we might properly appreciate the distinction made by Weber between proving oneself before a sect and communal or religious discipline. He noted that,

---

[1] This distinction between a church as an institution dispensing grace and a sect as a community of the pure, is an important element in Weber's sociology of religion; there is a very clear formulation of this distinction at the beginning of his essay *Hinduism and Buddhism* (Weber 1920–21 II: 6ff.). Weber was extremely pleased when Troeltsch adopted this distinction in his own work (1911a: 331–43).

while the sect did have the capacity to control and supervise its members, the discipline exercised by the church over its congregation was likewise capable of certifying the kind of behaviour expected on the part of the individual (2002: 103–4; 1948: 316–17). But Weber felt that there was an important difference: in the first case, discipline was sought and desired by the believer, while in the second case it was imposed externally, and so presumed mechanisms of authority and control that bore only on specific actions and events and not upon the conduct of life as a whole.

> According to all experience there is no stronger means of breeding traits than through the necessity of holding one's own in the circle of one's associates. The continuous and unobtrusive ethical discipline of the sects was, therefore, related to authoritarian church discipline as rational breeding and selection are related to ordering and forbidding. (1948: 320)[2]

This passage alludes to a third mechanism, rational "training" and, by extension, the application of strict discipline. This idea recurs in his discussion of the literate caste in China, whose work on the administrative problems of patrimonial princes was conducted with a practical and political rationalism of immense scope (Weber 1920–21: 398–99). A position among the literati was not hereditary, since it depended upon learned literary competence (ibid.: 396). The system of examination that opened the way into the literati was especially severe and rigorous. The rate of failure was high, and even success had implications for the individual's life as a whole:

> Even if the candidate had succeeded in passing the higher examinations with their rigorous assessment—in the assessment cells of the examination centres death from suicide was not unusual and was taken, according to the charismatic conception of the examination as a magical "trial", as a proof of the sinful turn of life of the person concerned—and if he did then enter office, ordered by his rank in the examination he had passed and by patronage, for the rest of his life he still remained under the supervision of the school. (ibid.: 416–17)

We shall come back to these remarks on schooling later, but first we have to consider how Weber might have continued his work into the eighteenth century. At the end of the *Protestant Ethic*, Weber announced

---

[2] In this passage from Weber, "breeding" and "discipline" are both translations of *Zucht* and *Züchtung*, which capture the sense of compulsion and domination. Weber could have used the term *Disziplin* but chose instead to associate the control of persons with that of animals. Where the English translation has "breeding" the French has *education*, which obscures this allusion. [KT]

what he would have to do in order to complete the work he had started in 1904:

> The task before us is rather to indicate the significance (only touched on in this sketch) of ascetic rationalism for the content of the *ethic* of the *social* economy, that is, for the type of organization and the functions of social communities, from the conventicler to the state. Then its relationship to humanist rationalism and its ideals and cultural influences, to the development of philosophical and scientific empiricism, and to technological development and the arts must be analyzed. Then finally its growth from the beginnings in the inner-worldly asceticism of the Middle Ages to its dissolution into pure utilitarianism must be charted *historically* and through the individual areas of expansion of ascetic religiosity. (2002: 121–22)

What happens once Puritanism turns into pure utilitarianism?[3] Must we think that the functioning of capitalism in the "iron age" has become a system in which actors do not need moral justification for their economic acts? Could we believe that they are able to pass into a sociodicy, a psychological support lending the rich and powerful a justification of what, in its absence, is only a statement of fact? We know that Weber responds to this question in the negative[4] when he directs attention to the ethical assurance that the seventeenth century bequeaths to the eighteenth:

---

[3] The link between theology and utilitarianism was very strong in the latter half of the eighteenth century. Elie Halévy emphasised that Jeremy Bentham's principles of utilitarian philosophy were popularised by two men of the church: Joseph Priestley, a dissenter, and William Paley, an Anglican (1901 I: 32–35). In his interesting anthology concerning religion and utilitarianism (1988), James E. Crimmins highlights six philosophers (four of whom were ordained) who founded their ethics upon the principle of utility. It could also be noted that the theological aspect of political economy—Smith's science of the legislator—is today increasingly recognised, both for the eighteenth century (Hill 2001; Dermange 2003) and for the nineteenth (Nelson 1991). Historically speaking, therefore, Weber's proposition can be seen as strongly connected to the manner in which utilitarian philosophy developed—a line of argument with which Troeltsch was in agreement (1911a: 95).

[4] "The fortunate person was rarely content with the mere fact of his own good fortune. He needed more than that, he wanted to have the *right* to it. He has to convince himself that he 'deserves' his good fortune, and, above all, that he deserves it in comparison to others. And he also needs to believe that the person who is not the recipient of similar good fortune receives only that which is fitting. Good fortune has to be 'legitimate'. If one understands by the general expression 'fortune' all the benefits of honour, power, possessions, and pleasure, then this is the most general rubric under which religion had to perform its service of legitimation: the theodicy of good fortune. Religion legitimates both the outward and internal interests of the rulers, the rich, the victorious, the healthy, in short, all those who enjoy good fortune. Theodicy, as religious legitimation, is firmly rooted in the deep (and 'pharisaic') needs of men and women, and in this sense it is easy to understand, even though it is often insufficiently considered in its effect" (Weber 2004: 60).

What that religiously vibrant era of the seventeenth century bequeathed to its utilitarian heir was, however, above all a tremendously clear—indeed, we can confidently say a *pharisaically* clear—conscience when it came to making money, provided only that it was lawfully done. The last remnant of "Deo placere non potest" disappeared. A *specifically middle-class ethic of the calling* arose. (ibid.: 118)

However, in *Protestant Ethic* Weber says very little more about the mechanisms through which such a good conscience might be maintained, diffused and justified once a religious foundation has lost its force. Instead, he emphasises the "mechanical" and "constraining" character of the capitalist system, once it has become established:

> *Today's* capitalist economic order is a monstrous cosmos, into which the individual is born and which in practice, for him, at least as an individual, is simply a given, an immutable shell, in which he is obliged to live. It forces on the individual, to the extent that he is caught up in the relationship of the "market", the norms of its economic activity. The manufacturer who consistently defies these norms will just as surely be forced out of business as the worker who cannot or will not conform will be thrown out of work. (ibid.: 13)

There is some pathos in this, leading Weber into a somewhat surprising position: that there is no longer any justification for this behaviour, leaving as sole support only agonistic passion (ibid.: 120–21).

On grounds that Weber himself provides, one can doubt whether such a position is tenable. First of all, the pharisaic need for legitimation remains, and this has its demands. For no longer is it so easy to produce credible, and hence admissible, legitimation, nor motivation to inner-worldly ascetic action.

Secondly, contemporary economic sociology has shown that, for example, competitive behaviour in financial markets has its own specific culture. Even in places devoted entirely to the pursuit of profit, traders persist in behaving in terms of a distinction between what is thought to be a legitimate pursuit of gain and that which is universally condemned as sheer opportunism (Abolafia 1996). Nonetheless, research in the Parisian market during the late 1990s showed just how many traders were interested in finding a justification for their considerable financial gains (Godechot 2000). This kind of finding is not limited to financial markets; the work of Neil Fligstein (1990) has demonstrated that industrial competition is strongly influenced by the state and by the negotiation of rules which establish the legal framework for industrial competition, as well as by the training provided by business schools. It is therefore difficult to agree with Weber when he talks in terms of a competitive process devoid of all moral and cultural support as a condition of existence for inhabitants of the "iron cage".

Thirdly, Weber was right when he listed science—in which the Puritans were, of course, especially interested (Merton 1938)—as a form of rational education which, right up to the present, has been a central vector of European modernity, and hence of utilitarianism. A sociological approach to this issue—and here Weber and Durkheim are clearly at one—would seek out the means by which the thought objects of the virtuosi of science, and of pedagogy and political economy, become mass phenomena: what social supports enable one to pass from an epoch where the "afterlife was everything" (Weber 2002: 105) to one in which the economic has taken over this role?

WEBER'S THESIS AND THE DURKHEIMIAN APPROACH

We saw in the previous chapter that Durkheim's lectures on the educational system dealt in part with the Reformation period, which Weber had studied. In this chapter we have seen that for Weber education was a "method", one social form among others furthering the rationalisation of existence, and that this method could become of central importance in fabricating the ethos of a dominant class (the Chinese literati). We have also seen that Weber thought education to be one of the important conduits through which the seventeenth century led up to the present day, alongside the discipline of sects.

At this point Durkheim's thinking on education and the sociology of knowledge extends Weber's work in an interesting direction. If we put together figures 7.1 and 8.1, where we synthesised Durkheim's analysis of Cartesianism and Weber's analysis of Protestantism, some structural similarities become apparent. First of all, Durkheim and Weber are equally concerned to define the social mechanisms (for Weber, saving the souls; for Durkheim, the schooling practices of the Jesuits) securing the diffusion of religious belief in the world. They also both emphasise the social mechanisms (for Weber, proving oneself before God or before the group as a constraint on the faithful; for Durkheim, academic competition) in operation at the level of individual behaviour. Finally, both emphasise the autonomy of the sphere with which they deal, since the abstract vision of classical rationalism is for Durkheim an involuntary emergent effect, while for Weber it is the bourgeois ethic of hard work. This structural similarity in their work can help strengthen the relationship drawn between religion and economy by contemporary economic sociology, which has not yet taken up Weber's interest in the historical origins of current socioeconomic conditions.

Individual Motivation, Values and Socioeconomic Behaviour

The Durkheimians did not ignore Weber's work, although so far as we know, he ignored theirs.[5] If there has never been a Durkheim-Weber dialogue, there is nevertheless one between the Durkheimians and Weber, and it should be no surprise that it involves the second research programme in economic sociology. Beyond this, the common features of the two approaches were long ago noted by Talcott Parsons (1949) and Raymond Aron (1967).

It is, however, problematic to think in terms of a true dialogue. Durkheim abandoned political economy very quickly and turned his efforts to a lengthy, and not entirely successful, effort in the institutionalisation of sociology (Karady 1976, 1979), while Weber, trained primarily as a lawyer, became a professor of political economy and his appreciation of the institutionalisation of sociology was accordingly partial. Moreover, the First World War introduced a lasting and major caesura in normal scholarly communications between France and Germany, quite apart from the usual effects of scholarly rivalry.[6] Finally, dialogue was made difficult because of differences in the methods employed; the attention that Weber paid to psychology, the meaning agents gave to their actions, could only distance Durkheim and the Durkheimians from this kind of "finalist" sociology (to use their terminology), all the more so given that the notion of involuntary outcomes from goal-directed action failed to fit into their analytical framework.

---

[5] A survey of the leading periodicals in political economy and sociology between 1900 and 1930, and covering Britain, France, Italy and the United States, showed that Durkheimian publications were much more open to Weber's work than any of the other publications (Steiner 1992). It seems at least reckless for Grossein (2000: i) to complain that a Durkheimian like Granet failed to cite Weber in his book *La religion des chinois*—a book lacking both bibliography and footnotes, so that no sources are named at all. Whereas nobody comments on the fact that Weber, who read French perfectly well, never cited any of the work on the sociology of religion published in *L'année sociologique* (with the minor exception of Bouglé's text on castes, which is mentioned in the bibliographic introduction to *Hinduism and Buddhism* [Weber 1920–21 II: 1]). Aron has written that Mauss told him that he had seen a complete set of the *Année* in Weber's office (Aron 1967: 545), but Weber was in any case notoriously parsimonious with his acknowledgements.

[6] In this regard, a letter from Mauss to Roger Bastide of 3 November 1936 is of interest: "I have received your little book [*Eléments de sociologie religieuse*]. One of those whose work you especially favour, Max Weber, was someone with whom Durkheim, Hubert and myself had the least contact. Of course, while he was happy to borrow from our work, what he did during the war—a time when everything was excusable—gave rise to some irritation. But he restricted himself to expressing opinions, many of which are suggestive, and some valuable, but none of which, without exception, are proven. This regard for Max Weber is also one of the things that bothers me about the large book by my cousin, Raymond Aron" (cited in Grossein 2000: i).

Nonetheless, we can identify the opening up of a dialogue in the first series of the *Année sociologique* (Steiner 1992), continued and developed between the wars by Halbwachs and Mauss (Marcel 2000). Halbwachs was particularly interested in Weber's work between the wars (Craig 1983: 280–81), as can be seen from several articles and reviews[7] as well as from the number of reviews devoted to works that discussed Weber's principal thesis.[8] Halbwachs also drew on Weber to bring social representations and economic behaviour together, or in other words, to realign the quantitative with the subjective approach to the social.

Let us begin with the text that Halbwachs devoted to the updating and rectification of Durkheim's account of suicide. As we know, Durkheim rejected the motivations of an actor as an explanatory base and instead pointed to large-scale collective forces. Halbwachs challenged this from the first:

> We will make two arguments against this very well-defined distinction between motivation and cause. Durkheim's thesis would seem plausible if there were no relationship at all between the action of such motivations and the outcome of juddering collective sentiment. But this is *not* the case. (1930:12)

He argues that motivations are not randomly distributed in society, but depend upon the circumstances of social structure, the position that the individual has in it and the forms through which individual situations and sentiments can be expressed in a given society.[9] By making a connection between social structure and individual motivation and taking the latter seriously, Halbwachs placed himself in between Durkheim and Weber. On the one hand, he argued for the linkage of psychology and

---

[7] Halbwachs's role here is extremely important; he published two articles on Weber and the thesis of the *Protestant Ethic* (1925, 1929) and signed four of the five reviews related to Weber's work which appeared in the first volume of the second series of *L'année* in 1925. His interest in Weber's sociological writings did not wane; reference to Weber remains frequent in his subsequent work, as well as in his teaching at the Ecole Polytechnique (Halbwachs 1937: 391). There are also lengthy disquisitions on Weber in his study of social classes (Halbwachs 1955: ch. 3).

[8] In the *Annales sociologiques*, Halbwachs reviewed R. H. Tawney's *Religion and the Rise of Capitalism*, Bernard Groethuysen's *Origines de l'esprit bourgeois en France*, H. M. Robertson's *Aspects of the Rise of Economic Individualism: A Criticism of Max Weber* and Amintore Fanfani's *Saggi di storia economica*. Simiand reviewed Henri Sée's *Les origines du capitalisme moderne* and another book by Fanfani, *Le origini dello spirito capitalisco in Italia*.

[9] This particular idea is developed particularly in a posthumously published article dealing with the expression of emotion: "Our emotions are subject to a genuine social discipline, such that with events of a particular kind, and in circumstances that often arise, it is society which directs how we are to behave" (Halbwachs 1947: 167). That should certainly be related to Mauss's piece entitled "The Obligatory Expression of Sentiment" (1921).

statistics; on the other, he emphasised changes in the values of this or that social group and the greater or lesser proximity of individuals to the values considered central to society. In this he went beyond a simple distinction between elite and mass, since values can be simultaneously multiple and hierarchised.

This line of thought can also be found in his commentary on the relationship between Protestantism and capitalism. Halbwachs rejects Veblen's argument that the success of Anglo-American industry is owed to an "instinct for workmanship" (1921; 1925: 253; 1955: 107), favouring instead Weber's explanation in terms of how moral qualities, initially thought to be humble, became central to a social group:

> The sole condition for the birth of the capitalist regime is that it [a morality founded in a vocation][10] was imposed not on some individuals, but upon a group, which is to say that it took the form of collective thought. It was necessary that it be presented as a morality accepted by a grouping of men. (Halbwachs 1925: 137)

The notion of motivation plays the role of a social cause in explaining individual behaviour, in that these motivations can be related to an axiological structure from which classes are more or less distanced:

> [General motivations such as ambition, saving, family spirit, etc.] are in everyone, for they are rooted in the group of which the individual is a member, and their form and intensity follow from conditions peculiar to the group, and in its relationship with other groups. We therefore invite the reader to join a scientific excursion through the social world. . . . We must fix our attention upon the diversity of human groups, identify the dominant collective representations in these groupings, their force and scope, and their limits. (Halbwachs 1955: 57–58)

The Durkheimian aspect of this proposition is obvious, where the accent falls upon the morality of the professional group as a collective representation; and so it is at the level of the group that motivations must be understood and statistically objectified. This applies in particular to economic representations, for these have a dual nature, elaborated by Halbwachs in respect of needs: "Needs, psychologists tell us, are psychic dispositions of a qualitative kind. However, they are susceptible to measurement, especially in their collective form. All that has to be done is to observe what is spent, and what importance is given to that which is

[10] The affinity here between Durkheim's focus upon professional groups and Weber's upon *Beruf* (calling, vocation, profession), requires emphasis, since what is usually translated into English as "calling" in *The Protestant Ethic* and as "vocation" in his later two lectures on politics and science is in fact the same term, *Beruf*. [KT]

bought" (ibid.: 166). These arguments are related to Halbwachs's interpretation of Weber's work, which, apart from the "conceptual theory of
economic sociology" to be found in the first two chapters of *Economy
and Society*, is treated by Halbwachs as "a kind of descriptive and concrete sociology serving as the point of departure and the experimental
foundation for abstract exposition" (1929: 86). He places a great deal of
emphasis upon the historical and empirical aspect of Weber's studies,[11]
and he does not fail to comment upon the statistical table with which
Weber begins *Protestant Ethic*. This is not mere anecdotal evidence, for
Weber's own procedures and arguments are not opposed to statistical
methods, even at the methodological level: Weber sees in statistics a
means of validating the causal imputations of a universal sociology
(Weber 1947: 85).

It is evident that Mauss shared Halbwachs's views here, despite the
reservations he expressed about Weber (see note 6, above). During the
interwar years, Mauss was a keen advocate of a convergence between
sociology and psychology (1924e), which involves therefore a diminution of the traditional objection Durkheim had made in respect of "finalist" sociologies. This development was linked with favourable public
statements regarding Weber, whether related to the convergence between
sociology and more specific domains, such as politics and economics
(Mauss 1927b: 291), or to his comprehensive methodology (Mauss 1934:
304).

Education, Morality and Life Conduct

The convergence with which we are here concerned involves, firstly, the
moral dimension of the religious and, secondly and conversely, the religious dimension of morality, as in Durkheim. If it is true that Weber was
careful to mark out the religious domain—which was the sole preoccupation of Protestant reformers, and not the moral reform of individuals—
the transition from Puritanism to utilitarianism was matched by an increasing preoccupation with morality from the point in the eighteenth
century where the influence of the religious life began to wane. It is at this
stage that Durkheim's approach can extend our understanding of the
hold of the economic vision of the world over men and women, introducing other mechanisms that provide a rational orientation for living a
practical life.

---

[11] "The generality of his views [on charisma and rationalisation] should not be allowed
to obscure the very large mass of factual material to be found in this work. This historical
and comparative study of all civilisations currently accessible to us uniquely extends our
economic horizon" (Halbwachs 1929: 87).

The relation of morality to religion is at the centre of the lecture Durkheim gave at the French Society for Philosophy in 1906.[12] The first step in his analysis involved a reference to Kant, so that he might define morality in terms of duty and obligation. He recapitulated the Durkheimian approach to the social, which becomes manifest in the existence of a sanction, and the notion of a positive sanction allowed Durkheim to add the desirability of a moral rule to the Kantian definition. This addition led Durkheim to consider the oppositions existing between utility and morality, the good and obligation, so that he might define the opposition between the economic and the moral as a tension, similar to the one that exists within the sacred, which is associated with both desire and fear—a theme that we have also seen at work in the opposition of gift and exchange, where Mauss deliberately makes use of the oxymoron "exchange-gift". The desirability of duty is not of the same kind as that which relates the individual to scarce and useful goods, but Durkheim does not skirt the key point that a constraining rule could be desired, even if this involved "a degree of hardship, some effort" (1906: 64). If, therefore, there is some kind of similarity between eudemonism and the moral life, Durkheim reassesses his antiutilitarian argument as follows:

> One can never derive obligation from what is desirable, since the specific character of obligation does, in some respect, do violence to desire. It is also impossible to derive obligation from the good, or vice versa, deduce altruism from egoism. (ibid.: 67)

This convergence with the sacred leads him to bring together morality and religion, then to develop a rationalist explanation of each of these, opening out into the sociology of collective ideation that he had called for since 1898.[13] Durkheim saw a close link between morality and religion, and it seemed to him impossible to understand the first without making reference to the second:[14]

---

[12] The text of this lecture and the following discussion was edited and published by Bouglé in *Sociologie et philosophie* (1924). That text is incomplete and includes a number of errors.

[13] At the end of his article on representations, Durkheim stated: "Regarding the processes through which these second-order social products [collective representations] are formed, while there is some analogy with that which we observe in the individual consciousness, it does have its own particular physiognomy. . . . There is a whole area of sociology that would need to investigate the laws of collective ideation where, so far, nothing has been done at all" (1898b: 45).

[14] The sacred character of morality is a central point in Durkheim's line of argument, and he reemphasised this in responding to a question from the auditorium: "Yes, I certainly seek to maintain the sacred character of morality, and I seek to maintain it not because it seems to me to meet this or that hope that I share, but because it is conveyed by facts themselves. Since morality appears everywhere in history marked by religion, it is impossible to entirely

Over the centuries, the moral life and the religious life have been inti-
mately connected, and even fused together; and still today one has to
say that this close union remains embedded in the consciousness of the
majority. . . . When two orders of facts have been so closely connected
for so long, when there has been such long-lasting kinship, it is impossible to completely disentangle them such that one becomes entirely
separate from the other. . . . Therefore, there has to be morality in religion and religion in morality. And indeed, today's morality is steeped
in religiosity. It is not that the foundation of religiosity has remained
unchanged, for it is certain that moral religiosity has tended to become
quite different from theological religiosity. The sacred character of
morality is not such that it should be left untouched by criticism, as
religion is. (ibid.: 69)

The writings that Durkheim devoted to education and ethics when he
arrived in Paris in 1902 gave him the chance to develop this issue. He
argued at some length that morality had, since the sixteenth century, been
subject to a process of secularisation. He related this process to the introduction of obligations into Christian religion which were increasingly
oriented toward man instead of toward God, then to Protestantism and
the marked decline in the practice of religious cults and, finally, to spiri-
tualist philosophy (1902–3/1961: 6–7), which implicitly opened the way
to a new ideal, the cult of the individual. This rapid historical *tour
d'horizon* introduced the idea of a profound similarity between morality
and religion in respect of the sequence: regulation of conduct, authority
and discipline. The first is one of the essential functions of morality (ibid.:
27), and the allusions he makes to anomie ("the evil of the infinite") and
to *effervescence* in the course of these lectures call to mind the arguments
of *Suicide*. Regulation cannot intervene without there being an authority
behind the rules which individuals accept—Durkheim's definition here
(ibid.: 87, 91) is surprisingly close to Weber's definition of charisma—an
authority to which individuals consciously submit themselves, for morality is more than a simple habit. Durkheim here defines moral conduct in
terms that would not be foreign to Weber, distinguishing axiological rationality from end-oriented rationality:

Here, for the act to be everything it should be, for the rule to be obeyed
as it ought to be, it is necessary for us to yield, not in order to avoid
disagreeable results or some moral or material punishment, but very

---

disentangle it from this character; it would otherwise cease to be itself. . . . Morality would
not be morality if it no longer had anything of a religious character in it. And the horror
that crime prompts is on every point comparable to that which sacrilege prompts among
believers" (1906: 101).

simply because we ought to, regardless of the consequences our conduct may have for us. One must obey a moral precept out of respect for it and for this reason alone. (ibid.: 30)

Regulatory authority therefore determines ends (ibid.: 47–48), ends which symbolise the collective, the social (ibid.: 61, 81–82). Religion and society belong to a collective level, having authority over the individual by regulating his behaviour through a discipline. But in religion authority is based upon transcendence, while the ideal upon which modern morality is founded requires that the individual be autonomous, that he accept discipline voluntarily.

Durkheim goes on to draw a parallel between the priest and the secular schoolteacher (ibid.: 155); there is a homology between the two functions to the extent that they play a central part in the methodical transmission of moral values. If the first draws upon transcendence and mysticism, the second invokes only an immanent reality (society), drawing upon rationalism, a principle opening a path to the autonomy of the will. Given these differences, he then traces a homology between the pairs priest-God and schoolteacher-society (1902d: 68), for in both cases there is the same objective: to form a new type of man, who undergoes a methodical education intended to imbue him with a certain ethos[15]—excepting the case of instantaneous conversion, as irrational and mystical for Weber as it is for Durkheim.

There is also something else that can be drawn from this passage by way of a sociological consideration of the schooling system. Here Durkheim had come very close to the issues that Weber had investigated in the *Protestant Ethic*, especially when Durkheim deals with the impact of the Jesuits on the French teaching system. In the previous chapter, we examined the *content* of this education, seeking its impact on the content of representations related to classical rationalism. But Durkheim was also very much concerned to reveal the social mechanism located within the *form* of such teaching.

In his survey of Renaissance pedagogic doctrine, Durkheim examined the views of Rabelais (erudition and the pursuit of science as hubris) and Erasmus (humanism), showing that they were both markedly aristocratic in character, honour and glory being the ordering principles (Durkheim 1904–5: 245–50). This aristocratic style of teaching created a distance vis

---

[15] "[Christianity] took the view that to form a man one need not imbue his mind with particular ideas, or give him specific routine; rather such forming meant creating in him a general will and mental disposition, lending him a general perspective upon the world" (Durkheim 1904–5: 37). Hence: "To preach is to educate" (ibid.: 30), for in both cases—Christianity or the modern school—it involved the same thing, the notion of duty (ibid.: 241–42; 1961: 6, 24–25).

à vis the *vie sérieuse*, and Durkheim considered that even Montaigne's "pedagogic nihilism" was incapable of significantly altering the situation. The Jesuits were also part of this history, but in their case one enters the domain of "practice", the institutional inscription of pedagogic ideas without which the latter are, sociologically, nothing. Nonetheless, the case of the Jesuits poses a major problem, since while they prompted resistance on the part of all those powers—the state, the clergy, the university, the *parlements*—that mattered at that time (ibid.: 269), it has to be said that they had enormous success among the elites, who entrusted them with the education of their children. Durkheim asks: To what did they owe their success? The answer cannot be found in the content of their teaching, which Durkheim thought to be a pale shadow of the humanist programme, suited only to the defence of Catholicism. The answer lay rather in the form taken by their teaching. This had two characteristics: firstly, the Jesuits instituted the principle of a continuous and personal contact between master and pupil; secondly, they instituted the principle of emulation among pupils (ibid.: 296–98).

The class was transformed into a specifically social milieu, with a principle of authority (the master omnipresent and in continuous personal relationship with his pupils) that secured discipline and regularity of conduct and a permanent motivation spurring each pupil and each group of pupils (emulation as competition). This translated into a finely graded hierarchy ranking both pupils and groups of pupils according to their school performance. This condition of permanent scholarly competition led to a situation in which pupils were obliged to constantly show their effort, in order to confirm their place in the group and maintain it: "The condition of perpetual competition in which the pupils lived spurred them to stretch their intelligence and their will, this becoming a necessity for them. At the same time, the close supervision to which they were subject made shirking less easy. They felt themselves guided, supported, encouraged. Everything induced them to display effort" (ibid.: 300). This new form of social functioning is related to the rise of the individual in seventeenth-century Europe: education was to connect the individual as such with his "*amour propre*, in the sense of personal dignity" (ibid.: 302).

Durkheim's approach here converges with that of Weber. The modern schooling system is based on a social mechanism that emphasises the need to affirm oneself within the group as the means of forming the modern ethic. The schooling system that the Jesuits created set up a mechanism of affirmation and confirmation of (scholarly) value of the individual before a group of his peers. By contrasting the discipline of the Church with the process of proving oneself before the sect, Weber called attention to the character of "voluntary submission" involved in the mechanism as well as the role of personal interest in self-affirmation before one's peers. Durkheim, for his part, contrasted religious discipline, with its mystical character, imposed upon reason from without, to school discipline, with its desired and desirable morality that seeks to promote the freedom of individual action within the collective and operates through an *amour propre* akin to self-interest.

As a social mechanism permanently at work, scholarly competition forms an ethos which endures beyond the period of school attendance and effects a lasting alteration to individual behaviour. Bourdieu examined this point in the chapters he devoted to the preparatory classes and examinations for the *grandes écoles* (1989).

Although Bourdieu's work was intended to disclose the relationships between the schooling system and the legitimation of domination in contemporary France,[16] he was led to treat the schooling system as a social mechanism producing a methodical rationalisation of life. He dealt with the preparatory classes and examinations—and also, of course, if rather allusively, with the formation of any elite whose selection involves ascetic and competitive isolation—as a sacred order separated from the profane, where university students were marked off from those who had not completed higher education (ibid.: 140, 166). Bourdieu noted in the preparatory classes a number of traits of "methodical" schooling which parallel those that Durkheim highlighted in the Jesuit colleges. The preparatory class institutes a "logic of urgency" (ibid.: 117) which, associated with the anxiety created by the examination (ibid.: 121), leads to heightened scholarly productivity—compared with that of the university student (ibid.: 109, 132–33, 137–37)—that is an intensive use of time (ibid.: 114–15) to which one can apply to the letter, directly, several of the sayings that Weber took from Franklin's *Poor Richard's Almanac* regarding time as a scarce resource and as a touchstone for the conduct of a rational

---

[16] Bourdieu conceived the schooling system in a quite specific way. He opposed the notion that it could be studied as a technique for the transmission of knowledge and instead placed all the emphasis on its symbolic function (the legitimation of domination being produced by, and underwriting, school knowledge) (1989: 101–2). As a result, he denied all technical validity in the mastering of knowledge, or any specific intellectual quality in those who acquired it, a proposition so difficult to maintain that he was compelled to retreat when referring to Weber, who accepted the idea that strong qualitative differences between individuals exist, involving a constant increase in the technical knowledge required of any individual (1989: 535 n. 6). This strategy is explained by the fact that Bourdieu gives priority in his sample to the arts preparatory classes (with which he is clearly familiar at first hand) to the detriment of the scientific classes. Such a thesis represents a general problem encountered in the previous chapter: can one reduce intellectual rationalisation to a *symbolic phenomenon*, or should one consider that rationalisation incorporates a *technical dimension of the practical teaching of nature* as an essential element? To put it bluntly, one does not select the same individuals when asking them to master Tacitus or Poincaré, because the material content of these symbolic forms is not without sociological significance.

life. This competitive mechanism is very close to what Durkheim describes for the seventeenth century; an examination is an essential procedure of self-confirmation whereby success lifts the anxiety of the scholar
and qualifies the individual for life—which is why Bourdieu coined the
term "state nobility". Entry into this modern "nobility" allows the individual to participate symbolically, as in Weber's description of the Puritan
sect, in the success of all other members of the same *grande école*, however distant a particular individual might be from the social success in
which he participates through one of his peers. The mechanism identified
by Durkheim remains at work in contemporary schooling and always
produces, if one follows Bourdieu, a result in terms of the rationalisation
of life.

One last thing has to be said. In the Weberian argument, the faithful
seeks unceasingly signs of his religious security, and this leads to the constant reproduction of this ascetic work upon him and upon the world.
The examination process, by contrast, does not extend through life in
this way; instead, it has a different effect, which Bourdieu isolates in the
term "state nobility": the process separates candidates from other pupils
and in a more or less definitive way. "Successful examination candidate"
has fixed and unchanging validity for the remainder of the individual's
life, and this condition opens up two possible kinds of behaviour. First of
all, in conformity with the Weberian idea of proving oneself, the individual is obliged to avoid discredit, to maintain his "scholarly rank" so
that success in the examination can have an impact upon the practical
rationalisation of life beyond the immediate period of schooling. Secondly, recapitulating the argument advanced by Troeltsch, the impact of
the examination comes to provide "scholarly security" that can never be
lost, whatever the circumstances, lending an enduring confidence and
legitimacy to the individual in carrying out his business. The individual is
therefore able to devote himself to activity in the world, strengthened by
a quality acquired at an early age. Pragmatically irrational, this assurance
provides great power to the graduate.

By taking this route through the sociology of the schooling system,
Durkheim's approach advances in a very similar direction to that of Weber,
demonstrating how the intellectual transformations taking place in Europe since the Renaissance are inscribed and end up creating a new type
of character, characterised by an individualism whose activity is oriented
by and towards economy and science. Durkheim's analysis permits the
isolation of a social mechanism (scholarly competition) whose presence
remains undimmed. Moreover, the fact that Durkheim follows the approach of the humanists complements Weber's study, who in the closing
pages of the *Protestant Ethic* suggests a similar evolution by fixing attention on the point at which there is a transition from religion to morality,

that is, from one representation of duty to another. But Weber did not elaborate his remarks. It is worth devoting some more time here to an examination of an exemplary case that provides an explanation of the modern economic ethos.

Rationality and the "Imitation of One's God"

Durkheim considers that the essence of religious morality is rooted in the individual's desire to resemble his God:

> God is not only conceived of as a lawmaker and the guardian of the moral order: he also represents an ideal which the individual strives to realize. To become like God, to seek to live in God's image, to merge with Him; such is the basic principle of all religious morality. (1902–3/1961: 103–4)

This general affirmation is exactly confirmed if one considers the way in which, in the late seventeenth and early eighteenth centuries, some *virtuosi* of religious rationalisation who were also major scientists established a connection between purely religious imperatives and the daily practice of individuals. This linkage of the religious and scientific domains allows us to make a connection between the social sphere at the heart of seventeenth-century European thought and what would become the big issue of the nineteenth century: science and the technical mastery of the world.[17] Leibniz played a key role in this, and we will here link his work to that of Malebranche, to which it is closely related.

The two writers do not belong to the sphere of Puritanism in Weber's sense; Leibniz is a Lutheran and Malebranche a Catholic, a member of the Order of Oratorians. These confessional associations explain why they felt the need to discuss the rationality of divine action.[18] Calvinist predestination conceived divine creation—the ineffable decree—as beyond all human understanding, which consequently does away with the problem of theodicy associated with Leibniz's name. The problem concerns the existence of evil in a world created by an infinitely benevolent God, and the originality of the solution put forward by Leibniz and Malebranche lies in their use of the most advanced contemporary mathematics to explain the rational nature of divine action.[19]

[17] Apart from the fact that reformed religion played a powerful role in the positive valuation of science through natural philosophy, both in Britain and on the Continent, as Merton has demonstrated (1938).

[18] Troeltsch (1911b: 106) remarks that Leibniz was more Catholic than Calvinist, or even than Lutheran (see also 1911a: 636).

[19] The expression used by Leibniz in opposing Hobbes shows that the interpretation here is not in any respect retrospective: "Mr. Hobbes claims that the wisdom attributed to God

Malebranche published his work before Leibniz, his interpretation of the creation placing emphasis on the "simplicity of paths". God is constrained by his perfection to act according to the simplicity of paths, which characterises the Order to which God himself is subordinated.

> An excellent worker must proportion his action to his work, he does nothing by complex means that he can do by simpler, and he never works without a goal, and he never engages in useless effort. From that it must be concluded that God, discovering in the infinite treasure of his wisdom an infinity of possible worlds as the necessary outcomes of the laws of movement that he could establish, determines to create that which could be produced and preserved by the simplest of laws, or which must be the most perfect in relation to the simplicity of the paths necessary to its production and preservation. (1680: 185 §13)

This is a remarkable argument: God created the most perfect of possible worlds, most perfect with respect to the constraints that his rationality imposes upon him; he chooses a small number of simple paths, having compared and weighed all the options (ibid.: 245 §7). Of course, God could have created a world more perfect in respect of the net outcome—with less evil from the human point of view—but he could only achieve this by employing a large number of special laws or by multiplying miracles—in other words, by creating a world less perfect if one takes account of the process of producing the world itself.

Leibniz shares the views of Malebranche regarding the simplicity of paths and its meaning in terms of the rationality of divine action, but he diverges from Malebranche on the issue of occasional causes (God does not intervene directly but allows the laws of nature that he created to run their course), favouring instead the notion of a preestablished harmony which allows one to restrict the "supernatural in the beginning of things" (1710: 43). For Leibniz, divine action, and hence human action, is not determined by a priori truths, truths which are the concern of logic and mathematics and which are characterised by the fact that their negation is either impossible or contradictory. Action is determined by a posteriori truths, those of which one can say that they define causal relations in the world which God has created but have no logical necessity since God could have arranged things differently. In other words, God cannot make A be A and not-A at the same time (a logical contradiction), but he could arrange that kinetic energy be expressed other than in the formula $\frac{1}{2} mv^2$. Since the course of the world is not predetermined, if there is

---

does not involve a logical discussion of the relation of means to ends, but that it is an incomprehensible attitude, attributed to an incomprehensible nature so that it might be honoured." (1710: 385).

freedom of action one needs to know by what rules action occurs—the action of God and, by extension, the action of men, who are so many monads, so many "little gods" (ibid.: 147). The originality of the Leibnizean solution lies in the use he makes of mathematical tools, which he develops at the same time as Newton (differential and integral calculus), to define the "principle of fitness" or the "choice of the best", which is to say, the best proportion between the result and the cost of an action.[20]

> However, this supreme wisdom, joined to a kindness no less infinite than that, cannot avoid choosing the best. For just as a lesser evil is a kind of good, so a lesser good is a kind of evil; it presents an obstacle to a greater good; and it would be something for God to correct in his actions, if he had the means of doing better. And just as in mathematics when there is no maximum, nor minimum, nothing finally distinct, everything is equal; or when that cannot be, nothing at all is done; one can say as far as perfect wisdom is concerned, which is no less regulated than mathematics, that if there were no best (*optimum*) among all possible worlds, God would not have made any." (ibid.: §8)

In other words, Leibniz pushes Malebranche's argument by making an analogy with the mathematics which permit the expression of instrumental rationality in the form of a problem of constrained optimisation. And this form of rationality is human rationality—Leibniz treats rationality, or at the very least wisdom, as a human quality, that is, it is human to the extent that it approaches that of the Creator, for it is a moral necessity that "the wisest be obliged to choose the best" (ibid.: §230)

This brings us back to Durkheim's argument that the essence of religious morality is to be found in the imitation of its God. It is interesting to find this argument in the writings of Cartesian philosophers, advocates of the classical rationalism that Durkheim respected, even if he considered their approach superseded or inadequate as a way of accounting for the social. It is also interesting to find this argument within the debate over rationalisation of the religious conception of the world, and to see how the linkage of religion to science could be made, a linkage with which Weber wanted to finish his book on the Protestant ethic. But again, it is important to find here a consideration whose *material* content (and there is nothing ineluctable about this content) can be found in the way in which classical rationalism comes to be employed in the physical sciences; in the engineering sciences, which from the nineteenth century on contributed increasingly to the practical transformation of the world; and in political economy, after which utilitarian economists, smitten with mathematics,

---

[20] This point is highlighted in Halbwachs's text dedicated to the work of Leibniz (1907: ch. 5).

reunited the elements (rationality, mathematics and utilitarianism) that can be found in the work of Leibniz.

Attention should be drawn to the fact that defining rationality by the mathematical technique of optimisation is not limited to the level of instrumental rationality, since it equally belongs to the level of axiology. If one agrees that there is nothing more desirable for the individual than to act in imitation of God, how can one escape the idea that rational action defined in terms of constrained optimisation is that which is most fair and most desirable, as well as most efficient? In other words, the principles of economic and technical rationality have as much to do with justice, the good, and the love of God as they have to do with efficiency. From this perspective, the transition from religion to morality was eased by the route which led through utilitarianism.

THE ECONOMIC ETHOS IN THE "IRON AGE" AND POLITICAL ECONOMY

The "elective affinity" between the Protestant ethic and the spirit of capitalism depends, according to Max Weber, on the general affirmation that an economic behaviour can only manifest itself as a mass phenomenon if it is considered legitimate. On the cusp of the modern world, from the sixteenth to the seventeenth centuries, this legitimation could only be diffused, Weber argued, as the most expansive form of belief: religion.

There is no reason to believe that this need for legitimation, made up in its pharisaic form of the theodicy of good fortune, ceases when Puritanism transforms itself into utilitarianism and religion in Europe cedes its function to a secularised morality (McIntyre 1988; Schneewind 1998) in which virtue replaces faith (interest taking the place of virtue). Nonetheless, from the eighteenth century onwards, the elements of the problems are modified in respect of a central issue that Weber sought to demonstrate. In effect, the *creation* of a religious doctrine valorising activity in the world via the rational conduct of life is very different from the maintenance and adaptation of such a form of conduct. If the reference to religion is in the nineteenth and twentieth centuries neither possible to mobilise nor necessary, what are the institutions that allow the production, in new forms, of the values and beliefs capable of overcoming the "psychological barriers" to the maintenance and transformation of rational conduct once this is directly associated with, and valorised by, economic activity?

The Reproduction of the Economic Ethos

Two texts which explicitly develop some of Weber's ideas (Bendix 1956; Boltanski & Chiapello 1999) have advanced the idea that an economic vocational ethic continued to develop once it had formed among Puritan sects. Bendix is interested in the forms of justification of industrialisation, presenting a comparative study of Russia and Britain in the nineteenth century, and America and the Soviet Union in the twentieth. Boltanski and Chiapello examine the differences between the spirit of capitalism of the 1960s and 1970s and that which developed in France during the 1990s.[21]

As Boltanski and Chiapello rightly say, "systemic constraints upon actors are insufficient in themselves to sustain their engagement. The constraint has to be interiorised and justified" (1999: 45). It is here that either ideology intervenes, understood as "All ideas which are espoused by or for those who exercise authority in economic enterprises, and which seek to explain and justify that authority" (Bendix 1956: 2, n. 1) or the spirit of capitalism as understood by Boltanski and Chiapello, "a framework of beliefs associated with the capitalist order which contribute to the justification and support of this order, legitimating modes of action and dispositions consistent with it" (1999: 46, see also 42)

Both studies are directed to the systems for justifying the position of economic elites as well as to the systems capable of mobilising the energies of persons directly implicated in economic activity. The material employed involves texts widely diffused in society—such as the "New Thought" movement discussed by Bendix (1956: 259–63) or texts more specific to the industrial milieu (professional engineering and management journals) or business literature (the manuals and popularisations studied by Boltanski and Chiapello [1999: 93–228]). They both also emphasise the notion that capitalism cannot function without ideological support, conceived as a discourse lending a meaning to the action and participation of a number of actors, in the absence of which political and economic institutions cannot function.

The Durkheimian intuition is that the schooling system plays a decisive role when it becomes a central institution through which the cognitive capital embodied in the individual is produced, through the transmission of knowledge from one generation to the next; it also plays a role as an instrument for rationalising the conduct of life, at least for those involved in the mechanism producing schooling values of the sort described by Bourdieu in his study of French preparatory classes. It should, however, be noted that the *material content* of education has also to be taken into account, since the mathematical principles of optimisation and those of

---

[21] We leave here to one side the work of Grœthuysen (1927), which is devoted to the problem of legitimation of bourgeois capitalist economic activity in seventeenth-century France. This study is, however, of interest, showing how (Catholic) religion ceded its position to Enlightenment ethics, such that the bourgeois Christian gradually became simply a "gentleman" (*honnête homme*).

economic theory are at the core of the economic constructs which are valorised by, and valorise, the vocational framework.

This does not at all involve a duplication of Weber's findings, since the methods employed by rational education cannot be the same as those used in Puritan sects, added to which these methods engage rather differently with the rationalisation of life conduct. This enables us to develop Weber's ideas through the use of what we have discovered in Durkheim and the Durkheimians. How, to use terms very similar to those of Weber, has the economic ethos of the "human type" characteristic of modern economic and technical society been diffused and altered? How, to use the terms that Mauss employed in concluding *The Gift*, can one say that *homo œconomicus* in the form of a "calculating machine" is before us? In other words, how can this type be modelled through emerging representations of economic activity and knowledge disseminated by educational systems as they have existed since the nineteenth century?

The Market, Industry and Political Economy

Those activities which we call "economic" have two aspects: market activity (and the economic theory that corresponds to it, the theory of markets) and industrial activity (and industrial science, physical theory applied by the engineer to production). The junction between these two aspects is not so simple to achieve as it might seem; it took until the second half of the nineteenth century for it to be realised on an intellectual level, and then until the second half of the twentieth for it to propagate fully throughout the academic world and daily life, including in the agents active in the fields of commerce and industry.

The practical rationality at work in economic activity works through economists as teachers and advisers, whether of princes or of firms; but it also includes engineers, since it is through their work that economic practice is inscribed in the industrial domain. These socially valorised representations transmit and lend shape to rational conduct through an elective affinity with the immanent economic representations which impose rationality upon everyday economic life, as Weber argued. Taking account of this dual dimension has considerable significance for the sociology of economic knowledge once one includes its moral aspect, its material content and the vectors through which it diffuses, and its temporality, all of which have over the last half-century rendered this duality a mass phenomenon. In concluding this chapter, we will sketch out the broad outlines of the sociological interpretation of economic discourse that emerges from the Durkheimian and Weberian problematic.

Firstly, economic discourse has a moral content and contributes to the formation of an ideal (the optimal management of the common good of a specific social group) justifying the deployment of economic activity and implying both political rationalisation (Hirschman 1977: 67–86) and social rationalisation, if only through a struggle against indolence, corruption and poverty (Grœthuysen 1927: conclusion). Many studies have noted the importance of moral considerations in the social sciences, identifying a kind of common ground which is of interest for the history of political economy (Hirschman 1984b). Following Hirschman and Nelson, it can be said that this ideal has much to do with the alliance between economic development and technical progress as a means employed by man to master both nature and society.

The moral dimension of economic rationality can be related directly to its religious foundation. If the rationality of the perfect consequentialist is that of the God of Leibniz's *Theodicy*, an actor whose knowledge is direct, perfect and costless, and if the ideal of wisdom rests in an ever closer approximation to this form of behaviour, then it is plain that instrumental rationality is not simply desirable in a technical sense—the criterion of efficiency—but also desirable in a moral sense—the criterion of justice. For what could rationally be more desirable than to imitate the behaviour of one's God, infinitely good and infinitely far-seeing? If one then introduces a supplementary intermediate proposition into this chain of reasoning, what is morally more desirable than conduct conforming to the rational measures taken by the benevolent and well-informed persons of the legislator's bureaucratic apparatus? Political economy had sought to constitute, or renew, itself through Smith's use of the Legislator, who would become the principal representative of the utilitarian calculator, rationally guiding the individuals whose destinies were in his charge to the "greatest happiness of the greatest number" (Bentham).

Secondly, we cannot follow Boltanski and Chiapello (1999: 47–55) when they argue that political economy is the ideology of capitalism, but then rule it out on grounds of the alleged weakness of its influence. We have explained elsewhere (Steiner 1998) why there is no reason to stand by this sketchy account, which is based on a very partial evaluation of contemporary economic discourse. Why should one not treat management discourse—itself the distant heir of French *management*, or the science of the wise government of a household, and of *œconomie politique* from the sixteenth to the eighteenth century—as part of economic discourse? While it might be a discourse involving different agents (managers, directors, and those who teach them) used for different ends (defining legitimate economic practices and gaining the adherence of employees), this does not remove it from the domain of economic discourse any more than the literature of *exempla* introduced by Weber can be stripped of its religious character by comparison with the writings of Luther and Calvin. Moreover, if one takes account of the sources used by Bendix, who also introduces writing on self-help and self-improvement (the "New Thought" movement or evangelical catechisms used among the British working classes), professional writing and management publications such as those of well-known industrial reformers (Robert Owen, Andrew Ure, Frederick Taylor or Elton Mayo), or the major texts of economic theory (Senior or Malthus, but also Francis Place), one is very close to the Durkheimian rule, that once something is defined as a social object (economic knowledge), it is necessary to take into account *all* the forms which it assumes.

Economic discourse has to be dealt with in this way: it runs from the heights of the most abstract economic theory to the widely read business press of the day. The statements of abstract economics, expressed in mathematics, reflect the endeavours of agents in the market seeking to derive the best deal for themselves, maximising their gain while constrained by the resources at their disposition. But this initial redefinition of the material to be treated as economic discourse is inadequate, since it assimilates economic discourse to the behaviour of a dealer; it is entirely commercial in scope. There is a second form of economic activity that we need to take into account: that of industry. The definition of economic discourse has to be extended to cover the engineers who direct production.

David Landes's *Unbound Prometheus* (2003) set up an ideal-typical opposition between British and German engineers, noting that early British engineers had not received any specific technical training, and that until the mid-nineteenth century Britain had no systematic programme for training engineers comparable to that existing in continental Europe, especially in France and Germany.[22] British entrepreneurs did not regard their engineers very highly and were largely indifferent to theoretical knowledge and the technical and product innovations it made possible (Landes 2003: 131). Engineers were far more highly regarded in the German industrial world, which had a strong sense of the utility of science and technology. Landes contrasts the British entrepreneur, oriented toward the market with an accounting mindset and seeking to maximise returns from short-run fluctuations of incomings and outgoings, with the German engineer, backed up by industrialists and bankers, among whom the new had a premium not because it "paid", as the British said, but because it worked better. There was a good and a bad way of doing things, and the good way was the scientific way, the mechanised way (ibid. 2003: 354).

---

[22] In France there was the Ecole des ponts et chaussées, and the Ecole des mines. For a review of the French engineering schools, see Schinn 1978, Weiss 1982, Picon 1992, Belhoste, Dalmedico & Picon 1994. For Germany, see Gispen 1989.

Of course, the opposition between the two types should not be pushed too far, since there is always a *tension* in economic activity between production and valorisation, between productive techniques and commercial techniques. The engineer, fired by technological novelty and endowed with knowledge of the applied science necessary for production, sooner or later will run up against commercial constraints. This is exactly one of the issues in industrial science that was addressed at the beginning of the nineteenth century (Weiss 1982; Vatin 1994, 1998): while engineering calculation is not unlike economic calculation, since it seems to maximise a return, it also depends upon commercial conditions, such as the costs of energy, machinery and human labour.[23]

Engineers and their industrial connection are a social category typical of the nineteenth century. They intervene in the day-to-day practical work of administration (both in the public and private sectors), just as Comte understood in the mid-1820s. (Because of his training in the Ecole polytechnique, he was well placed to understand this relationship.)[24] The engineer was master of the mathematical tools for optimisation necessary for the practical rationalisation of economic activity in the formal sense first stated by Leibniz, and was able to valorise as a practical norm and economic ideal the rationalisation of life. That the economists and the engineer ended up profoundly resembling each other with regard to their mastery of mathematical language and the associated training first became evident in the French case of the engineer-economist (Etner 1987), but became general in the twentieth century. An especially striking example of this can be found among financial traders who graduated from the best engineering schools, and whose training in mathematics and physics was used primarily for the valorisation of derivatives trading (Godechot 2001). Conversely, contemporary mathematical economists call for the development of engineering practices within economics when the design of market microstructures is involved (Roth 2002).

---

[23] François Vatin's study of human labour and the work done by machinery (1994)—the concept of work in physical science is elaborated by analogy with that of economy as used by French engineers—shows the connections between technology and economy in the training and, above all, the activity of the engineer. But that is not entirely new, as Hélène Vérin notes in her study of engineering practice in the seventeenth and eighteenth centuries: fortification called for a combination of military and architectural techniques with economic techniques (1993).

[24] In his treatment of the organisation of science and of scientists, Comte introduced a subdivision within the category "scientists" to give a place to engineers. They were considered to be a "distinct corporation, serving as a permanent and regular intermediary between scientists (*savants*) and industrialists for all special works" (1825: 173; see also 1830–42 I: 670–72).

Seen in these terms, the sociology of economic knowledge sketched out programmatically by Durkheim remains a significant intellectual resource. Linked to Weber's work on the relationship between the "spirit" of capitalism and the social organisation of belief, it presents us with a sociology of economic knowledge embedded within an understanding of training and schooling that goes to the heart of the system of values embodied by contemporary economic life.

Conclusion

Starting out from the two programmes that Durkheim developed in seeking to come to terms with the sociology of the economy, we have shown how the studies conducted by Halbwachs, Mauss and Simiand—to name only his three most important collaborators—reworked his early insights. This approach has allowed us to highlight the importance of economic sociology and positive economics in the writings of Simiand and Halbwachs, and relate this to Mauss's writings on the anthropology of religions and the social history of economic categories. During the interwar years, from Mauss's *The Gift* in 1925 to Simiand's "Money as a Social Reality" of 1934, the work of the Durkheimians converged upon a dialogue with Durkheim's two research programmes in such a way as to reunite them.

In chapters 1–6, Durkheimian economic sociology has been presented as a methodological critique of political economy, taking account of the importance of representations in the understanding and conceptualisation of market coordination; but this was also a means of comparing the modern exchange mechanism with that of the gift exchange. This work is of enduring relevance to the sociology of the economy and to materially rational economic knowledge, terms that are here preferred to those of heterodox economics as developed by the regulation school, especially when it is a matter of the monetary and financial problems in which Mauss and Simiand were interested and the stream of thinking associated with the theory and practice of the gift relationship.

The final two chapters have been devoted to two general findings. First, since Durkheimian economic sociology emphasises the role of representations and that of the sociology of knowledge, the sociology of economic knowledge comes to play a large part in it. Particular attention is given to the schooling system in the organisation of modern society; Durkheimian economic sociology is consequently oriented towards a "social history of economic categories" (Mauss)—or in other words, an investigation of the manner in which economic categories have propagated in such a way that modern man has become a "calculating machine". The economic sociology of Halbwachs, Mauss and Simiand draws attention to a public which, at that time, had barely emerged but which has since proliferated: experts and management consultants whose knowledge and economic skills are a key element in market functioning, especially when the problem of market coordination is reconceived as the "coordination of impressions", to use Simiand's phrase. This demonstrates how important the study of economic culture is, not only with regard to its content but also with regard to the form in which it is taken up, that is, its social effects. Contemporary economic sociology has already engaged with such issues.

The introduction of Max Weber highlights parallels with the work of Durkheim in respect of the social mechanisms through which obligations are created and maintained; a "method" or "conduct of life" guiding the individual to a rationalisation of the existence of an "elective affinity" with the spirit of capitalism. Durkheim's sociology of knowledge and of the schooling system provides a means of extending Weber's analysis beyond the seventeenth century and into the eighteenth and nineteenth, with the onward march of a process of secularisation that completes the argument initiated in *Protestant Ethic* and opens up a fresh perspective upon contemporary work in economic sociology.

The Durkheimians approached the schooling system as a means of sustaining the reproduction of an economic ethos, initially unsought and unintended but then increasingly conceived as an intended outcome, a valorised and valorising result. The economic discourse which became part of this process came to fuel economic life and was no longer simply a more or less adequate reflection of this life. Here again the pertinence of Durkheimian thinking to contemporary research is evident. But this also opens up a basic question concerning the manner in which sociology deals with economic discourse. Is the encounter between a vision of the modern world and economic belief solely a "miraculous" outcome, a magical relationship of adequacy between belief and action, a magnification of the symbolic and performative function of belief? Or does it not also enter into a very concrete and practical element of practical rationality (embodied in the engineers and managers engaged in the "industrial" dimension of economic life), which makes up an inescapable element of the rationality which economic discourse has put at the core of its message? This is a rationality which is at the heart of the rational economic discourse produced by the academic economist, as it is in the practice of engineers or economic agents, as much in its technical as in its ethical aspects. Seen in this light, the question that remains unsettled relates to the need to study simultaneously economic discourse and the beliefs that it produces as dimensions of technicity and ethics on the one hand and the symbolic on the other.

The Durkheimian approach thus throws renewed emphasis upon the importance of the Weberian problem of *Menschentum*, of a type of individual that, through social selection mechanisms, is favoured by a given form of society and for whom, therefore, a given form of ideal is provided.

References

WORKS FROM DURKHEIM AND THE DURKHEIMIANS

L'année sociologique, first series (1897–1913). 13 vols. Paris: Alcan. Cited as *AS*
   I 1–13.
Notes critiques—Sciences sociales (1900–1906). Paris: Société nouvelle de librai-
   rie et d'édition.
L'année sociologique, second series (1925–27). 2 vols. Paris: Alcan. Cited as *AS* II.
Annales sociologiques (1934–40). Series D, Economic Sociology, 4 vols.; series B,
   Religious Sociology, 2 vols. Paris: Alcan. Cited as *AS* III B–D.

Bouglé, Célestin

(1894) *Les sciences sociales en Allemagne: Le conflit des methodes.* Paris: Alcan,
   1912.
(1899) *Les idées égalitaires: Etude sociologique.* Paris: Alcan, 1925.
(1907) "Les castes et la vie économique". *Revue d'économie politique* 20(1):
   81–96, 20(2): 194–206 and 21(2): 271–82.
(1908a) *Essai sur le régime des castes.* Paris: Alcan, 1935.
(1908b) "Marxisme et sociologie". *Revue de métaphysique et de morale* 16:
   723–50.
(1914) *Qu'est-ce que la sociologie ?* Paris: Alcan.
(1922) *Leçons de sociologie sur l'évolution des valeurs.* Paris: Armand Colin.
(1934) "La sociologie économique en France". *Zeitschrift für Sozialforschung*
   3(3): 383–408.
(1935) *Cours de sociologie économique.* Paris: Centre de documentation universitaire.
(1936) "La méthodologie de François Simiand et la sociologie". *Annales sociologiques*, series A, 1: 5–28.
(1938) *Bilan de la sociologie française.* Paris: Alcan.

Bourgin, Hubert

(1905) "Essai sur une forme d'industrie: L'industrie de la boucherie à Paris au
   XIXe siècle". *L'année sociologique* 8: 1–117.
(1907) *L'industrie de la boucherie dans le département de l'Oise au 19ème siècle.*
   Paris: Honoré Champion.
(1924) *L'industrie et le marché: Essai sur le développement industriel.* Paris: Alcan.
——— & Georges Bourgin (1920). *L'industrie sidérurgique en France au début
   de la revolution.* Paris: Imprimerie nationale.

Davy, Georges

(1922) *La foi jurée: Etude sociologique du problème du contrat: La formation du
   lien contractual.* Paris: Alcan.

Durkheim, Emile

(1885a) Review of Ludwig Gumplowicz, *Grundriss der Soziologie*. In Durkheim 1975 I: 344–54.

(1885b) Review of Alfred Fouillée, *La propriété sociale et la démocratie*. In Durkheim 1970: 171–83.

(1885c) "Organisation et vie du corps social selon Schäffle". In Durkheim 1975 I: 355–77.

(1886a) "Les études de sciences sociales". In Durkheim 1970: 184–214.

(1886b) Review of Guillaume de Greef, *Introduction à la sociologie*. In Durkheim 1975 I: 37–43.

(1887) "La science positive de la morale en Allemagne". In Durkheim 1975 I: 267–343.

(1888a) "Cours de science sociale: Leçon d'ouverture". In Durkheim 1970: 77–110.

(1888b) "Le programme économique de M. Schäffle". In Durkheim 1975 I: 377–83.

(1889) Review of Friedrich Tönnies, *Gemeinschaft und Gesellschaft*. In Durkheim 1975 I: 383–90.

(1893/1984) *De la division du travail social*. Paris: Presses universitaires de France, 1973. *The Division of Labour in Society*. Translated by W. D. Halls. Basingstoke: Palgrave.

(1894/1982) *Les règles de la méthode sociologique*. Paris: Presses universitaires de France, 1977. *The Rules of Sociological Method*. Translated by Steven Lukes. New York: Free Press.

(1895) "L'état actuel des études sociologiques en France". In Durkheim 1975 I: 73–108.

(1895–96) *Le socialisme: Sa définition, ses débuts, la doctrine saint-simonienne*. Paris: Presses universitaires de France, 1971.

(1897a/2006) *Le suicide: Etude de sociologie*. Paris: Presses universitaires de France, 1976. *On Suicide*. Translated by Robin Buss. London: Penguin Books.

(1897b) Review of Gaston Richard, *Le socialisme et la science sociale*. In Durkheim 1970: 236–44.

(1897c) Review of Antonio Labriola, *Essai sur la conception matérialiste de l'histoire*. In Durkheim 1970: 245–54.

(1898a) "De la définition des phénomènes religieux". In Durkheim 1969: 140–65.

(1898b) "Représentations individuelles et représentations collectives". In Durkheim 1924: 1–48.

(1898–1900/2001) *Leçons de sociologie, physique des mœurs et du droit*. Edited by Hüseyin Nail Kubali. Paris: Presses universitaires de France, 1969. *Professional Ethics and Civil Morals*. Translated by Cornelia Brookfield. London: Routledge.

(1900a) "La sociologie en France au XIXe siècle". In Durkheim 1970: 111–36.

(1900b) "La sociologie et son domaine scientifique". In Durkheim 1975 I: 13–36.

(1901a) Review of Georg Simmel, *Philosophie de l'argent*. In Durkheim 1975 I: 178–82.

(1901b) "Préface à la seconde édition". In Durkheim 1894: xi–xxiv.

(1902a) "Préface à la seconde edition: Quelques remarques sur les groupements professionnels". In Durkheim 1893: i–xxxvi.

(1902b) "Sur le totémisme". In Durkheim 1969: 315–52.

(1902c) Review of Georg Simmel, *Philosophie des Geldes*. In Durkheim 1969: 358–62.

(1902d) "L'éducation, sa nature et son rôle". In Durkheim 1922: 41–68.

(1902e) "Nature et méthode de la pédagogie". In Durkheim 1922: 69–90.

(1902–3/1961) *L'éducation morale*. Paris: Presses universitaires de France, 1974. *Moral Education: A Study in the Theory and Application of the Sociology of Education*. Translated by Everett K. Wilson & Hermann Schnurer. New York: Free Press.

(1904) "La sociologie et les sciences sociales". In Durkheim 1975 I: 166–69.

(1904–5) *L'évolution pédagogique en France*. Paris: Presses universitaires de France, 1969.

(1905) "L'évolution et le rôle de l'enseignement secondaire en France". In Durkheim 1922: 113–30.

(1906) "La détermination du fait moral". In Durkheim 1924: 48–116.

(1908a) "Intervention à un débat organisé à la société d'économie politique". *Bulletin de la Société d'économie politique* 3: 60–73, session of 4 April.

(1908b) "Remarques sur la méthode en sociologie". In Durkheim 1975 I: 58–63.

(1909a/2004) "Sociologie et sciences sociales". In Durkheim 1970: 136–59. "Sociology and the Social Sciences." In *Readings from Emile Durkheim*, revised edition, edited and translated by Kenneth Thompson. London: Routledge.

(1909b) "Sociologie religieuse et théorie de la connaissance". In Durkheim 1975 I: 184–88.

(1910) "L'enseignement de la morale à l'école primaire". *Revue française de sociologie* (1992) 33(4): 611–23.

(1911a) "Jugements de valeur et jugements de réalité". In Durkheim 1924: 117–41.

(1911b) "Pédagogie et sociologie". In Durkheim 1922: 91–112.

(1912/1995) *Les formes élémentaires de la vie religieuse*. Paris: Presses universitaires de France, 1968. *The Elementary Forms of Religious Life*. Translated by Karen E. Fields. New York: Free Press.

(1913) "Le problème religieux et la dualité de la nature humaine". In Durkheim 1975 II: 23–59.

(1913–14) *Pragmatisme et sociologie*. Edited by Armand Cuvillier. Paris: Vrin, 1955.

(1915) "La sociologie". In Durkheim 1975 I: 109–18.

(1917) "Une définition de la société". In Durkheim 1975 I: 71.

(1922) *Education et sociologie*. Paris: Presses universitaires de France, 1985.

(1924) *Sociologie et philosophie*. Paris: Presses universitaires de France, 1963.

(1969) *Journal sociologique*. Edited by Jean Duvignaud. Paris: Presses universitaires de France.

(1970) *La science sociale et l'action*. Edited by Jean-Claude Filloux. Paris: Presses universitaires de France.

(1975) *Textes*. 3 vols. Edited by Victor Karady. Paris: Minuit.

(1998) *Lettres à Marcel Mauss*. Edited by Philippe Besnard & Marcel Fournier. Paris: Presses universitaires de France.

——— & Paul Fauconnet, (1903) "Sociologie et sciences sociales". In Durkheim 1975 I: 121–59.

——— & Mauss, Marcel (1903) "De quelques formes primitives de classification". In Durkheim 1969: 394–461.

Fauconnet, Paul

(1908) "La méthode sociologique appliquée à l'étude des faits économiques: A propos d'un livre récent". *Revue de synthèse historique* 47(2): 181–87.

(1928) *La responsabilité: Etude de sociologie*. 2nd edition. Paris: Alcan.

Granet, Marcel

(1922) *La religion des chinois*. Paris: Presses universitaires de France, 1951.

Halbwachs, Maurice

(1905a) "Remarques sur la position sociologique du problème des classes". In Halbwachs 1972: 41–57.

(1905b) "Les besoins et les tendances dans l'économie sociale". In Halbwachs 1972: 27–40.

(1905c) "La ville capitaliste selon Sombart". *Revue d'économie politique* 19(7): 736–47.

(1907) *Leibniz*. Paris: Mellotée, 1928.

(1908) "Notes et discussions: La théorie économique du salaire". *Revue du mois*, November, 608–11.

(1909) *Les expropriations et le prix des terrains à Paris (1860–1900)*. Paris: Cornély.

(1912) *La classe ouvrière et les niveaux de vie: Recherches sur la hiérarchie des besoins dans les sociétés industrielles*, Paris & New York: Gordon & Breach, 1970.

(1913) *La théorie de l'homme moyen: Essai sur Quetelet et la statistique morale*. Paris: Alcan.

(1918) "Le *Traité de sociologie générale* de M. Vilfredo Pareto". *Revue d'économie politique* 32(5): 578–85.

(1920a) "Science économique et sociologie: Le *Traité de sociologie générale* de M. Vilfredo Pareto". *Revue d'économie politique* 34(4): 467–75.

(1920b) "Matière et société". In Halbwachs 1972: 58–94.

(1921a) "L'instinct ouvrier dans l'art industriel". *Revue philosophique*, 91: 214–33.

(1921b) "Revenus et dépenses des ménages de travailleurs: Une enquête officielle d'avant-guerre". *Revue d'économie politique* 35(1): 50–59.

(1923) "L'expérimentation statistique et les probabilités". In Halbwachs 1972: 275–307.

(1925) "Les origines puritaines du capitalisme d'après Weber". *Revue d'histoire et de philosophie religieuses* 5: 132–57.

(1929) "Max Weber: Un homme, une œuvre". *Annales d'histoire économique et sociale* 1: 81–88.

(1930) *Les causes du suicide*. Paris: Alcan.

(1931) "L'œuvre scientifique de quelques économistes étrangers: Friedrich von Gottl-Ottlidenfield". *Revue d'économie politique* 45(1): 37–60.

(1933a) *L'évolution des besoins dans les classes ouvrières*. Paris: Alcan.

(1933b) "La loi en sociologie". In Halbwachs 1972: 308–28.

(1935a) "La morphologie religieuse". In Halbwachs 1972: 225–30.

(1935b) "La statistique en sociologie". In Halbwachs 1972: 329–48.

(1936) "La méthodologie de François Simiand: Un empirisme rationaliste". In Halbwachs 1972: 346–89.

(1937) "Le point de vue du sociologue". In Halbwachs 1972: 390–408.

(1938a) *Morphologie sociale*. Paris: Armand Colin.

(1938b) "La psychologie collective du raisonnement". In Halbwachs 1972: 131–51.

(1939a) "Les caractéristiques des classes moyennes". In Halbwachs 1972: 95–111.

(1939b) "Genre de vie: Consommations et besoins". *Revue d'économie politique* 53(1): 439–55.

(1940) *Sociologie économique et démographie*. Paris: Hermann & Cie.

(1947) "L'expression des émotions et la société". In Halbwachs 1972: 164–73.

(1955) *Esquisse d'une psychologie des classes sociales*. Paris: Marcel Rivière.

(1972) *Classes sociales et morphologies*. Edited by Victor Karady. Paris: Minuit.

Maunier, René

(1908) "Vie religieuse et vie économique : La division du travail". *Revue internationale de sociologie*, offprint: 1–80.

(1910a) *L'origine et la fonction économique des villes: Etude de morphologie sociale*. Paris: Giard & Brière.

(1910b) *L'économie politique et la sociologie*. Paris: Giard.

(1912) Review of Simiand, *La méthode positive en science économique*. *Revue internationale de sociologie* 20(4): 313.

(1927a) "Recherches sur les échanges rituels en Afrique du Nord". *L'année sociologique*, new series, 2: 11–97.

(1927b) Review of *L'année sociologique*. *Revue philosophique* 104: 303–11.

(1930) *Mélanges de sociologie Nord-Africaine*. Paris: Alcan.

(1937) "Les groupes d'intérêts et l'idée de contrat en Afrique du Nord". *Annales sociologiques*, series C, 2: 35–61.

Mauss, Marcel

(1899) *Essai sur la nature et la fonction du sacrifice*. In Mauss 1969 I: 193–307.

(1909) *La prière*. In Mauss 1969 I: 357–477.

(1914) "Les origines de la notion de monnaie". In Mauss 1969 II: 106–12.

(1920a) *La nation*. In Mauss 1969 III: 573–634.

(1920b) "La chaire de la coopération au Collège de France". In Mauss 1997: 367–69.

(1921) "L'expression obligatoire des sentiments". In Mauss 1969 III: 269–78.

(1922) "Les changes". In Mauss 1997: 477–504.

(1924a) "Gift-gift". In Mauss 1969 III: 46–51.

(1924b/1992) "Appréciation sociologique du bolchevisme". In Mauss 1997:

537–66. "A Sociological Assessment of Bolshevism (1924–5)". Translated by Ben Brewster. In Mike Gane, *The Radical Sociology of Durkheim and Mauss*. 165–220. London: Routledge.

(1924c) "Les changes". In Mauss 1997: 567–664.

(1924d) "Les changes". In Mauss 1997: 665–91.

(1924e) "Rapports réels et pratiques de la psychologie et de la sociologie". In Mauss 1950: 283–308.

(1925a/1954) *Essai sur le don: Forme et raison de l'échange dans les sociétés archaïques*. In Mauss 1950: 143–279. *The Gift: Forms and Functions of Exchange in Archaic Societies*. Translated by Ian Cunnison. New York: Free Press.

(1925b) "*In memoriam*: L'œuvre inédite de Durkheim et de ses collaborateurs". In Mauss 1969 III: 473–99.

(1925c) "Socialisme et bolchevisme". In Mauss 1997: 699–721.

(1927a/) *Divisions et proportions des divisions de la sociologie*. In Mauss 1969 III: 178–245. "Sociology: Its Divisions and Their Relative Weightings". In Mauss, *Two Essays*, 31–89. Edited by Mike Gane; translated by William Jeffrey. New York: Berghahn Books.

(1927b) "Note de méthode sur l'extension de la sociologie, énoncé de quelques principes à propos d'un livre récent". In Mauss 1969 III: 283–97.

(1928) Introduction to Durkheim 1895–96: 27–31.

(1930) "L'œuvre de Mauss par lui-même". *Revue française de sociologie* 20(1) (1979): 209–20.

(1933) "La sociologie en France depuis 1914". In Mauss 1969 III: 436–50.

(1934) "Fragment d'un plan de sociologie générale descriptive". In Mauss 1969 III: 303–58.

(1936) "Les techniques de corps". In Mauss 1950: 363–86.

(1937) Introduction to Durkheim 1898–1900. In Mauss 1969 III: 500–04.

(1938) "Une catégorie de l'esprit humain: La notion de personne, celle de 'moi'". In Mauss 1950: 331–62.

(1947) *Manuel d'ethnographie*. Edited by Denise Paulme. Paris: Payot.

(1950) *Sociologie et anthropologie*. Edited by Georges Gurvitch. Paris: Presses universitaires de France, 1980.

(1969) *Œuvres*. 3 vols. Edited by Victor Karady. Paris: Minuit.

(1997) *Ecrits politiques*. Edited by Marcel Fournier. Paris: Fayard.

——— & Paul Fauconnet, (1901/2005) "Sociologie". In Mauss 1969 III: 139–77. "Sociology". In Mauss, *Two Essays*, 1–30. Edited by Mike Gane; translated by William Jeffrey. New York: Berghahn Books. 1–30.

——— & Henri Hubert, (1904) *Esquisse d'une théorie générale de la magie*. In Mauss 1950: 1–141.

——— & Henri Hubert, (1906) "Introduction à l'analyse de quelques phénomènes religieux". In Mauss 1969 I: 3–39.

——— & Henri Beuchat, (1906) *Essai sur les variations saisonnières des sociétés Eskimos: Etude de morphologie sociale*. In Mauss 1950: 389–477.

Simiand, François

(1898) "L'année sociologique française". *Revue de métaphysique et de morale* 6: 608–53.

(1902) "Essai sur le prix du charbon en France et au 19e siècle". *L'année sociologique*, 6: 1–81.

(1903) "Méthode historique et science sociale: Etude critique à propos des ouvrages récents de M. Lacombe et M. Seignobos". In Simiand 1987: 113–69.

(1906) "La causalité en histoire". In Simiand 1987: 209–41.

(1907) *Le salaire des ouvriers des mines de charbon en France: Contribution à la théorie économique du salaire*. Paris: Cornély.

(1909) "La théorie économique du salaire et l'économie politique traditionnelle". *Revue du mois*, March: 346–49.

(1912) *La méthode positive en science économique*. Paris: Alcan.

(1922) *Statistique et experience: Remarques de méthode*. Paris: Rivière.

(1929–31) *Cours d'économie politique*. Paris: Domat-Montchrestien.

(1930a) "Les théories économiques du salaire: Examen critique". *Revue d'économie politique* 44(5): 1281–97.

(1930b) "La théorie expérimentale en science économique positive". *Revue philosophique* 110(9–10): 161–76.

(1930–32) *Recherches sur le mouvement général des prix du XVIe au XIXe siècle*. Paris: Domat-Montchrestien.

(1931) "A propos de *Le salaire, l'évolution sociale et la monnaie*". *Revue d'économie politique* 45(5): 1169–89.

(1932a) *Le salaire, l'évolution sociale et la monnaie: Essai de théorie expérimentale du salaire*. Paris: Alcan.

(1932b) *Les fluctuations économiques à longue période et la crise mondiale*. Paris: Alcan.

(1934a) *Inflation et stabilisation alternées: Le développement économique des Etats-Unis (des origines coloniales au temps présent)*. Paris: Domat-Montchrestien.

(1934b) "La monnaie, réalité sociale". *Annales sociologiques*, series D, 1: 1–86.

(1934c) *De l'échange primitif à l'économie complexe*. Paris: Editions de la pensée ouvrière.

(1937) "La psychologie sociale des crises et des fluctuations de courte durée". *Annales sociologiques*, series D, 2: 3–32.

(1987) *Méthode historique et sciences sociales*. Compiled & edited by Marina Cedronio. Amsterdam: Editions des archives contemporaines.

SECONDARY LITERATURE

Abolafia, Mitchell (1996) *Making Markets: Opportunism and Restraint on Wall Street*. Cambridge, Mass.: Harvard University Press.

Abraham-Frois, Gilbert, & Françoise Larbre (1998) "La diffusion de la *Théorie générale* dans le milieu universitaire français: Retard ou spécificité ?". *Revue d'économie politique* 108(1): 109–27.

Aftalion, Albert (1938) *Cours de statistique*. Edited by J. Lhomme & J. Priou. Paris: Presses universitaires de France.

——— (1940) *Monnaie, prix et change: Expériences récentes et théorie*. 2nd edition. Paris: Sirey.

Aglietta, Michel (1976) *Régulation et crises du capitalisme: L'expérience américaine*. Paris: Calmann-Lévy.

Aglietta, Michel, & André Orléan (1982) *La violence de la monnaie*. Paris: Presses universitaires de France.

——, eds. (1998) *La monnaie souveraine*. Paris: Odile Jacob.

—— (2002) *La monnaie entre violence et confiance*. Paris: Odile Jacob.

Aimard, Guy (1962) *Durkheim et la science économique*. Paris: Presses universitaires de France.

Alexander, Jeffrey (1982) *Theoretical Logic in Sociology. The Antinomies of Classical Thought: Marx and Durkheim*. Berkeley: University of California Press.

—— (1990) "The sacred and the profane. Information machine: Discourse about the computer as ideology". *Archives de sciences sociales des religions* 69(1): 161–71.

Ansart, Pierre (1969) *Marx et l'anarchisme*. Paris: Presses universitaires de France.

—— (1970) *Sociologie de Saint-Simon*. Paris: Presses universitaires de France.

Arena, Richard, & Anna Maricic (1988) "Les réactions françaises à la *Théorie générale* (1936–1951): La recherche d'une dynamique économique". *Cahiers d'économie politique* 14–15: 15–41.

Aron, Raymond (1967) *Les étapes de la pensée sociologique: Montesquieu, Comte, Marx, Tocqueville, Durkheim, Pareto et Weber*. Paris: Gallimard.

Assoun, Paul-Laurent (1976) "Emile Durkheim et les socialistes de la chaire". *Revue française de sciences politiques* 26(5): 957–82.

Augello, Massimo, & Marco Guidi, eds. (2002) *The Spread of Political Economy and the Professionalisation of Economics: Economic Societies in Europe, America and Japan in the Nineteenth Century*. London: Routledge.

Balibar, Etienne (1993) *La philosophie de Marx*. Paris: La découverte, 2001.

Bastiat, Frédéric (1850) *Harmonies économiques*. Paris: Guillaumin, 1881.

Baudelot, Christian, & Roger Establet (1994) *Maurice Halbwachs: Consommation et société*. Paris: Presses universitaires de France.

Baudrillart, Henri (1883) *Des rapports de l'économie politique et de la morale*. Paris: Guillaumin.

—— (1891) "Morale (Accord de la morale et de l'économie politique)". In Say & Chailley 1891 II: 341–49.

Beckert, Jens (1997) "Contract and Social Justice: Emile Durkheim's theory of integration in modern societies". In W. Pickering, ed., *Emile Durkheim: Critical Assessments of Leading Sociologists, Third Series*, 4: 290–311. London: Routledge, 2001.

Becquemont, Daniel, & Laurent Mucchielli (1998) *Le cas Spencer: Religion, science et politique*. Paris: Presses universitaires de France.

Belhoste, Bruno, Amy Dahan Dalmedico & Antoine Picon, eds. (1994) *La formation polytechnicienne 1794–1994*. Paris: Dunod.

Bellah, Robert N. (1990) "Morale, religion et société dans l'œuvre de Durkheim". *Archives de Sciences Sociales des Religions* 69(1): 9–25.

Belot, Gustave (1903) "Analyse et comptes rendus: Emile Durkheim, *L'Année sociologique*", vol. 5. *Revue philosophique* 55(1): 96–103.

Bendix, Reinhard (1950) *Work and Authority in Industry: Ideologies of Management in the Course of Industrialization*. Berkeley: University of California Press.

Bernès, Marcel (1895) "Review of Durkheim, *Règles de la méthode sociologique*". *Revue d'économie politique* 9(2): 186–89.

Besnard, Philippe (1970) *Capitalisme et protestantisme: La controverse post-weberienne*. Paris: Armand Colin.

—— (1973) "Durkheim et les femmes ou le *Suicide* inachevé". *Revue française de sociologie* 14(1): 27–61.

—— (1979) "La formation de l'équipe de *L'Année sociologique*". *Revue française de sociologie* 20(1): 7–31.

—— (1983) "The Epistemological Polemic: François Simiand". In P. Besnard ed., *The Sociological Domain: The Durkheimians and the Founding of French Sociology*, 248–62. Cambridge & Paris: Cambridge University Press / Editions de la Maison des sciences de l'homme.

—— (1985) "La polémique autour de la *Foi jurée*". *Revue française de sociologie* 26(2): 247–57.

—— (1987) *L'anomie: Ses usages et ses fonctions dans la discipline sociologique depuis Durkheim*. Paris: Presses universitaires de France.

—— (1993) "Les pathologies des sociétés modernes". In Besnard, Borlandi & Vogt 1993: 197–211.

—— (1998) "Le centenaire d'une entreprise fondatrice". *L'année sociologique* 48(1): 9–25.

Besnard, Philippe, Massimo Borlandi & Paul Vogt, eds. (1993) *Division du travail et lien social: Durkheim un siècle après*, Paris: Presses universitaires de France.

Bianchini, Marco (1982) *Bonheur public et méthode géométrique*. French translation. Paris: INED, 2002.

Blay, Michel, & Robert Halleux, eds. (1998) *La science classique, XVIe–XVIIIe siècles: Dictionnaire critique*. Paris: Flammarion.

Block, Maurice (1897) *Les progrès de l'économie politique depuis Adam Smith*. Paris: Guillaumin.

Boltanski, Luc, & Eve Chiapello (1999) *Le nouvel esprit du capitalisme*. Paris: Gallimard.

Boltanski, Luc, & Laurent Thévenot (1991) *De la justification: Les économies de la grandeur*. Paris: Gallimard.

Borlandi, Massimo (1993) "Durkheim lecteur de Spencer". In Besnard, Borlandi & Vogt 1993: 67–109.

—— (1995) "Les faits sociaux comme produits de l'association entre les individus". In Borlandi & Mucchielli 1995: 139–64.

—— (1998) "Durkheim, les durkheimiens et la sociologie générale". *L'année sociologique* 48(1): 27–65.

Borlandi, Massimo, & Laurent Mucchielli, eds. (1995) *La sociologie et sa méthode: Les Règles de Durkheim un siècle après*. Paris: L'Harmattan.

Bosco, Augusto (1897) Review of Durkheim, *Le Suicide*. *Rivisita italiana di sociologia*, 376–83.

Boudon, Raymond (1991) "Durkheim et Weber: Convergences de méthode". In Boudon 1998: 93–136.

Boudon, Raymond (1995) "*L'éthique protestante* de Max Weber: Bilan de la discussion". In Boudon 1998: 55–92.

——— (1998) *Etudes sur les sociologues classiques*. Paris: Presses universitaires de France.

——— (1999) "Les *Formes élémentaires de la vie religieuse*: Une théorie toujours vivante". *L'année sociologique* 49(1): 149–98.

——— (2000) "Max Weber: La 'rationalité axiologique' et la rationalisation de la vie morale". In Boudon 1998: 201–46.

——— (2001) "La rationalité du religieux selon Max Weber". *L'année sociologique* 51(1): 9–50.

Bouet, H. (1901) Review of Durkheim, *Règles de la méthode sociologique*. *Journal des économistes* 48 December: 130–31.

Bourdieu, Pierre (1971a) "Une interprétation de la théorie de la religion selon Max Weber". *Archives européennes de sociologie* 12(1): 3–21.

——— (1971b) "Le marché des biens symboliques". *L'année sociologique* 22: 49–126.

——— (1972) *Esquisse d'une théorie de la pratique*. Geneva: Droz.

——— (1980) *Le sens pratique*. Paris: Minuit.

——— (1989) *La noblesse d'état: Grandes écoles et esprit de corps*. Paris: Minuit.

——— (1994) *Raisons pratiques: Sur la théorie de l'action*. Paris: Le Seuil.

——— (1997a) *Méditations pascaliennes*. Paris: Le Seuil.

——— (1997b) "Le champ économique". *Actes de la recherche en sciences sociales* 119: 48–66.

——— (2000) *Les structures sociales de l'économie*. Paris: Le Seuil.

——— (2001) *Science de la science et réflexivité*. Paris: Raisons d'agir.

Bowley, Arthur L. (1907) Review of Simiand, *Le salaire des ouvriers des mines de charbon en France*. *Journal of the Royal Statistical Society* 70 (September): 508–9.

Boyer, Robert (1976) "La croissance française de l'après-guerre et les modèles macroéconomiques". *Revue économique* 27(5): 882–939.

——— (1978) "Les salaires en longue période". *Economie et statistiques* 103: 99–118.

——— (1979) "La crise actuelle: Une mise en perspective historique. Quelques réflexions à partir d'une analyse du capitalisme français en longue période". *Critiques de l'économie politique* 7–8: 3–113.

——— (1986) *La théorie de la régulation: Une analyse critique*. Paris: La découverte.

——— (1989) "Economie et histoire: Vers de nouvelles alliances?" *Annales ESC* 60(6): 1397–1426.

——— (1995) "Du fordisme canonique à une variété de modes de développement". In Boyer & Saillard 1995: 369–77.

Boyer, Robert, & André Orléan (1993) "Les transformations des conventions salariales entre théorie et histoire". *Revue économique* 42(2): 233–72.

Boyer, Robert, & Jacques Mistral (1983) "Le temps present: La crise. D'une analyse historique à une vue prospective". *Annales ESC* 54(3): 483–506.

Boyer, Robert, & Yves Saillard, eds. (1995) *Théorie de la regulation: L'état des savoirs*. Paris: La découverte.

Breton, Yves (1991) "Les économistes français et les questions de méthode". In Breton & Lutfalla 1991: 389–419.

Breton, Yves, & Michel Lutfalla, eds. (1991) *L'économie politique en France au XIXe siècle*. Paris: Economica.

Breton, Yves, Anton Broder & Michel Lutfalla, eds. (1997) *La longue stagnation en France: L'autre grande dépression 1873–1897*. Paris: Economica.

Bücher, Karl (1896) *Etudes d'histoire et d'économie politique*. French translation. Paris: Alcan, 1901.

Caillé, Alain (1986) *Splendeurs et misères des sciences sociales: Esquisse d'une mythologie*. Geneva: Droz.

——— (2000) *Anthropologie du don*. Paris: Desclée de Brouwer.

Calabresi, Guido, & Philip Bobbit (1968) *Tragic Choices: The Conflicts Society Confronts in the Allocation of Tragically Scarce Resources*. New York: Norton.

Callon, Michel (1996) "Introduction: The embeddedness of economic market in economics". In M. Callon, ed., *The Laws of the Market*. Oxford: Blackwell.

Cardi, François, & Joëlle Plantier eds. (1993) *Durkheim sociologue de l'éducation*. Paris: L'Harmattan.

Cartelier, Jean (1995) *La monnaie*. Paris: Flammarion.

Cartelier, Jean, & Michel De Vroey (1989) "L'approche de la regulation: Un nouveau paradigme?" *Economies et sociétés* 4: 63–87.

Cauwès, Paul (1881) *Précis du cours d'économie politique*. Paris: Larose & Forcel.

——— (1893) *Cours d'économie politique*. Paris: Larose & Forcel.

Cazeneuve, Jean (1968) *Sociologie de Marcel Mauss*. Paris: Presses universitaires de France.

Cefaï, Daniel, & Alain Mahé (1998) "Echanges rituels de don, obligation et contrat. Mauss, Davy et Maunier: Trois perspectives de sociologie juridique". *L'année sociologique* 48(1): 209–28.

Charle, Christophe (1980) "Entretiens avec Ernest Labrousse". *Actes de la recherche en sciences sociales* 32–33: 111–25.

Cherkaoui, Mohamed (1998) *Naissance d'une science sociale: La sociologie selon Durkheim*. Geneva: Droz.

——— (2003) "Les transitions micro-macro: Apports et limites de la théorie du choix rationnel dans les *Foundations of Social Theory*". *Revue française de sociologie* 43(2): 231–54.

Clark, Terry N. (1968) "The Structure and Functions of a Research Institute: The *Année sociologique*". *Archives européennes de sociologie* 9(1): 72–91.

Coats, Bob, ed. (2000) *The Development of Economics in Western Europe since 1945*. London: Routledge.

Cochoy, Frank (2002) *Une sociologie du packaging; ou, L'âne de Buridan face au marché*. Paris: Presses universitaires de France.

Cohen, Bernard I. (1990) "Some Documentary Reflections on the Dissemination and Reception of the 'Merton Thesis'". In J. Clark, C. Modgil & S. Modgil, eds., *Robert K. Merton: Consensus and Controversy*, 307–48. London: Falmer Press.

Coleman, James S. (1986) "Social Theory, Social Research and a Theory of Action". *American Journal of Sociology* 91(6): 1309–35.

Coleman, James S. (1989) "Weber and the Protestant Ethic: A Comment on Hernes". *Rationality and Society* 1(2): 291–94.

———— (1990) *Foundations of Social Theory*. Cambridge, Mass.: Harvard Belknap Press.

Colini, Stephan, Donald Winch & John Burrow (1983) *That Noble Science of Politics: A Study in Nineteenth Century Intellectual History*. Cambridge: Cambridge University Press.

Colson, Clément (1908) "La théorie économique du salaire et l'économie politique traditionnelle". *Revue du mois*, December, 728–30.

———— (1909) "Réponse à MM. Halbwachs et Simiand". *Revue du mois*, March, 349–52.

Comte, Auguste (1818) "Deux lettres à Saint-Simon". In Comte 1970: 439–50.

———— (1819) "Du budget". In Comte 1970: 113–39.

———— (1822) *Plan des travaux scientifiques nécessaires pour réorganiser la société*. In Comte 1851–54 IV: 47–136.

———— (1825) *Considérations philosophiques sur les sciences et les savants*. In Comte 1851–54 IV: 137–75.

———— (1826) *Considérations sur le pouvoir spiritual*. In Comte 1851–4 IV: 176–215.

———— (1828a) Review of J-B. Bidaut, *Du monopole qui s'établit dans les arts industriels et dans le commerce"*. In Comte 1970: 171–74.

———— (1828b) "Review of col. Swan, *Courtes observations sur l'état actuel du commerce et des finances de l'Europe"*. In Comte 1970: 175–78.

———— (1828c) "Economie politique: Revue industrielle". In Comte 1970: 179–93.

———— (1830–42) *Cours de philosophie positive*. Paris: Hermann, 1975.

———— (1851–54) *Système de politique positive; ou, Traité de sociologie instituant la religion de l'humanité*. 3rd edition. Paris: Larousse, 1890.

———— (1852) *Catéchisme positiviste; ou, Sommaire exposition de la religion universelle*. Paris: Garnier frères, 1922.

———— (1970) *Auguste Comte: Ecrits de jeunesse 1816–1828*. Paris & The Hague: Mouton.

Corning, Peter A. (1982) "Durkheim and Spencer". *British Journal of Sociology* 33(3): 359–82.

Constant, Benjamin (1814) *De l'esprit de conquête et de l'usurpation dans leurs rapports avec la civilisation européenne*. In *Œuvres de Benjamin Constant*. Paris: Gallimard, 1957.

Coquelin, Charles (1852) "Crises commerciales". In Coquelin & Guillaumin 1852 I: 526–34.

Coquelin, Charles, & Gilbert-Urbain Guillaumin, eds. (1852) *Dictionnaire de l'économie politique*. Paris: Guillaumin.

Cordonnier, Laurent (1997) *Coopération et réciprocité*. Paris: Presses universitaires de France.

Cournot, Antoine-Augustin (1838) *Recherches sur les principes mathématiques de la théorie des richesses*. Paris: Calman-Lévy, 1974.

Craig, John E. (1979) "Maurice Halbwachs à Strasbourg". *Revue française de sociologie* 20(1): 273–92.

Crimmins, James E., ed. (1998) *Utilitarians and Religion*. Bristol: Thoemmes Press.

Damalas, Bernard (1947) *L'œuvre scientifique de François Simiand*. Paris: Presses universitaires de France.

Demeulenaere, Pierre (1996) *Homo œconomicus: Enquête sur la constitution d'un paradigme*. Paris: Presses universitaires de France.

Denis, Henri (1938) *Les récentes théories monétaires en France: Idée quantitative et conflit des methodes*. Paris: Sirey.

Dermange, François (2003) *Le dieu du marché: Ethique, économie et théologie dans l'œuvre d'Adam Smith*. Geneva: Labor & Fides.

Desrosières, Alain (1993) *La politique des grands nombres: Histoire de la raison statistique*. Paris: La découverte.

DiMaggio, Paul, & Hugh Louch (1998) "Socially Embedded Consumer Transactions: For What Kind of Purchases Do People Most Often Use Networks?" *American Sociological Review* 63(5): 619–37.

Disselkamp, Annette (1994) *L'Ethique protestante de Max Weber*. Paris: Presses universitaires de France.

Dockès, Pierre (1993) "Les recettes fordistes et les marmites de l'histoire (1907–1993)". *Revue économique* 44(3): 485–527.

Dubar, Claude (1969) "La méthode de Marcel Mauss". *Revue française de sociologie* 10(4): 515–21.

Dumont, Louis (1977) *Homo Æqualis: Genèse et épanouissement de l'idéologie économique*. Paris: Gallimard.

Dunoyer, Charles (1845) *De la liberté du travail; ou, Simple exposé des conditions dans lesquelles les forces humaines s'exercent avec le plus de puissance*. Paris: Guillaumin.

——— (1852) "Gouvernement". In Coquelin & Guillaumin 1852 I: 835–41.

Duval, Julien (2000) "Conversions et concessions à l'économie". *Actes de la recherche en sciences sociales* 116–17: 3–32.

Esping-Andersen, Gøsta (1990) *Les trois mondes de l'Etat-providence: Essai sur le capitalisme moderne*. French translation. Paris: Presses universitaires de France.

Etner, François (1987) *Histoire du calcul économique en France*. Paris: Economica.

Favereau, Olivier (1988) "La *Théorie générale*: De l'économie conventionnelle à l'économie des conventions". *Cahiers d'économie politique* 14–15: 197–220.

——— (1995) "Régulation et conventions". In Boyer & Saillard 1995: 511–20.

Filloux, Jean-Claude (1977) *Durkheim et le socialisme*. Geneva: Droz.

——— (1994) *Durkheim et l'éducation*. Paris: Presses universitaires de France.

Fischman, Marianne, & Emeric Lendjel (2000) "La contribution d'X-Crise à l'émergence de l'économétrie en France dans les années trente". *Revue européenne des sciences sociales* 118: 115–34.

Fligstein, Neil (1990) *The Transformation of Corporate Control*. Cambridge, Mass.: Harvard University Press.

Fourgeaud, André (1929) *La rationalisation: Etats Unis–Allemagne*. Paris: Payot.

Fournier, Marcel (1994) *Marcel Mauss*. Paris: Fayard.

——— (1997) "Marcel Mauss, le savant et le citoyen". In Mauss 1997: 7–59.

Friot, Bernard (1998) "Quelles règles pour le salaire socialisé ? Les enseignements de l'échec de Jean Marchal". *Economies et sociétés* 20(3): 79–103.

Frobert, Ludovic (2000) *Le travail de François Simiand*. Paris: Economica.

Fustel de Coulange, Numa (1864) *La cité antique: Etude sur le culte, le droit, les institutions de la Grèce et de Rome*. 13th edition. Paris: Hachette 1890.

Gane, Mickaël (1988) *On Durkheim's Rules of Sociological Methods*. London: Routledge.

———, ed. (1992) *The Radical Sociology of Durkheim and Mauss*. London: Routledge.

Garnier, Joseph (1880) *Traité d'économie politique sociale ou industrielle*. 8th edition. Paris: Garnier-Guillaumin.

Geiger, Roger L. (1981) "René Worms et l'organisation de la sociologie". *Revue française de sociologie* 22(3): 345–60.

Gide, Charles (1894) *Principes d'économie politique*. Paris: Larose & Forcel.

——— (1898) Review of *L'année sociologique*. *Revue d'économie politique* 12(6): 969–70.

——— (1903) Review of Simiand, *Essai sur le prix du charbon en France*. *Revue d'économie politique* 17(2): 191.

——— (1908) Review of Simiand, *Le salaire des ouvriers des mines de charbon en France*. *Revue d'économie politique* 22(1): 72–74.

——— (1911) *Cours d'économie politique*. Paris: Sirey.

——— (1914) Review of *L'année sociologique*. *Revue d'économie politique* 28(2): 245.

Giddens, Anthony (1971) *Capitalism and Modern Social Theory: An Analysis of the Writings of Marx, Durkheim and Max Weber*. Cambridge: Cambridge University Press.

Gillard, Lucien (1996) "Le dilemme productivité-répartition". In Gillard & Rosier 1996: 177–93.

Gillard, Lucien & Michel Rosier, eds. (1996) *François Simiand (1873–1935): Sociologie-histoire-économie*. Amsterdam: Editions des archives contemporaines.

Gislain, Jean-Jacques, & Philippe Steiner (1995) *La sociologie économique (1890–1920): Durkheim, Pareto, Schumpeter, Simiand, Veblen et Weber*. Paris: Presses universitaires de France.

——— (1999) "American Institutionalism and French Positive Political Economy: Some Connections". *History of Political Economy* 31(2): 273–96.

Godbout, Jack T. (2000) *Le don, la dette et l'identité: "Homo donator" versus "homo œconomicus"*, Paris: La découverte.

Godbout, Jack T. & Alain Caillé (1992) *L'esprit du don*. Paris: La découverte, 2000.

Godechot, Olivier (2001) *Les traders: Essai de sociologie des marchés financiers*. Paris: La découverte.

Godelier, Maurice (1996) *L'énigme du don*. Paris: Fayard.

Gouhier, Henri (1941) *La jeunesse d'Auguste Comte et la formation du positivisme*. Paris: Vrin, 1970.

Granovetter, Mark (1990) "The Old and the New Economic Sociology: A History and an Agenda". In R. Friedland & A. F. Robertson, eds., *Beyond the Marketplace: Rethinking Economy and Society*, 89–112. Chicago: Aldine.

Grimmer-Solem, Erik, & Roberto Romani (1998) "The Historical School, 1870–1900: A Cross-National Reassessment". *History of European Ideas* 24(4–5): 267–99.

——— (1999) "In search of full empirical reality: Historical political economy, 1870–1900". *European Journal of the History of Economic Thought*, 6(3): 333–64.

Grœthuysen, Bernard (1927) *Origines de l'esprit bourgeois en France: L'église et la bourgeoisie*. Paris: Gallimard, 1977.

Grossein, Jean-Pierre (1996) "Présentation". In Weber 1996: 51–129.

——— (1999) "Peut-on lire en français *L'éthique protestante et l'esprit du capitalisme?*" *Archives européennes de sociologie* 40(1): 125–47.

——— (2000) "Présentation". In Weber 1920c: i–xxv.

——— (2002) "Une nouvelle traduction de l'*Ethique protestante et l'esprit du capitalisme*" *Revue française de sociologie* 43(3): 653–71.

Guglielmi, Jean-Louis (1945) *Essai sur le développement de la théorie du salaire*. Paris: Sirey.

Guitton, Henri (1938) *Economie Rationnelle, Economie Positive, Economie Synthétique: De Walras à Moore*. Paris: Sirey.

Hacking, Ian (1999) *Entre science et réalité: La construction sociale de quoi?* French translation. Paris: La découverte, 2001.

Halévy, Elie (1901) *La formation du radicalisme philosophique*, Paris: Presses universitaires de France, 1995.

Halleux, Robert (1998) "Ingénieurs". In Blay & Halleux 1998: 51–60.

Hayek, Friedrich (1948) *Individualism and the Economic Order*. Chicago: University of Chicago Press.

——— (1952) *The Counter-Revolution of Science: Studies in the Abuse of Reason*. Indianapolis: Liberty Press, 1979.

Heilbron, Johan (1985) "Les métamorphoses du durkheimisme, 1920–1940". *Revue française de sociologie* 26(1): 203–32.

——— (1990) *The Rise of Social Theory*. English translation. Oxford: Polity Press.

——— (1993) "Ce que Durkheim doit à Comte". In Besnard, Borlandi & Vogt 1993: 59–66.

——— (2001) "Economic sociology in France". *European Societies* 3(1): 41–67.

Hénaff, Marcel (2002) *Le prix de la vérité: Le don, l'argent, la philosophie*. Paris: Seuil.

Henry, Michel (1976) *Marx: Une philosophie de l'économie*. Paris: Gallimard.

Héran, François (1987) "L'institution démotivée: De Fustel de Coulanges à Durkheim et au-delà". *Revue française de sociologie* 28(1): 67–98.

——— (1988) "De *La cité antique* à la sociologie des institutions". *Revue de synthèse* 3–4: 363–90.

Hernes, Gudmund (1989a) "The Logic of *The Protestant Ethic*". *Rationality and Society* 1(1): 123–62.

——— (1989b) "Response to Coleman". *Rationality and Society* 1(2): 295–300.

Hervieux-Léger, Danièle, & Jean-Paul Willaime (2001) *Sociologies et religion: Approches classiques*. Paris: Presses universitaires de France.

Higgs, Henry, ed. (1894) *Palgrave's Dictionary of Political Economy*. London: Macmillan.

Hill, Lisa (2001) "The Hidden Theology of Adam Smith". *European Journal of the History of Economic Thought* 8(1): 1–29.

Hirschhorn, Monique (1988) *Max Weber et la sociologie française*. Paris: L'Harmattan.

Hirschman, Albert O. (1970) *Défection et prise de parole*. French translation. Paris: Le Seuil, 1995.

———— (1977) *Les passions et les interest: Justifications politiques du capitalisme avant son apogee*. French translation. Paris: Presses universitaires de France 1980.

———— (1984a) "Against Parsimony: Three Easy Ways of Complicating Some Categories of Economic Discourse". *American Economic Review* 74 (May): 89–96.

———— (1984b) *L'économie comme science morale et politique*. French translation. Paris: Galimard/Le Seuil.

Iacono, Alfonso (1992) *Le fétichisme: Histoire d'un concept*. Paris: Presses universitaires de France.

Isambert, François-André (1990) "Durkheim: Une science de la morale pour une morale laïque". *Archives de sciences sociales des religions* 69(1): 129–46.

———— (1992) "Une religion de l'homme? Sur trois interprétations de la religion dans la pensée de Durkheim". *Revue française de sociologie* 32(2): 443–62.

Jeanneney, Jean-Marcel (1936) *Essai sur le mouvement des prix en France depuis la stabilisation monétaire (1927–1935)*. Paris: Sirey.

———— (1996) "Souvenirs de François Simiand". In Gillard & Rosier 1996: 267–68.

Joas, Hans (1994) "La théorie de l'action chez Durkheim et chez Weber: Le problème de la créativité". In J. Coenen-Huther & M. Hirschhorn, eds., *Durkheim, Weber: Vers la fin des malentendus*, 53–71. Paris: L'Harmattan.

Jones, Robert A. (1974) "Durkheim's Response to Spencer: An Essay toward Historicism in the Historiography of Sociology". *Sociological Quarterly* 15 (summer): 341–58.

———— (1993) "La science positive de la morale en France: Les sources allemandes de la *Division du travail social*". In Besnard, Borlandi & Vogt 1891: 11–42.

———— (1999) *The Development of Durkheim's Social Realism*. Cambridge: Cambridge University Press.

Juglar, Clément (1891) "Crises commerciales". In Say & Chailley 1891 I: 641–50.

Karady, Victor (1976) "Durkheim, les sciences sociales et l'Université: Bilan d'un semi-échec". *Revue française de sociologie* 17(2): 267–312.

———— (1979) "Stratégies de réussite et modes de faire valoir de la sociologie chez les durkheimiens". *Revue française de sociologie* 20(1): 49–82.

Karsenty, Bruno (1994) *Marcel Mauss: Le fait social total*. Paris: Presses universitaires de France.

———— (1997) *L'homme total: Sociologie, anthropologie et philosophie chez Marcel Mauss*. Paris: Presses universitaires de France.

Kirat, Thierry (1990) "Taylorisme et rationalisation du travail en France et en Allemagne dans l'entre-deux-guerres". *Revue d'économie politique* 100(1): 58–82.

Knight, Frank H. (1921) *Risk, Uncertainty and Profits*. London: London School of Economics, 1935.

Kubali, Hüseyin Nail (1950) "Avant-propos". In Durkheim 1898–1900: 5–7.

Kuhn, Thomas S. (1970) *The Structure of Scientific Revolutions*. 2nd edition. Chicago: University of Chicago Press.

Kuisel, Richard F. (1981) *Le capitalisme et l'Etat en France: Modernisation et dirigisme au XXe siècle*. French translation. Paris: Gallimard, 1984.

Lacroix, Bernard (1981) *Durkheim et le politique*. Paris: Presses de la fondation nationale des sciences politiques.

——— (1990) "Aux origines des sciences sociales françaises: Politique, société et temporalité dans l'œuvre de Durkheim". *Archives de sciences sociales des religions* 69(1): 109–27.

Lacroix, Bernard, & Béatrice Landerer (1972) "Durkheim, Sismondi et les socialistes de la chaire". *L'année sociologique* 23: 159–204.

Ladrière, Paul (2001) *Pour une sociologie de l'éthique*. Paris: Presses universitaires de France.

Landes, David (1962) *The Unbound Prometheus: Technological Change and Industrial Development in Western Europe from 1750 to the Present*. Cambridge: Cambridge University Press, 2003.

Landry, Adolphe (1907) "Quelques travaux récents de théorie économique". *Revue d'économie politique* 21(6): 687–711.

Lapidus, André (1992) "Une introduction à la pensée économique médiévale". In A. Béraud & G. Faccarello, eds., *Nouvelle histoire de la pensée économique*, 1: 24–70. Paris: La découverte.

Lebaron, Frédéric (2000) *La croyance économique: Les économistes entre science et politique*. Paris: Seuil.

——— (2003) *Les fondements symboliques de l'ordre économique*. Habilitation thesis, Paris VII.

Lefort, Claude (1951) "L'échange et la lutte des hommes". In Lefort 1978, *Les formes de l'histoire*, 15–29. Paris: Gallimard.

Leibniz, Gottfried-Wilhelm (1710) *Essais de théodicée: Sur la bonté de Dieu, la liberté de l'homme et l'origine du mal*. Paris: Flammarion, 1969.

Leroy-Beaulieu, Paul (1884) *Le collectivisme: Examen critique du nouveau socialisme*. Paris: Guillaumin.

——— (1896) *Traité théorique et pratique d'économie politique*. 3rd edition. Paris: Guillaumin, 1906.

Levan-Lemesle, Lucette (1986) "De la société d'économie politique aux Facultés de Droit: Caractères et paradoxes de l'institutionnalisation de l'économie politique en France". *Œconomia* 6: 223–37.

——— (1991) "L'institutionnalisation de l'économie politique en France". In Breton & Lutfalla 1991: 356–88.

Lévi-Strauss, Claude (1947) "La sociologie française". In G. Gurvitch & W. E. Moore, eds., *La sociologie au XXe siècle II: Les études sociologiques dans les différents pays*, 513–45. Paris: Presses universitaires de France.

——— (1950) "Introduction à l'œuvre de Marcel Mauss". In Mauss 1950: ix–lii.

Liesse, André (1891) "Sociologie". In Say & Chailley 1891 II: 890–900.

Llobera, Joseph R. (1980) "Durkheim, the Durkheimians and Their Collective Misrepresentation of Marx". *Social Science Information* 19(2): 385–411.

Lockwood, David (1964) "System Integration and Social Integration". In G. K. Zollschan & W. Hirsch, eds., *Exploration in Social Change*, 244–57. New York: Houghton Mifflin.

Logue, William (1993) "Durkheim et les économistes français". In Besnard, Borlandi & Vogt 1993: 43–58.

Lordon, Frédéric (1997) *Les quadratures de la politique économique: Les infortunes de la vertu.* Paris: Albin Michel.

Lukes, Steven (1973) *Emile Durkheim: His Life and Work. A Historical and Critical Study.* London: Penguin Press.

Lutfalla, Georges (1934) "Essai critique sur la détermination statistique des courbes d'offre et de demande". *Annales sociologiques*, series D, 1: 87–117.

———— (1949) "Quelques tâches présentes de la sociologie économique". *L'année sociologique*, 3rd series, 2: 649–60.

MacIntyre, Alasdair (1988) *Quelle justice? Quelle rationalité?* French translation. Paris: Presses universitaires de France, 1993.

Mahé, Alain (1998) "Un disciple méconnu de Marcel Mauss: René Maunier". In R. Maunier, *Recherches sur les échanges rituels en Afrique du Nord.* Paris: Bouchène, 1998.

Mailfer, Henri-Charles (1883) "Le positivisme devant la morale, le droit et l'économie politique". *Journal des économistes* 69 (September): 317–39.

Malebranche, Nicolas (1680) *Traité de la nature et de la grace.* Paris: Vrin, 1958.

Malinowski, Bronislaw (1921) "The Primitive Economics of the Trobriand Islanders", *Economic Journal* 31(1): 1–16.

———— (1923) *Les argonautes du pacifique occidental.* French translation. Paris: Galllimard, 1989.

Marcel, Jean-Christophe (1998) "Jean Stoetzel élève de Maurice Halbwachs: Les origines françaises de la théorie des opinions". *L'année sociologique* 48(2): 319–51.

———— (2001) *Le durkheimisme dans l'entre-deux-guerres.* Paris: Presses universitaires de France.

March, Lucien (1903) "Bibliographie—François Simiand, *Essai sur le prix du charbon en France au 19ème siècle*". *Journal de la société statistique de Paris* 2: 68–70.

———— (1908) "Quelques observations sur les procédés et sur certains enseignements des statistiques de salaires: A propos des récentes communications de MM. G. Cadoux et F. Simiand". *Journal de la société statistique de Paris* 5: 149–60.

Marchal, André (1943) *Economie politique et technique statistique.* Paris: LGDJ.

———— (1952–55) *Méthode scientifique et science économique.* Paris: Librairie de Médicis.

———— (1953) *La pensée économique en France depuis 1945.* Paris: Presses universitaires de France.

———— (1959) *Systèmes et structures économiques.* Paris: Presses universitaires de France.

Marchal, Jean (1942) *Rendements fiscaux et conjoncture: Contribution à la théorie de la sensibilité des impôts,* Paris: Librairie de Médicis.

———— (1952) "Approches et catégories à utiliser pour une théorie réaliste de la répartition". *Revue économique* 3(2): 147–82.

Marchal, Jean, & Jacques Lecaillon (1959) *La répartition du revenu national.* Paris: Génin.

Marjolin, René (1938) "Rationalité ou irrationalité des mouvements économiques de longue durée". *Annales sociologiques*, series D, 3: 1–38.

———— (1941) *Prix, monnaie et production: Essai sur les mouvements économiques de longue durée.* Paris: Presses universitaires de France.

———— (1947) "Gaëtan Pirou et François Simiand". *Revue d'économie politique* 61(4): 683–88.

———— (1986) *Le travail d'une vie: Mémoires 1911–1986.* Paris: Laffont.

Marx, Karl (1867) *Das Kapital: Kritik der politischen Oekonomie. Vol. 1 Der Produktionsprocess des Kapitals.* Hamburg: Otto Meissner.

———— (1893) *Le capital: Critique de l'économie politique.* Book 3. French translation. Paris: Editions sociales, 1969.

———— (1905–10) *Théories sur la plus-value.* French translation. Paris: Editions sociales, 1974–78.

Merton, Robert K. (1938) *Science, Technology and Society in Seventeenth-Century England.* New York: Harper Torchbooks, 1970.

———— (1957) *Eléments de théorie et de méthode sociologique.* French translation. Paris: Plon, 1965.

Mill, John Stuart (1842) *A System of Logic, Ratiocinative and Inductive.* In *The Collected Works of John Stuart Mill*, vols. 7–8. Indiana: Liberty Press, 2006.

———— (1844) *Essays on Some Unsettled Questions of Political Economy.* Bristol: Thoemmes Press, 1992.

———— (1848) *Principles of Political Economy.* New York: Colonial Press, 1900.

———— (1865) *Auguste Comte et le positivisme.* French translation. Paris: Alcan, 1898.

———— (1899) *Lettres inédites de John Stuart Mill à Auguste Comte avec les réponses de Comte.* Paris: Alcan.

Mirowski, Philip (1992) "The How, the When and the Why of Mathematical Expression in the History of Economic Analysis". *Journal of Economic Perspectives* 6(2): 145–57.

———— (2002) *Machine Dreams: Economics Becomes a Cyborg Science.* Cambridge: Cambridge University Press.

Mongin, Philippe (2000) "La méthodologie économique au 20ème siècle: Les controverses en théorie de l'entreprise et la théorie des préférences révélées". In A. Béraud & G. Faccarello, eds., *Nouvelle histoire de la pensée économique*, 3: 340–78. Paris: La découverte.

Moore, Henri L. (1911) *Laws of Wages: An Essay in Statistical Economics.* New York: Kelley, 1967.

———— (1929) *Synthetic Economics.* New York: Kelley, 1967.

Morgan, Mary S., & Malcolm Rutherford (1998) "American Economics: The Character of the Transformation". In M. S. Morgan & M. Rutherford, eds., *From Interwar Pluralism to Postwar Neoclassicism*, 1–26. Durham, N.C.: Duke University Press.

Morrisson, Christian (2000) "L'économie historique dans la *Revue économique*: Du programme à la réalisation". *Revue économique* 51(5): 1059–78.

Mottez, Bernard (1966) *Systèmes de salaire et politiques patronales: Essai sur l'évolution des pratiques et des idéologies patronales*: Paris: CNRS.

Mucchielli, Laurent (1998) *La découverte du social: Naissance de la sociologie en France*. Paris: La découverte.

Murray, Robert A. (1912a) "Un critico dell'economia matematica". *Rivista italiana di sociologia*, 77–84.

——— (1912b) Review of Simiand, *La méthode positive en science économique*. *L'indépendance: Chronique bi-mensuelle* 2 February: 449–53.

Nandan, Yash (1974) *Le maître, les doctrines, les membres et le magnum opus: Une étude critique et analytique de l'école durkheimienne et de "L'Année sociologique"*. PhD thesis, Paris V.

Nau, Heino H., & Philippe Steiner (2002) "Schmoller, Durkheim and Old European Institutionalist Economics". *Journal of Economic Issues* 36(4): 1005–24.

Nelson, Robert H. (1991) *Reaching for Heaven on Earth: The Theological Meaning of Economics*, Lanham: Rowman & Littlefield.

——— (2001) *Economics as Religion: From Samuelson to Chicago and Beyond*. University Park: Pennsylvania State University Press.

Nicolaï, André (1960) *Comportement économique et structures sociales*. Paris: L'Harmattan, 1999.

Orléan, André (1992a) "La monnaie comme lien social: Etude de *Philosophie de l'argent* de Georg Simmel". *Genèses* 8: 86–107.

——— (1992b) "Contagion des opinions et fonctionnement des marchés financiers". *Revue économique* 43(4): 685–98.

——— (1998) "La monnaie auto-référentielle: Réflexions sur les évolutions monétaires contemporaines". In Aglietta & Orléan 1982: 359–86.

——— (2002) "Pour une nouvelle approche des interactions financières: L'èconomie des conventions face à la sociologie économique". In I. Huault, ed., *La construction sociale de l'entreprise; Autour des travaux de Mark Granovetter*, 207–29. Colombelle: Editions management & sociétés.

———, ed. (1994) *Analyse économique des conventions*. Paris: Presses universitaires de France.

Pagano, A. (1909) Review of Durkheim, *De la méthode dans les sciences. Rivista Italiana di sociologia*: 210–19.

Paoletti, Giovanni (1992) "Durkheim à l'Ecole normale supérieure: Lectures de jeunesse". *Etudes durkheimiennes/Durkheim Studies* 4: 7–21.

——— (2000) "Representation and Belief: Durkheim's Rationalism and the Kantian Tradition". In W. Pickering, ed., *Durkheim and Representations*, 118–35. London: Routledge.

——— (2002a) "Il quadrato di Durkheim: La definizione del legame sociale e suoi critici". In M. Rosati & A. Santambrogio, eds., *Emile Durkheim: Contributi ad una rilettura critica*, 235–61. Roma: Meltemi.

——— (2002b) "Durkheim et le problème de l'objectivité: Une lecture des *Formes élémentaires de la vie religieuse*". *Revue française de sociologie* 43(3): 437–59.

——— (2003) *Durkheim et la philosophie: Histoires, généalogies, themes*. PhD thesis, Institut d'etudes politiques de Paris.

Pareto, Vilfredo (1896–97) *Cours d'économie politique*. In *Œuvres complètes de Vilfredo Pareto*, vol.1. Geneva: Droz, 1964.

————— (1898) "Le suicide". In *Œuvres complètes de Vilfredo Pareto*, 6: 122–24. Geneva: Droz.

————— (1902–3) *Les systèmes socialistes*. In *Œuvres complètes de Vilfredo Pareto*, vol. 5. Geneva: Droz.

————— (1909) *Manuel d'économie politique*. In *Œuvres complètes de Vilfredo Pareto*, vol. 7. Geneva: Droz.

————— (1917) *Traité de sociologie générale*. In *Œuvres complètes de Vilfredo Pareto*, vol. 12. Geneva: Droz, 1968.

Parodi, Dominique (1907) "Morale et sociologie". *Revue d'économie politique* 21(2): 241–70.

Parsons, Talcott (1949) *The Structure of Social Action*. 2nd edition. Glencoe: Free Press.

————— (1959) "Durkheim's Contribution to the Theory of Integration of Social Systems". In *Sociological Theory and Modern Society*, 3–34. New York: Free Press, 1967.

Pénin, Marc (1998) *Charles Gide 1847–1932: L'esprit critique*. Paris: L'Harmattan.

Perroux, François (1960) *Economie et société: Contrainte—Echange—Don*. Paris: Presses universitaires de France.

————— (1973) *Pouvoir et économie*. Paris: Dunod.

Petit, Annie (1995a) "De Comte à Durkheim : Un héritage ambivalent". In Borlandi & Mucchielli 1995: 49–70.

————— (1995b) "Durkheim critique de Mill". In Borlandi & Mucchielli 1995: 71–100.

Pfefferkorn, René (1997) "Maurice Halbwachs et l'économie politique". In C. de Montlibert, ed., *Maurice Halbwachs 1877–1945*. Strasbourg: Presses universitaires de Strasbourg.

Pickering, William S. F. (1984) *Durkheim's Sociology of Religion: Themes and Theories*. London: Routledge & Kegan Paul.

————— (1993) "L'évolution de la religion". In Besnard, Borlandi & Vogt 1993: 185–96.

————— (2000) "What Do Representations Represent? The Issue of Reality". In W. Pickering, ed., *Durkheim and Representations*. 98–117. London: Routledge.

Picon, Antoine (1992) *L'invention de l'ingénieur moderne: L'Ecole des ponts et chaussées 1747–1851*. Paris: Presses de l'École nationale des ponts et chaussées.

Pirou, Gaëtan (1929) *Doctrines sociales et sciences économiques*. Paris: Recueil Sirey.

————— (1932) "Une théorie positive du salaire". *Revue d'économie politique* 46(6): 1265–87.

————— (1936) Preface to Jeanneney 1936: ix–xv.

————— (1937) "Economie dynamique et théorie abstraite". *Revue d'économie politique* 51(4): 1177–91.

————— (1938) Preface to Guitton 1938: v–x.

————— (1939) *Traité d'économie politique: Introduction à l'étude de l'économie politique*. Paris: Sirey.

————— (1942) Preface to Marchal 1942: 9–11.

Poggi, Gianfranco (1983) *Calvinism and the Capitalist Spirit: Max Weber's Protestant Ethic*. London: Macmillan.

Polanyi, Karl (1944) *La grande transformation: Aux origines politiques et économiques de notre temps*. French translation. Paris: Gallimard, 1983.

———— (1977) *The Livelihood of Man*, New York: Academic Press

Polier, Léon (1911) *Cours d'économie politique: 1ère et 2ème année de licence*. Toulouse.

Pouch, Thierry (2001) *Les économistes français et le marxisme: Apogée et déclin d'un discours critique (1950–2000)*. Rennes: Presses universitaires de Rennes.

Pradelle, Michèle de (1996) *Les vendredis de Carpentras: Faire son marché en Provence ou ailleurs*. Paris: Fayard.

Proudhon, Pierre-Joseph (1846) *Système des contradictions économiques; ou, Philosophie de la misère*. In *Œuvres complètes de P-J. Proudhon: Nouvelle edition*. Paris: Rivière, 1923.

Puynode, Gustave du (1893) Review of Durkheim, *De la division du travail social*. *Journal des économistes* 15 (August): 287–92.

Quételet, Adolphe (1835) *Sur l'homme et le développement de ses facultés; ou, Essai de physique sociale*. Paris: Fayard, 1991.

Racine, Luc (1991) "L'obligation de rendre les présents et l'esprit de la chose donnée: De Marcel Mauss à René Maunier". *Diogène* 154: 69–94.

Raffalovitch, Arthur (1885) "Le socialisme de M. Schäffle". *Journal des économistes* 29 (March): 389–97.

Ratansi, Piyo (1990) "Puritanism and Science: The 'Merton Thesis' after Fifty Years". In J. Clark, C. Modgil & S. Modgil, eds., *Robert K. Merton: Consensus and Controversy*, 351–69. London: Falmer Press.

Richebé, Nathalie (2002) "Les réactions des salariés à la 'logique compétence': Vers un renouveau de l'échange salarial ". *Revue française de sociologie* 43(1): 99–126.

Robertson, Dennis (1954) "What Does the Economist Economize?" In D. Robertson, *Economic Commentaries*, 147–54. London: Stapple Press, 1955.

Rogers, J. D. (1894) "Social Science". In Higgs 1894 III: 428–30.

Roquet, Léon (1897) Review of Durkheim, *Le Suicide*. *Journal des économistes* 32 (November): 284–86.

Rosier, Michel (1996) "Le "monétarisme social"". In Gillard & Rosier 1996: 215–26.

Roth, Alvin E. (2002) "The Economist as Engineer: Game Theory, Experimentation, and Computation as Tools for Design Economics". *Econometrica* 70(4): 1341–78.

Royer, Clémence (1891) "Positivisme". In Say & Chailley 1891 II: 529–40.

Rousseau, Jean-Jacques (1762) *Du contrat social; ou, Principes du droit politique*. In *Œuvres complètes de J.-J. Rousseau*, vol. 3. Paris: Gallimard, 1964.

Rutherford, Malcolm (2000) "Institutionalism between the Wars". *Journal of Economic Issues* 34 (June): 291–303.

Sahlins, Marshall (1972) *Age de pierre, âge d'abondance: L'économie des sociétés primitives*. French translation, Paris: Gallimard, 1976.

———— (1976) *Au cœur des sociétés: Raison utilitaire et raison culturelle*. French translation. Paris: Gallimard, 1980.

Saint-Marc, Henri (1893) Review of Durkheim, *De la division du travail social*. *Revue d'économie politique* 7(4): 862–70.

Saint-Simon, Henri (1817) *Lettres de Henri Saint-Simon à un Américain*. In *Œuvres de Saint-Simon*, vol.1. Paris: Anthropos, 1966.

Samuelson, Paul A. (1947) *Foundations of Economic Analysis*. Cambridge, Mass.: Harvard University Press.

Say, Jean-Baptiste (1794) *Abrégé de la vie de Franklin*. In *Œuvres morales et politiques*, vol. 5 of *Œuvres complètes de J.-B. Say*, 165–82. Paris: Economica, 2003.

——— (1819) *Cours à l'Athénée Royal*. In J-B. Say, *Cours d'économie politique et autres essays*. Paris: Flammarion, 1996.

Say, Léon, & Joseph Chailley eds. (1891) *Nouveau dictionnaire de l'économie politique*. Paris: Guillaumin.

Schäffle, Albert (1874) *La quintessence du socialisme*. French translation. Paris: Société nouvelle de librairie & d'édition, 1904.

Schmoller, Gustav (1883) "Gli scritti di C. Menger e di W. Dilthey sulla metodologia delle scienze politiche et sociali". Italian translation. *Quaderni di storia dell'economia politica*, 1988, 141–64.

——— (1894a) Review of Durkheim, *De la division du travail social*. *Jahrbuch für Gesetzgebung und Volkswirtschaft* 18(1): 286–89.

——— (1894b) " L'économie politique, sa théorie et sa méthode". *Revue d'économie politique* 8(2): 105–40, 8(4): 339–63 and 8(5): 462–79.

——— (1897) *Politique sociale et économie politique*. French translation. Paris: Giard & Brière, 1902.

——— (1899) *Principes d'économie politique*. French translation. Paris: Giard & Brière, 1900–1904.

Schneewind, Jerome B. (1997) *The Invention of Autonomy: A History of Modern Moral Philosophy*. Cambridge: Cambridge University Press.

Schumpeter, Joseph A. (1914) "La méthode 'positive' en économie", French translation in Gillard & Rosier 1996: 137–42.

——— (1954) *History of Economic Analysis*. London: Allen & Unwin.

Servet, Jean-Michel, et al. (1999) *Une économie sans argent: Les systèmes d'echange local*. Paris: Seuil.

Shinn, Terry (1978) "Des Corps de l'Etat au secteur industriel: Genèse de la profession d'ingénieur, 1750–1920". *Revue française de sociologie* 19(1): 39–71.

Simmel, Georg (1900) *Philosophie de l'argent*. French translation. Paris: Presses universitaires de France, 1987.

——— (1912) *La religion*. French translation. Courtry: Circé 1998.

Sismondi, Jean-Charles Léonard, Simonde de (1826) *Nouveaux principes d'économie politique*. 2nd edition, Paris: Calman-Lévy, 1971.

Small, Albion (1902) Review of Durkheim, *De la division du travail social*. *American Journal of Sociology*, 567–68.

Smelser, Neil J., & Richard Swedberg, eds. (1994) *Handbook of Economic Sociology*. Princeton: Princeton University Press.

Smith, Adam (1776) *An Inquiry into the Nature and the Causes of the Wealth of Nations*. Indianapolis: Liberty Press, 1981.

Smith, Philip, & Jeffrey C. Alexander (1996) "Durkheim's Religious Revival". *American Journal of Sociology* 102(2): 585–92.

Sombart, Werner (1913) *Le bourgeois: Contribution à l'histoire morale et intellectuelle de l'homme économique moderne.* French translation. Paris: Payot, 1966.

Spencer, Herbert (1876–85) *Principes de sociologie.* French translation, Paris: Alcan, 1908–10.

——— (1897) *Les institutions professionnelles et industrielles.* French translation. Paris: Guillaumin & Co., 1898.

Steiner, Philippe (1992) "*L'Année sociologique* et la réception de l'œuvre de Max Weber". *Archives européennes de sociologie* 33(2): 329–49.

——— (1994) *La sociologie de Durkheim.* Paris: La découverte.

——— (1998) *Sociologie de la connaissance économique: Essai sur les rationalisations de la connaissance économique (1750–1850).* Paris: Presses universitaires de France.

——— (1999) *La sociologie économique.* Paris: La découverte.

——— (2000a) "La *Revue économique* 1950–1980: La marche vers l'orthodoxie académique?" *Revue économique* 51(5): 1009–58.

——— (2000b) "Marx et la sociologie économique". *Cahiers internationaux de sociologie* 108(1): 57–77.

——— (2001a) "Le marché et les "marchandises fictives": Don de sang et don d'organes". *Revue française de sociologie* 42(2): 357–74.

——— (2001b) "The Sociology of Economic Knowledge". *European Journal of Social Theory* 4(4): 443–58.

——— (2005) "Pourquoi la sociologie économique est-elle si développée en France?" *L'année sociologique* 55(2): 391–415.

——— (2008) "L'héritage au 19ème siècle en France: Loi, intérêt de sentiment et intérêts économiques". *Revue économique* 59(1): 75–97.

——— (2010) *La transplantation d'organes: Un commerce nouveau entre les êtres humains.* Paris: Gallimard.

Swedberg, Richard, ed. (1990) *Economics and Sociology: Redefining Their Boundaries. Conversations with Economists and Sociologists.* Princeton: Princeton University Press.

——— (1996) "Analyzing the Economy: On the Contribution of James Coleman". In J. Clark, ed., *James S. Coleman*, 313–28. Bristol: Falmer Press.

——— (1998) *Max Weber and the Idea of Economic Sociology.* Princeton: Princeton University Press.

Swiedinek, O. von (1911) Review of Simiand, *Le salaire des ouvriers des mines de charbon en France. Jahrbuch für Gesetzgebung verwaltung und Volkswirtschaft* 35(3): 460–63.

Tarde, Gabriel (1888) "Les deux sens de la valeur". *Revue d'économie politique* 2(3): 526–40 and 2(4): 561–76.

——— (1893) *La logique sociale.* Le Plessy-Robinson: Synthelabo, 1999.

——— (1902) *Psychologie économique.* Paris: Alcan.

Tarot, Camille (1999) *De Durkheim à Mauss: L'invention du symbolique. Sociologie et science des religions.* Paris: La découverte.

Testart, Alain (1998) "Uncertainties of the "Obligation to Reciprocate": A Critique of Mauss". In W. James & N. Allen, eds., *Marcel Mauss: A Centenary Tribute.* Oxford: Berghahn Books.

——— (2001) "Echanges marchands, échanges non-marchands". *Revue française de sociologie* 42(4): 719–48.

Thompson, Kenneth, ed. (2004) *Readings from Emile Durkheim*. London: Routledge.

Titmuss, Richard (1970) *The Gift Relationship: From Blood to Social Policy*. London: LSE books.

Tocqueville, Alexis de (1835) *De la démocratie en Amérique*. In *Œuvres complètes d'Alexis de Tocqueville*, vol. 1, bk. 1. Paris: Gallimard, 1951. *Democracy in America*. Edited by Isaac Kramnick. London: Penguin Books, 2003.

——— (1840) *De la démocratie en Amérique*. In *Œuvres complètes d'Alexis de Tocqueville*, vol. 1, bk. 2. Paris: Gallimard, 1951. *Democracy in America*. Edited by Isaac Kramnick. London: Penguin Books, 2003.

Tracy, Antoine, Louis Claude, Destutt de (1823) *Traité d'économie politique*. Paris: Bouguet & Lévi.

Troeltsch, Ernst (1911a) *The Social Teaching of the Christian Churches*. English translation. London: Allen & Unwin, 1931.

——— (1911b) *Protestantisme et modernité*. French translation. Paris: Gallimard, 1991.

——— (1913) "Religion, économie et société". In Troeltsch 1911b: 133–47.

Turner, J. H. (1985) *Herbert Spencer: A Renewed Appreciation*. Beverly Hills: Sage.

Turner, Steven (1996) "Durkheim among the Statisticians". *Journal of the History of the Behavioral Sciences* 32(4): 354–78.

Vatin, François (1994) *Le travail: Physique et économie*. Paris: Presses universitaires de France.

——— (1998) *Economie politique et économie naturelle chez Antoine-Augustin Cournot*. Paris: Presses universitaires de France.

Vérin, Hélène (1993) *La gloire des ingénieurs: L'intelligence technique du XVIe au XVIIIe siècle*. Paris: Albin Michel.

——— (1998) "Ingénieurs du Roi". In Blay & Halleux 1998: 61–68.

Vogt, Paul W. (1979) "Un durkheimien ambivalent : Célestin Bouglé, 1870–1940". *Revue française de sociologie* 20(1): 123–39.

Wagner, Adolf (1892) *Les fondements de l'économie politique*. French translation. Paris: Giard & Brière, 1904.

Walras Léon (1896) *Etudes d'économie sociale*. In *Œuvres économiques complètes*, vol. 9. Paris: Economica, 1990.

——— (1900) *Eléments d'économie politique pure*. 4th edition. In *Œuvres économiques complètes*, vol. 8, Paris: Economica, 1988.

Ward, Lester F. (1902) "Contemporary Sociology III". *American Journal of Sociology*, 749–62.

Watts Miller, William (1994) "Les deux préfaces: Science morale et réforme morale". In Besnard, Borlandi & Vogt 1993: 147–64.

Webb, Sidney, & Beatrice Webb (1901) *Industrial Democracy*. London: Clark.

Weber, Max (1905) *L'éthique protestante et l'esprit du capitalisme*. French translation. Paris: Gallimard, 2003.

——— (1906) "Les sectes protestantes et l'esprit du capitalisme". In Weber 1964: 257–93.

Weber, Max (1907) *Critique of Stammler*. English translation. Berkeley: University of California Press.

—— (1907–10) "Anticritiques". In Weber 1905: 321–446.

—— (1915) Introduction to *L'Ethique économique des religions mondiales*. In Weber 1996: 329–78.

—— (1916–17) *Hindouisme et Bouddhisme*. French translation. Paris: Flammarion, 2003.

—— (1920a) "Avant-propos". In Weber 1996: 489–508.

—— (1920b) *Le judaïsme antique*. French translation. Paris: Plon, 1971.

—— (1920c) *Confucianisme et taoïsme*. French translation. Paris: Gallimard, 2000.

—— (1920d) "Considération intermédiaire: Théorie des degrés et des orientations du refus du religieux du monde". In Weber 1996: 410–60.

—— (1920e) *Le judaïsme antique*. French translation. Paris: Plon, 1970.

—— (1920–21) *Gesammelte Aufsätze zur Religionssoziologie*. 3 vols. Tübingen: J.C.B. Mohr.

—— (1921) *Economie et société*. French translation. Paris: Plon, 1971.

—— (1922) *Wirtschaft und Gesellschaft*. Tübingen: J.C.B. Mohr.

—— (1923) *General Economic History*. French translation. Glencoe: Free Press, 1951.

—— (1947) *Theory of Social and Economic Organization*. Translated by A. M. Henderson & Talcott Parsons. London: William Hodge.

—— (1964) *L'éthique protestante et l'esprit du capitalisme*. French translation. Paris: Plon.

—— (1948) "The Protestant Sects and the Spirit of Capitalism". In H. H. Gerth & C. Wright Mills, eds. *From Max Weber*, 302–22. London: Routledge.

—— (1996) *Sociologie des religions*. French translation. Paris: Gallimard.

—— (2002) *The Protestant Ethic and the "Spirit" of Capitalism*. Translated and edited by Peter Baehr & Gordon C. Wells. London: Penguin Books.

—— (2004a) "Intermediate Reflection on the Economic Ethic of the World Religions". In S. Whimster, ed., *Essential Weber*, 215–44. London: Routledge.

Weiller, Jean, & Bruno Carrier (1994) *L'économie non-conformiste en France au XIXe siècle*. Paris: Presses universitaires de France.

Weiss, John H. (1982) *The Making of the Technological Man: The Social Origins of French Engineering Education*. Cambridge, Mass.: MIT Press.

Wolfesperger, Alain (1977) "De la contestation de l'orthodoxie à la tentation du sociologisme chez les économistes". *Revue française de sociologie* 18(3): 397–434.

Wuthnow, Robert (1994) "Religion and Economic Life". In Smelser & Swedberg 1994: 620–46.

Yamashita, Masayuki (1995) "La sociologie française entre Auguste Comte et Emile Durkheim: Emile Littré et ses collaborateurs". *L'année sociologique* 45(1): 83–115.

Yamey, B. S. (1949) "Scientific Bookkeeping and The Rise of Capitalism". *Economic History Review* 1(2–3): 99–113.

Yamey, B. S., H.C. Edey & Hugh W. Thomson (1963) *Accounting in England and Scotland: 1543–1800*. London: Sweet & Maxwell.

Index